KU-693-055

KINGSTON COLLEGE

00096970

The Short Oxford History of Europe

The Eighteenth Century

The Short Oxford History of Europe

General Editor: T. C. W. Blanning

The Short Oxford History of Europe

General Editor: T. C. W. Blanning

The Eighteenth Century

Europe 1688–1815

Edited by T. C. W. Blanning

OXFORD

UNIVERSITY PRESS

OXFORD
UNIVERSITY PRESS

Great Clarendon Street, Oxford OX2 6DP

Oxford University Press is a department of the University of Oxford.
It furthers the University's objective of excellence in research, scholarship,
and education by publishing worldwide in

Oxford New York

Athens Auckland Bangkok Bogotá Buenos Aires Calcutta
Cape Town Chennai Dar es Salaam Delhi Florence Hong Kong Istanbul
Karachi Kuala Lumpur Madrid Melbourne Mexico City Mumbai
Nairobi Paris São Paulo Singapore Taipei Tokyo Toronto Warsaw

with associated companies in Berlin Ibadan

Oxford is a registered trade mark of Oxford University Press
in the UK and in certain other countries

Published in the United States
by Oxford University Press Inc., New York

© Oxford University Press, 2000

All rights reserved. No part of this publication may be reproduced,
stored in a retrieval system, or transmitted, in any form or by any means,
without the prior permission in writing of Oxford University Press,
or as expressly permitted by law, or under terms agreed with the appropriate
reprographics rights organizations. Enquiries concerning reproduction
outside the scope of the above should be sent to the Rights Department,
Oxford University Press, at the address above

You must not circulate this book in any other binding or cover
and you must impose this same condition on any acquirer

British Library Cataloging in Publication Data

Data available

Library of Congress Cataloguing in Publication Data

Data available

ISBN 0–19–873181–7 (Hbk)
ISBN 0–19–873120–5 (Pbk)

1 3 5 7 9 10 8 6 4 2

Typeset in Minion
by RefineCatch Limited, Bungay, Suffolk
Printed in Great Britain by
T. J. International Ltd., Padstow, Cornwall

KINGSTON COLLEGE
LEARNING RESOURCES CENTRE

Class No.	990.2 BLA
Acc. No.	00096900
	2/01
...or No.	

General Editor's Preface

The problems of writing a satisfactory general history of Europe are many, but the most intractable is clearly the reconciliation of depth with breadth. The historian who can write with equal authority about every part of the continent in all its various aspects has not yet been born. Two main solutions have been tried in the past: either a single scholar has attempted to go it alone, presenting an unashamedly personal view of a period, or teams of specialists have been enlisted to write what are in effect anthologies. The first offers a coherent perspective but unequal coverage, the second sacrifices unity for the sake of expertise. This new series is underpinned by the belief that it is this second way that has the fewest disadvantages and that even those can be diminished if not neutralized by close cooperation between the individual contributors under the directing supervision of the volume editor. All the contributors to every volume in this series have read each other's chapters, have met to discuss problems of overlap and omission, and have then redrafted as part of a truly collective exercise. To strengthen coherence further, the editor has written an introduction and conclusion, weaving the separate strands together to form a single cord. In this exercise, the brevity promised by the adjective 'short' in the series' title has been an asset. The need to be concise has concentrated everyone's minds on what really mattered in the period. No attempt has been made to cover every angle of every topic in every country. What this volume does provide is a short but sharp and deep entry into the history of Europe in the period in all its most important aspects.

Sidney Sussex College   T. C. W. Blanning
Cambridge

Contents

List of contributors

DEREK BEALES held the Chair of Modern History at Cambridge from 1980 to 1997 and is a Fellow of Sidney Sussex College. He is also a Fellow of the British Academy. He has written on nineteenth-century Britain and Italy and on the Habsburg Monarchy in the eighteenth century, especially on Joseph II. The first volume of his biography of the latter was published in 1987. He is currently engaged on volume II of that work and on a book on the monasteries of Catholic Europe before, during, and after the French Revolution.

T. C. W. BLANNING is Professor of Modern European History at the University of Cambridge and a Fellow of Sidney Sussex College. He is also a Fellow of the British Academy. His recent works include *Joseph II* (1994), *The French Revolutionary Wars 1787–1802* (1996), and *The French Revolution: Class War or Culture Clash?* (1997). He has also edited *The Oxford Illustrated History of Modern Europe* (1996) and *The Rise and Fall of the French Revolution* (1996); as well as (with David Cannadine) *History and Biography: Essays in Honour of Derek Beales* (1996) and (with Peter Wende) *Reform in Great Britain and Germany 1750–1850* (1999).

CHRISTOF DIPPER is Professor of Modern and Contemporary History at the University of Darmstadt and editor-in-chief of *Neue Politische Literatur*. His recent publications include *Deutsche Geschichte 1648–1789* (2nd edn., 1994), *1848–1949 im Überblick: Ein Jahrhundert deutscher Geschichte* (CD-ROM 1997), and (with Ulrich Speck) *1848—Revolution in Deutschland* (1998).

JOHN A. LYNN is Professor of History at the University of Illinois at Urbana-Champaign and adjunct Professor of History at the Ohio State University. His major works include *The Bayonets of the Republic: Motivation and Tactics in the Army of Revolutionary France, 1791–94* (rev. edn., 1996), *Giant of the Grand Siècle: The French Army, 1610–1715* (1997), and *The Wars of Louis XIV, 1667–1714* (1999). He is currently writing a book of essays on war and culture.

P. J. MARSHALL, formerly Rhodes Professor of Imperial History at King's College, is a Fellow of the British Academy. Among many other publications, he has edited *The Oxford History of the British Empire*, ii. *The Eighteenth Century*.

SHEILAGH OGILVIE is Reader in Economic History at the University of Cambridge. Her recent books include *State Corporatism and Proto-Industry* (1997), *Germany: A New Social and Economic History*, ii. *1630–1800* (1996), and (with Markus Cerman) *European Proto-Industrialization* (1996). She is currently writing a book on the economic history of Bohemia in the early modern period.

JULIAN SWANN lectures on Early Modern Europe at Birkbeck College, University of London. He is the author of *Politics and the Parlement of Paris under Louis XV, 1754–1774* (1995) and is currently writing a history of the Estates General of Burgundy, 1661–1790.

Introduction: the beneficiaries and casualties of expansion

T. C. W. Blanning

If no single concept or metaphor can summarize adequately an epoch lasting a century, the one word that best bridges all aspects of the eighteenth century is 'expansion'. It features prominently in each of the six chapters that follow. Whether it is the size of armies, literacy rates, state intervention, the acreage of overseas empires, industrialization, or just the number of Europeans on the planet, the figures for 1800 are appreciably higher than those for 1700. In this respect, the eighteenth century forms the hinge between the old world and the new, for by its end the degree of change was not only detectable, it was also seen to be irreversible. For example, until very late in the day, it was commonly if erroneously believed that the population of the world had been steadily falling since classical times. So deluded governments pursued policies of demographic mercantilism by competing fiercely for the supposedly dwindling stock, obstructing emigration and encouraging immigration. As Europe's population actually increased by forty to fifty million during the course of the century, the discrepancy between perception and reality eventually demanded a rethink. Two years before the century ended, Thomas Malthus's *Essay on the Principle of Population as it Affects the Future*

Improvement of Society announced a new era in which *over-population* would be seen as the main problem.

For the sake of conceptual clarity, we have had to organize this volume in six layers, but are aware of course that these were not discrete entities. Europe always was more like a tub of tutti-frutti than a slice of Neapolitan (an appropriate simile, for ice cream was the period's invention, being usually credited to the Parisian café-owner Tortoni). Indeed, this was more than ever the case in the eighteenth century, as the traditional 'society of orders' with its legally ring-fenced corporations started to dissolve into more fluid and mobile classes. Readers looking for an account of the major changes in—say—the European economy in the eighteenth century will certainly find a self-contained account in Chapter 3, but they should be aware that the developments described and analysed by Sheilagh Ogilvie both affected and were affected by contemporary events and forces charted elsewhere.

There is no single thread that will unravel the complex tapestry, rather a multitude of frayed ends, any one of which will lead the reader into the web of interlocking, interacting phenomena. Selection of which to follow may be left to serendipity (a concept also invented in the eighteenth century, by Horace Walpole in 1754), but will probably owe much to one's personal hierarchy of historical causation. Subscription to the 'primacy of foreign policy', for example, will focus attention on the thread of international conflict. In this quarter, the eighteenth century can be said to have begun in 1688 or 1689. It was in 1688 that the 'Glorious Revolution' brought William of Orange to the English throne and thus began the 'Second Hundred Years War' with France. It was to end only in 1815 with the Battle of Waterloo. It was in 1689 that Tsar Peter I seized power and began a drive to make Russia the dominant power in eastern Europe. It was to end only 300 years later, in 1989.

These two prolonged if intermittent struggles clearly had a profound impact not just on the states directly involved but also on the entire continent and indeed the world. The French and the British fought in North America, in the Caribbean, in Africa, in India, and on the high seas. The degree of exertion involved created a 'military fiscal state' in Britain, but eventually proved too much for French absolutism, plunging it into terminal crisis in the late 1780s. Although the triumphant resurgence of French power under the Revolution and Napoleon proved to be short-lived, it was strong enough to redraw the map of Europe so radically that the old order could never be fully restored. At the other end of the continent, changes of no less importance occurred. Peter the Great's conquest of the Swedish empire in the Baltic and subjection of Poland made Russia a permanent part of Europe for the first time, an achievement symbolized by the creation of a brand-new capital called St Petersburg on a green-field (or rather brown-swamp) site on the Gulf of Finland. Russian armies wintered in Mecklenburg in 1716, reached the Rhine in 1735, campaigned in Holland in 1799, and marched into Paris in 1814.

No European unlucky enough to get in the way of these various armies would have made the mistake of some historians in supposing that 'foreign policy' can be isolated from other forms of human activity. Nor was its influence confined to inflicting murder, rape, and pillage. The need to raise ever larger armies—and ever larger amounts of taxation to finance them—made states reach out to touch both the rich man in his castle and the poor man at his gate. This acquisitive drive in support of territorial expansion also generated policies to expand the economy by maximizing returns from agriculture, trade, and industry, although not all of them achieved the desired result and many were self-defeating. Nor were religion and secular culture spared the effects of war. States also grasped the prelate in his palace and the parish priest in his vicarage, for the rolling acres of the Churches offered a temptation too rich to resist. The need to represent a state's power inspired the patronage of countless artists working in every media. As Peter Burke has observed in his book *The Fabrication of Louis XIV*, cultural policy was 'the continuation of war and diplomacy by other means'.

But eighteenth-century culture was, of course, much more than state propaganda. Indeed, it offers an attractive alternative point of entry for understanding the period. In western, northern, and central Europe at least, it was just then that the ability to read and write ceased to be the preserve of a small élite and became accepted as a desirable and realizable goal for everyone. By 1800 adult literacy rates exceeded 50 per cent in many places, and reactionaries such as the Austrian aristocrat Count Auersperg, who told Emperor Leopold II in 1790 that education should be confined to nobles and that 'the mass of the people must remain stupid and pious', were in a dwindling minority. It was a development that caused a seismic shift in European culture. If representational complexes exemplified by Versailles did not disappear overnight, the values they represented faced a growing challenge. To meet the requirements of the newly literate, a flood of novels, periodicals, pamphlets, and newspapers poured from the presses. In France, the number of titles doubled between mid-century and the outbreak of the Revolution, while in Germany it has been estimated that more than half a million publications of various kinds appeared during the course of the century.

Two characteristics of what can reasonably be called a cultural revolution should be noted. First, culture became increasingly commercialized. Access was no longer governed by royal, aristocratic, or clerical patrons but depended solely on the consumer's ability to pay. Of course 'culture as commodity' was not the invention of the eighteenth century—Londoners had paid for admission to Shakespeare's Globe Theatre, for example—but the scale and scope of the expansion constituted a real watershed in European history. Secondly, the increase in the number of active participants created a new kind of cultural space—the public sphere. Situated between the private world of the family and the official world of the state, the public sphere was a forum in which previously isolated individuals could come together to exchange information, ideas, and criticism. Whether communicating with each other at long range by subscribing to the same periodicals, or meeting face to face in a coffee house (very much an eighteenth-century phenomenon) or in one of the new voluntary associations, such as a reading club or Masonic lodge, the public acquired a collective weight far greater than the sum of its individual members.

It was from the public sphere that a new source of authority emerged to challenge the opinion-makers—or rather opinion-dictators—of the old regime: public opinion. By the middle of the eighteenth century, it was already clear that a new arbiter had emerged. In 1747, for example, La Font de Saint Yenne (usually regarded as the first modern art critic) wrote: 'It is only in the mouths of those firm and equitable men who compose the public . . . that we can find the language of truth.' Even the chief government censor in France, Malesherbes, recognized that in the literary world 'only the public is entitled to judge'. And not only in the literary world: having cut its teeth criticizing paintings or novels, the public moved on to politics. The timing of this transition naturally varied across Europe. First in the field were Britain and the Dutch Republic, for they had in common relatively high rates of literacy and urbanization and enjoyed a relatively liberal censorship regime. *Mutatis mutandis*, at the other extreme and the other end of Europe, it is next to impossible to find anything resembling a public sphere or public opinion in Russia before the nineteenth century. Yet even there the German-born Catherine the Great was at pains to cultivate a Russian image, out of deference to national sensitivities.

No less than war, the influence of public opinion was ubiquitous. Indeed, public opinion often had to be taken into account *before* states decided to go to war. Even before the French Revolution institutionalized public opinion as a determinant of foreign policy, its influence could make itself felt. It helped to propel a reluctant Sir Robert Walpole into making war in 1739 and helped to propel a reluctant George III into making peace in 1783. The developments that underpinned the emergence of public opinion were perhaps even more influential in promoting social and economic change, for they promoted that mobility which destabilized the static society of orders. As Sheilagh Ogilvie tells us below, 'societies constrained economies as much as economies revolutionized society', so this cultural shift had important economic consequences. So it did for Europe's relations with the rest of the world. On the one hand, it helped to generate a popular imperialism more ambitious than anything seen hitherto; on the other hand, it helped to make colonists less inclined to accept metropolitan subjection. In other words, by promoting literacy and thus the formation of public opinion as an alternative source of legitimacy, authoritarian governments were digging their own graves, both at home and abroad.

So, whether a political, social, economic, or cultural point of entry is chosen for access to the eighteenth century, the fluidity of these categories will soon become apparent. Within each of them too, boundaries were in a constant state of flux, as power relationships waxed and waned. This applied most obviously to the political map of the continent. In 1700 the second-largest country in Europe (after Russia) was Poland, yet in 1800 it no longer existed, excised by the partitions of 1772, 1793, and 1795. There was nothing inevitable about this collapse. In the previous century, as often as not it was the Poles who lorded it over the Russians, Prussia was a Polish fief, and it was the Polish King John Sobieski who raised the siege of Vienna by the Turks in 1683. Moreover, between 1697 and 1763 Poland was joined in personal union with Saxony, the most prosperous and progressive principality in the Holy Roman Empire.

The failure of Poland-Saxony to fulfil its potential to become the dominant power in central and eastern Europe tells us a good deal about what was needed for international success in the eighteenth century. A geographical explanation looks attractive but does not take us very far. Although Poland's location on the North European plain certainly meant that it lacked natural frontiers, it was no more vulnerable than Prussia, whose capital Berlin was captured twice during the Seven Years War. Nor does its socio-economic backwardness provide a satisfactory answer, for in this respect it was probably less handicapped than Russia. Poland possessed huge resources of raw materials for which western Europe had an acute and growing need, notably grain and 'naval stores' (construction materials for ships). Yet it was the Prussians, who took control of the River Vistula by the first and second partitions, and the Russians, who wrested control of the northern shore of the Black Sea from the Turks, who were the chief beneficiaries. However contingent it might appear, the accident of personality seems to have been decisive. While Russia under Peter the Great (1689–1725) and Prussia under Frederick William I (1713–40) and his even more formidable son Frederick the Great (1740–86) wrenched their countries into the first rank of European powers by subordinating everything to military power, the Saxon kings of Poland Augustus II (1697–1733) and Augustus III (1733–63) squandered their resources on self-indulgent display. In the process they created at Dresden one of the most glamorous courts, sophisticated cultures, and beautiful cities in Europe, but that counted for little when the Prussian armies arrived.

The military victories and diplomatic *coups* that transformed the map of eastern Europe were supported by—and were symptomatic of—a political development of a more structural kind: the emergence of the modern state, famously defined by Max Weber as 'that agency in society which has a monopoly of legitimate force'. It had a long history, dating back well before the Reformation, in the course of which three crucial axioms were formed: first, politics came to be regarded as a discrete realm, independent of theology; secondly, the supreme authority in any polity came to be regarded as independent of any international agency such as the papacy or the Holy Roman Empire; and, thirdly, that authority also claimed a monopoly of legislation and allegiance within its borders. The civil and religious wars of the sixteenth and seventeenth centuries completed the formation of a concept of sovereignty that may have been exercised by a human agency such as a king or a parliament but that ultimately resided in an abstraction: the state. It was the eighteenth century that saw its final emergence to become, as Quentin Skinner has put it, 'the master-noun of political argument'.

From this perspective, it was the ability to achieve a monopoly of legitimate force that determined political success in eighteenth-century Europe. At one end of the scale there was Poland, where the dispersion of authority was such that each member of the parliament (*Sejm*) could veto any measure under consideration or even dissolve the assembly and nullify its legislation. The elective nature of the monarchy and the legal right to form confederations encouraged foreign intervention to promote foreign interests. No wonder the Poles found it so difficult to mobilize even a fraction of their resources to defend their independence, let alone take a proactive role in European politics. Especially, it might be added, when they were confronted by such autocratic polities as Russia and Prussia, ruled by such autocratic personalities as Peter the Great or Frederick the Great, neither of whom were obliged to consult anyone. As Julian Swann shows in Chapter 1, the 'absolutists' were never as absolute in practice as they claimed to be in theory, but in the land of the blind the one-eyed man was king.

There was more than one way of seeing. A state directed by a single person's will was able to respond more quickly than one governed by a constitution, but it was not necessarily able to respond more effectively. That was the lesson delivered by the Dutch in the seventeenth century when they defeated the Spanish and by the British in the eighteenth century when they defeated the French. Concentration of decision-making was not enough. Especially at a time when both physical and symbolic communication were difficult, the ordinary subject's cheering capacity for obstruction through simple inertia could defeat the most imperious will. Only voluntary cooperation, especially from the social élites, could translate authority into action. Frederick the Great was effective not because he took decisions by himself but because the system he had inherited, and the example he set, encouraged his nobles and burghers to cooperate in providing the men and the money for his armies. Even more successful was the parliamentary regime developed by the British, albeit only after a prolonged period of upheaval in the previous century. Its combination of power, wealth, and liberty promoted a demographically second-rate country to world-power status.

As the ground moved beneath their feet, European rulers needed to be nimble if they were to keep their balance. After an unpromising start, the Spanish Bourbons probably made the most of their opportunities, consolidating their power at home while expanding their empire both in the New World and in Italy. Never again, however, were their armies to dominate and devastate western and central Europe. The same could be said of their old enemy and polar opposite, Sweden, which never recovered from defeat at Poltava at the hands of Peter the Great in 1709 and the consequent loss of its Baltic empire. More protracted was the decline of the Dutch Republic, gradually succumbing to British direction 'like a long boat which follows in the wake of the warship to which it is tied', as Frederick the Great put it. The most eminent casualty, of course, was the Bourbon dynasty in France, pale from anaemia long before its terminal haemorrhage at the end of the 1780s. By that time the three forms of legitimacy identified by Max Weber—traditional, legal, and charismatic—had been eroded by a fatal combination of impotence abroad and despotism at home. It is difficult not to be exasperated at the sight of Louis XV and XVI consistently declining opportunities to adapt to changing conditions, especially the rise of the public sphere. On the other hand, those who seized power from their flaccid hands with such confidence proved to be no more adept at political management, soaring higher but falling harder.

The other main casualty of the century would seem to be Christianity in general and the Catholic Church in particular. Challenged by rationalism, marginalized by secularization, and expropriated by states old and new, both ideology and institution were certainly on the defensive from c.1750. Yet, as Derek Beales demonstrates, there is better reason to dub the eighteenth century 'the Christian Century' than 'the Age of Reason'. It was a period marked by several powerful religious revivals, an increased popularity of religious literature, and undimmed religious controversy. Even the terrible wounds inflicted after 1789 were beneficial in the long run, for the Church that emerged was much more populist, much more ultramontane, and generally better equipped to survive in a more pluralist world. The guillotining of a king or the mass drowning of priests is the kind of atrocity (or exploit, according to taste) that catches the eye. Quantitatively, however, it was the anonymous toiling masses who were the most conspicuous beneficiaries or victims. As Sheilagh Ogilvie shows, economic change was slow and fitful: industrially speaking, as the last quarter of the century began, most parts of Europe had changed little in the previous 100 or even 200 years. Despite population growth, agricultural and commercial expansion, and improvements in transport, proto-industrialization could become fully-fledged industrialization only when strong governments combined with strong markets to break down the traditional political and social framework. Although a number of 'industrial landscapes' developed further in the course of the century, it was only in England that the necessary conditions for a real qualitative leap came together.

Thin and patchy, this economic expansion could not absorb the rapidly growing number of Europeans. The inelasticity of food production drove up prices, while the inelasticity of industry pushed down wages. The result was impoverishment for that large proportion of the population that was not self-sufficient. A new kind of poverty emerged, not a sudden affliction by famine, plague, or war but a permanent state of malnutrition and underemployment. It was also a vicious circle, for the undernourished were not so wretched as to be unable to produce the children who perpetuated their misery. They were also increasingly at the mercy of market forces, as capitalism eroded the traditional society of orders and its values. This was a process that went furthest and fastest in the west and centre of Europe. In the east, in Prussia, Poland, Russia, and the eastern provinces of the Habsburg Monarchy, most of the rural population was bound to the soil and their lords as serfs. Legally their position was greatly inferior to their counterparts in the west, but materially they may have been better off, thanks to the lower population density and hence greater availability of land.

Of course, there were also those who found this ill wind bracing rather than enervating. With the price of land trebling and the prestige attached to landownership undiminished, the enterprising could flourish mightily. A key group were the tenant farmers, to whom credit for most of the agricultural innovations of the period must be given. Perhaps best placed to make the most of the century's opportunities was the aristocrat who owned large estates rich in mineral resources, served by good communications and located in industrializing regions, and—perhaps most important of all—was blessed with the necessary intellectual and personal qualities to become an entrepreneur. In an ideal world, he would also marry into a family engaged in government finance, investment banking, and overseas commerce, the other fast lanes to wealth. He would need a conscience robust enough to allow him to forget the involuntary services performed by the seven million slaves transported from Africa to the Caribbean during the course of the century. He would also be well advised to be an Englishman and thus immune to the sudden visits from Nemesis in the shape of war or revolution, to which his continental colleagues were so prone, especially after 1789.

However one defines the period—does the 'long eighteenth century' of 1688–1815 make more sense than the short version of 1715–89, indeed can any two dates biting into the seamless web of history have meaning?—the scope and intensity of the changes described and analysed in this volume appear to be very striking. Yet it would be salutary to remember the observation of a character in *The Leopard* by Giuseppe Tomasi di Lampedusa (himself a duke and a prince) that 'everything must change so that everything may remain the same'. In the chapters that follow, the forces making for continuity have been given as much attention as those generating more glamorous change. In the conclusion, stock will be taken and the new disentangled from the old.

1

Politics and the state in eighteenth-century Europe

Julian Swann

The eighteenth century was a formative period in the development of both modern notions of politics and the idea of the state. In 1700 the majority of Europeans were subjects of hereditary rulers, who conceived of their state as a patrimony for whose conservation they were accountable only to God. Only four years later, Bishop Bossuet won the applause of Louis XIV for his *Politics Drawn from Holy Scripture*, arguably the definitive defence of divine-right monarchy. Yet, by 1793, the tomb of the Sun King had been desecrated and his unfortunate descendant guillotined by a republican regime. The French Revolution, with its ideology of national sovereignty and of the liberty and equality of the citizen, has been interpreted as an important landmark on the road to modern democratic government ever since. Nor were events in France an isolated phenomenon. The Americans had already thrown off the yoke of British rule, and, perhaps more significantly, founded a new republic whose political order was based upon a written constitution. They had been closely followed by Poland, which adopted its own ill-fated constitution in May 1791. A revival of political radicalism in Britain, the campaigns of the Dutch patriots, and the revolt of the Belgians against Joseph II all appeared to suggest that it was monarchy itself, and not just its divinely ordained status, that was in danger.

If the French Revolution was a terrible shock for the crowned heads of Europe, it was a long way from being their Nemesis. As the revolutionary armies sought to spread their gospel that 'all monarchs were tyrants', they discovered to their dismay that such an ideology fell on stony ground. The failure of the French to attract substantial support was more than just a reaction to the rapacity of their troops. The durability of the European old regime was also due, in large measure, to the ability of its rulers to respond effectively to an alternative conception of government. Since the Renaissance a new vision of the state as an abstract entity had been coming into view. Throughout most of the early modern period, the patrimonial and impersonal concepts of the state lived uneasily side by side, but by 1800 the balance had shifted decisively. Continuity in government was no longer simply a matter of hereditary right; instead the state was increasingly perceived as autonomous, independent of whomever happened to be ruling at any given moment. The state now represented the source of legitimate authority and governments acted in its name. As these ideas took root, they were accompanied by a change in philosophy regarding the ruler and the subject. The pious hope that the prince would treat his subjects in a paternalistic and Christian fashion was gradually superseded by a belief in the existence of a governing contract. In return for obedience from their subjects, rulers were now expected to take an interest in their happiness and well-being. The unspoken corollary was that failure could result in the breaking of that contract. With the exceptions of France and Poland, the map of the states and crowned heads of Europe in 1800 resembled that of a century earlier. Yet deeper currents were transforming the meaning of both politics and government and this chapter will assess their impact.

European states: monarchies, republics, and despotisms

In *The Spirit of the Laws*, probably the most influential political text of the eighteenth century, Montesquieu revised Aristotle's classical trilogy of monarchy, aristocracy, and democracy into a new formula of monarchy, republic, and despotism. His ideas found a receptive audience in literate circles from Lisbon to Moscow, and they supply a convenient starting place for an examination of European political systems. The continent was dominated by the absolute monarchs, exemplified by those of France, and including, amongst others, the rulers of Austria, Prussia, Spain, Portugal, Savoy, and Denmark. What these states had in common were hereditary princes whose authority was based upon a recognized line of succession. Although they claimed that their sovereignty was divinely sanctioned, there were theoretical limits to their power because they were expected to obey religious and natural law and, in particular, to respect the lives and property of their subjects. In practice, they were restrained by a host of corporate institutions including provincial estates, the Church, judicial bodies, and municipal councils. In addition, they were obliged to weigh very carefully the interests of social élites. The monarch was the point of unity in these corporate and particularist societies, which lacked any national representative body to challenge royal authority.

Where national parliaments existed, the authority of the ruler was often sharply reduced, and, when fortune favoured them, princes were quick to dispense with their services. The Portuguese crown offered a perfect example of this phenomenon by refusing to summon the Cortes for more than a century after 1698, once the discovery of Brazilian gold made the process of haggling over taxation superfluous. Without the independence provided by a personal El Dorado, English kings were less fortunate. The seventeenth century was particularly traumatic, witnessing civil war and the execution of Charles I and the subsequent overthrow of James II. Henri IV famously quipped that 'Paris is worth a Mass' when converting to Catholicism in order to secure his claim on the French throne, but after Charles II the Stuarts were either too principled or too stupid to follow his lead. The chief beneficiaries of their obstinacy were the members of the House of Hanover. What followed was an era of remarkable stability in British politics because of the general acceptance of the constitutional convention that sovereignty lay with the king in parliament. When both sides of the political equation were working in harmony, it proved possible to mobilize resources with an effectiveness unmatched by supposedly more absolute states elsewhere.

Sweden was perhaps closest to the British model and in the Riksdag it possessed a strong tradition of national representation. During the reigns of Karl XI and especially that of the mercurial Karl XII it seemed as if the crown had thrown off its shackles and established its absolutist credentials. At his coronation in 1697, Karl XII refused to sign the traditional accession charter and even had the audacity to crown himself in an unequivocal demonstration of his political intentions. The Riksdag was never summoned during his reign, but Sweden's deviation from its constitutional norm proved short-lived. Despite his military talents, Karl led his country to crushing defeat in the Great Northern War. When he died on campaign in 1718, he left no direct heir and the Riksdag filled the political vacuum with a vengeance. His successor, Ulrika Eleonora, was elected queen on the condition that she accept both an accession charter and the constitution of 1719. That document remained the basis of government throughout what became known as Sweden's 'age of liberty', and the monarch's prerogative was reduced to the 'right to eat and sleep'. The political pendulum swung back towards the crown in 1772 when an increasingly discredited system was overturned by Gustav III's remarkably popular royalist *coup*. It did not, however, mark the demise of the Riksdag and Sweden continued with a form of mixed government until the emergence of a fully democratic system in the twentieth century.

If Britain and Sweden provided working models of parliamentary monarchies, the Polish-Lithuanian Commonwealth offered a salutary lesson of another kind. Together with the rather peculiar examples of the papacy and the Holy Roman Empire, it represented one of the few surviving elective monarchies. On the death of the king the country entered into an interregnum prior to an elaborate election involving the whole of the numerous Polish nobility, the *szlachta*, which formed the political nation. Needless to say, the process was an almost open invitation to foreign powers to meddle in Polish affairs, and, after Peter I's victory in the Great Northern War, no king could hope to remain in Warsaw without Russian acquiescence. The royal election was, however, more of a symptom than the cause of Poland's frailty that would result in successive partitions of the kingdom and its extinction as a state by the end of the century.

Poland's sadly predictable disappearance from the political map in 1795 was followed a decade later by that of the Holy Roman Empire. It has led many to assume that the political structure of the empire was moribund. Certainly the eighteenth and nineteenth centuries belonged to states like Prussia that proved capable of fighting wars of territorial acquisition. The experience of the twentieth century has, however, prompted sober reflection on the desirability of such models and has inspired a fresh look at the Empire. Although the emperor was elected, the process involved none of the noble republican anarchy displayed in Poland. Instead, the nine electors, composed of the territorial princes of Bavaria, Bohemia, Hanover, the Palatinate, Prussia, and Saxony, plus their ecclesiastical counterparts from Mainz, Cologne, and Trier, consistently chose a Habsburg candidate. Only when an eligible male was lacking, as in 1740, did they opt for the Bavarian, Charles VII. A Habsburg emperor worked to the advantage of all. Having long since abandoned any hopes of moulding the Empire into a cohesive state, the Habsburgs, with the notable exception of Joseph II, had become defenders of the status quo. What this meant in practice was a willingness to protect the independence of the imperial cities, ecclesiastical states, and minor princes against the ambitions of more powerful neighbours.

The political systems of European monarchies were far from uniform, but, whether they lived under the absolute or parliamentary variety, most commentators were convinced that their government was in one way or another limited. For an élite schooled in Aristotle and fortified by Montesquieu there was an acute awareness that monarchy could degenerate into despotism. Whenever political theorists looked for a contemporary example of such a government, their eyes fell upon either the Ottoman sultans or the Russian tsars and tsarinas. Without doubt these genuinely autocratic monarchies were distinct from the other types we have so far examined. Neither had a stable or recognized succession and they were prey to bloodthirsty struggles for power. On securing the throne, a sultan normally murdered his brothers. In Moscow, a succession crisis followed the death of every eighteenth-century ruler, with the élite guards regiments acting in the same decisive fashion as the janissaries in Constantinople. No less a figure than Catherine II owed her crown to collusion in the overthrow and murder of her husband, Peter III. Russia had no tradition of constitutional government, nor had it developed the corporatist structures so common further west. Its rulers, like the sultans, presided over a truly autocratic government and their example was a fearsome reminder of the dangers of despotism.

The last major species of polity to be found in Europe was the republic. The Venetian and especially the Dutch republics were international states of some significance, but the majority were small city states such as Genoa, Lucca, or Geneva. Venice, and most of the smaller city states, had long lost any democratic component to their governments and were almost impermeable oligarchies. In the seven provinces of the Dutch Republic power was firmly in the hands of an oligarchy composed of the nobility and of the urban patricians or regents. Despite the overwhelming wealth and power of Holland, each province had equal representation at the Estates General. Holland tolerated a situation apparently to its disadvantage because of the presence of another force in the political equation, the provincial governors or stadholders. In William I, the Silent, and William III, the House of Orange had supplied the heroes of both the Dutch revolt and of the resistance to Louis XIV and it had long monopolized these offices. The stadholders possessed extensive powers of patronage, nominating military officers and appointing urban magistrates and provincial officials. Throughout its history, the Dutch state experienced almost permanent tension between the republican structure of its political system, defended most enthusiastically by the regents of Holland, and the potential for monarchy that the House of Orange represented. Scratch below the surface of any political crisis and the competing interests of the two parties are not hard to find.

Europe thus possessed a rich array of political systems, but what is striking from a modern perspective is the absence of any government based upon democratic consent. Eighteenth-century theorists frequently reflected upon the history of the ancient city states, but whatever their admiration for Athens or Rome they were convinced that a democratic system could never work in their own age. Should an attempt be made the only likely result was mob rule or anarchy. Even the great Jean-Jacques Rousseau, who preached the radical doctrine that sovereignty lay with the people in his celebrated *Contrat social*, was not convinced that his ideas could be applied to modern territorial states. Rare were visionaries like the Marquis d'Argenson who predicted 'that the House of Commons will one day govern England; in this way there will be a true democracy. Senators will be elected by every province and town, chosen by the plurality of all those capable of voting and for the duration of a parliament that will be fixed, no doubt, for three years.' For most of his contemporaries such ideas were utopian, and democracy was not recognized as a viable form of government.

High politics

Louis XIV died repenting that he had 'loved war too much'. It was an epitaph that could have been applied to most of his contemporaries, because war and its attendant military and diplomatic arts were the true sport of kings. The causes of conflict remained surprisingly traditional. As they reflected on their youthful impetuosity, both Louis XIV and Frederick II admitted pursuing personal glory on the battlefield. Dynastic issues were even more significant, and the wars of the Spanish, Polish, and Austrian successions provide firm evidence of the strength of patrimonial attitudes amongst European rulers. For the Habsburg emperor, Charles VI, the failure to produce a male heir meant that much of his diplomatic energy had to be directed into persuading the European powers to accept the Pragmatic Sanction by which his daughter, the future empress Maria Theresa, would succeed him. The Habsburgs also remained loyal to their traditional practice of ruling as a family. While Maria Theresa and her eldest son Joseph II shared power in Vienna, his younger brother, Leopold, ruled as Grand Duke of Tuscany and their uncle, Charles Alexander of Lorraine, presided over the court in Brussels. To the chagrin of numerous British statesmen, both George I and George II kept a similarly proprietorial eye on their native electorate of Hanover. Even the most cursory glance at the activities of the great peace conferences of Utrecht or Aix-la-Chapelle reveals the immense significance accorded to balancing the respective family interests of Habsburg and Bourbon. Nor did the Revolution mark a decisive break with this practice, as the comic-opera attempts of Napoleon to accommodate the regal ambitions of his relatives demonstrated.

The continuing weight of dynastic objectives in international affairs underlines a fundamental feature of eighteenth-century politics. It was the monarch who played a personal and usually decisive part in the formation of policy. The reigns of Karl XII, Frederick II, or Napoleon provide dramatic examples of the prince literally risking the future of the House and even the very existence of the state on the roll of the military dice. Less cavalier rulers were also expected to direct government themselves, or at least to appoint a minister to do so on their behalf. That the eighteenth century is remembered for the reigns of Catherine II, Charles III, Maria Theresa, or Joseph II is due, in part, to the dedication, energy, and intelligence that they brought to the task of government. The problems of Louis XV and Louis XVI were exacerbated by the pressure they faced to follow the trail blazed by the Sun King. Both men were indecisive and shy, lacking the character required to govern. More damaging was their unwillingness to return to an alternative model of kingship perfected by Louis XIII which involved ruling through a powerful first minister. The eighteenth century had its equivalents to Richelieu and Olivares, most strikingly the Marquis de Pombal. Dom José I of Portugal was not one of the continent's more enlightened rulers, but he had the good sense to appoint the ruthless and resourceful Pombal. Even in constitutional regimes the monarch was central to the political process and Robert Walpole, William Pitt, or Lord North needed to command the allegiance of their sovereign as well as that of parliament.

These examples make it tempting to assume that there was 'no politics beyond the public person of the king', as the theorists of absolutism argued. Certainly high politics, defined as that affecting the great issues of state such as war and peace, religion, taxation, and internal administration, makes no sense without reference to the sovereign. To influence the decision–making process it was necessary to gain access to the monarch and naturally enough the court was the central arena for political struggle. For the ruler, the court was simultaneously household, seat of government, and the stage upon which to project an image of majesty to awe both subjects and foreign rivals. The fifteenth-century Burgundian dukes had been consummate practitioners of this art and the ritual of the Habsburg court descended directly from them. At Versailles, however, Louis XIV had raised court spectacle to new heights and the image of the Sun King shone brightly throughout Europe. Elsewhere royal palaces reached a new level of splendour and the cost of the imperial court quintupled in the course of the fifty years after 1672. In 1701 a phenomenal 75 per cent of the expenditure of Max Emmanuel of Bavaria was lavished on the court and Ernest August of Hanover and Friedrich Karl Von Schönborn, prince-bishop of Würzburg, both topped 50 per cent.

Rulers of these comparatively minor states were engaged in a fierce cultural competition, designed to add honour and lustre to their dynasty. Further east, the great magnates of Hungary and Poland had their own palaces with the Esterházy, Radziwills, or Czartoryski, employing hundreds of dependent gentry in their households or private armies. They too sought to use display as a means of conducting their wider political strategies.

After the death of Frederick I, the personal idiosyncrasies of his successors ensured that Prussia never developed a court culture. For those seeking influence, access to the king was no less important than elsewhere, it was simply attained through other channels, notably the army or the highest offices of the bureaucracy. The militarization of monarchy, with Joseph II and Frederick II rarely seen out of uniform, was an invention of the eighteenth century that has been much copied by authoritarian rulers, but their rejection of the court was less influential. The shock of the French Revolution convinced many crowned heads of the need for power to be displayed, and the ever astute Napoleon created a court with its own guard, ceremonial, and ultimately nobility within a few years of seizing power in 1799.

High politics was a fight to win access to the monarch either directly or through his ministers or intimates. Achieving that aim alone was nearly impossible and court politics was dominated by factions. These cabals sought to manipulate the monarch not only by placing themselves or their creatures in the royal council, but also by monopolizing the offices of the household. Great aristocrats no more become gentlemen of the bedchamber out of subservience than they became grooms of the stool out of a desire to wipe the royal bottom. They accepted these appointments because contact with the prince was power and power meant offices, influence, and wealth for themselves and their families. With the men away from the court for long periods in the army or on official postings, responsibility devolved upon aristocratic women, many of whom personally directed the factions themselves.

Thanks to the efforts of Frederick William I, who created his celebrated General Directory in 1723, Prussia's military and fiscal administration was heavily centralized and came closest to a modern bureaucratic ethic. Prussia was also distinguished by the absence of a ministerial ethos and there was no Kaunitz, Struensee, or Choiseul sitting at the right hand of Frederick William or his successor. Indeed one expert has described ministerial tasks under Frederick II 'as being little more than secretarial'. Prussia was very much the exception. In general, eighteenth-century governments did not have clearly defined boundaries between the court and the government or bureaucracy. There was nothing incongruous about a palace having royal apartments squeezed alongside council chambers, or of state business being conducted in the king's bedchamber. Nor were ministers or other officers professionals in any modern sense. Many had actually bought or inherited their offices, especially in France where venality was most solidly entrenched, with everything from the office of judge to that of tester of spirituous liquors up for sale. Other individuals were simply too important to ignore and, for example, Maria Theresa suffered acute embarrassment trying to keep incompetent grandees, such as Prince Paul Anton Esterházy, from inflicting irreparable damage on her armies.

Ministers and leading state officials were overwhelmingly noble. This was, however, more than just the result of prejudice in favour of an élite social group because nobles were the most likely to have the education and training required for office. Indeed, too high a birth could be a disadvantage because monarchs feared mighty subjects who might outshine or even compete with themselves. It was not a coincidence that so many distinguished royal servants including Kaunitz, Pombal, Campomanes, and the majority of the French ministers of the eighteenth century came from the middling ranks of their respective nobilities. They could be entrusted with great responsibilities, be showered with signs of royal favour, and, unlike members of the great aristocratic houses, be disgraced without risk. Monarchs were not, of course, restricted to seeking advice from those who held ministerial office and they had numerous networks of informal counsel. They regularly consulted members of their extended family, courtiers, and respected generals, diplomats, or administrators. As we have seen, the Habsburgs ruled as a family and they were not alone. Louis XIV kept up a detailed and sensitive correspondence with his young grandson, Philip V, and for many years Louis XV was advised by his cousin, the Prince de Conti.

High politics was, therefore, a struggle for the ear of the monarch and for the goodwill of the power brokers who controlled access to his person and to the patronage dispensed in his name. At times it can appear as little more than a catalogue of intrigues, with power being sought as an end in itself. The most authoritative recent historian of pre-reform Prussia has, for example, written that Hardenberg's enthusiasm for opposing Napoleon was inspired by the realization that it was only way of stopping his rival, Haugwitz. Opponents of Cardinal de Fleury in France, headed by the Maréchal de Belle-Isle, vehemently advocated war against Austria in 1740 because the ageing cleric was known to be pacific. Backstabbing and infighting were common because ministers had no sense of collective responsibility. Individuals were summoned to advise the sovereign and they were under no obligation to concur with the opinions of others. Effective government was dependent upon a ruler with sufficient character to transform potentially destructive rivalries into creative ones.

In these political battles, both advancement and security depended as much upon factional and clientage ties as they did on individual talent. Factions formed around the heir to the throne and other members of the royal family as well as in the entourage of ministers. Nor was it a coincidence that royal mistresses, such as Madame de Maintenon or Madame de Pompadour, were simultaneously feted and loathed by fellow courtiers. Given the power a mistress could wield, there were constant attempts to plant a pliable favourite onto unsuspecting monarchs. Christiane Wilhelmine von Gravenitz provided a dramatic illustration of successful intrigue. She was introduced to Duke Eberhard Ludwig of Württemburg initially as part of a factional ruse to gain his confidence. The infatuated prince subsequently caused an international incident by contracting a bigamous marriage with her. Once the dust had settled, the family of Christiane Wilhelmine was set fair for a period of dominance in the duke's council and for a lucrative monopoly of his patronage. Such incidents were legion and the spoils of office could be immense. Robert Walpole amassed a colossal fortune during his time in power, and eighteenth-century rulers lavished titles, lands, and sinecures on their favourites.

We should, however, avoid reducing high politics to nothing more than a history of scavenging cliques. Serious differences about policy and the exercise of power did exist, even if they lacked the coherence of the ideological politics of conservatism, liberalism, and socialism that emerged with such force during the nineteenth century. The principal cause of conflict in high political circles was foreign policy. From the diplomatic revolution of 1756 until the Revolution, French court factions could be identified by their attitude to the infamous Austrian alliance. In Stockholm the political parties, the Hats and the Caps, also fought over foreign policy objectives. The Hats, generously funded by Versailles, berated their opponents for their pro-Russian policy, which, they claimed, had undermined the alliance with France. The Caps, not surprisingly, attracted funds from Russia and also from Britain. Nor was foreign policy the only source of political strife. In the age of Enlightenment religion had lost none of its power to divide. The courts of Lisbon, Madrid, Versailles, and Vienna, to name but a few, were all agitated by the campaign against the Jesuits. The grisly fate of the tsarevich, Alexei, who was arrested and tortured to death on the orders of his father, owed much to his sympathy for the Old Believers who were fomenting opposition to Peter I's religious reforms.

His tragic death offers a striking illustration of the seriousness of high politics and the price to be paid for open opposition to the sovereign. In Portugal, Pombal transformed an attempt on the life of José I into a vicious show trial of his aristocratic opponents, the Duke of Aveiron and the Marquesa de Távora Velho, whose illustrious titles were not enough to save them from torture and execution. The Dolgorukov clan in Russia suffered a similar fate after its abortive attempt to impose an accession charter on Empress Anna in 1730. In constitutional monarchies the death penalty for political crimes was not unknown. In Sweden, the bitter feuding between the parties led to the execution of Erik Brahe and seven others in 1756. French monarchs, despite their absolutist reputation and the presence of the notorious Bastille, were comparatively tolerant of the inherent factionalism of Versailles. Exile was the punishment reserved for ministers, courtiers, or members of the parlements who attracted the king's displeasure. For the élite, high political manœuvring was not a capital crime; that was one of the Revolution's more dubious innovations.

Factionalism was a natural product of a political culture that had not developed the concept of a 'loyal' opposition. To resist the will of the sovereign was treason, and to avoid exile, or even the block, it was necessary to tread carefully. The time-honoured solution was to declare that His Majesty had been deceived by false counsel and that resistance was in fact a legitimate attempt to bring truth to the feet of the throne. It was a risky strategy, which helps to explain why critics of a reigning monarch were prone to attach themselves to the entourage of a member of the royal family. Even in Britain, it was still considered politic for the 'opposition' to group itself around Frederick, prince of Wales, or after his death the future George III. Bute rose to power through this route, while in France the accession of Louis XVI brought a return to favour of Maurepas, who had been in disgrace for twenty-five years. There was nevertheless a clear distinction between absolute and constitutional monarchies. Like any of his continental cousins, George III could choose a favourite, but he could not keep him in power without the support of parliament.

Enlightened absolutism

If war and diplomacy remained the principal concerns of European rulers, there was a detectable broadening of their conception of government. In the course of the eighteenth century attention was increasingly focused upon the health, education, and happiness of the subject and it has led historians to identify a new species of monarch, the enlightened absolutist. It is easy to deny the existence of such an unlikely hybrid by arguing that this sudden interest in public welfare was a reaction to the need for fitter and better-educated soldiers and for the money to pay for them. Alternatively, it can be interpreted as a rational response to the spread of enlightened ideas, especially religious scepticism from France and Britain. Yet we need to be wary of such cynicism. The search for an increase in military effectiveness was not incompatible with a genuine desire to improve the life of the subject. Nor did monarchs initiate reforms because they feared the enlightened ideas emanating from Voltaire, Diderot, Hume, Rousseau, and their disciples. What the Enlightenment provided was the optimistic belief that, by applying the cool eye of reason to the affairs of state, governments could become stronger and more efficient. Not that it was necessary for an effective reformer to be enlightened in a cultural or intellectual sense. Frederick William I scored highly on the despotic scale, and yet he was incredibly successful in preparing Prussia for its phenomenal expansion during the eighteenth century.

In Germany the impetus for a more interventionist state sprang, in part, from the writings of the natural law philosophers, such as Samuel Pufendorf and Christian Grotius, and, especially, from the

Cameralist school. Cameralism was preoccupied with increasing state revenue and its theorists argued that a prosperous ruler required a numerous, healthy, and productive population. As a consequence, Cameralists encouraged policies that regulated not only the economy, but also the social and physical lives of the people. By the early eighteenth century, these ideas dominated the Protestant universities of Halle, Göttingen, and Leipzig. Cameralist influence was always strongest in the Protestant states, although the remarkable success of the Prussians after 1740 caused serious reflection elsewhere. The leading Austrian ministers of mid-century, Friedrich Wilhelm Haugwitz and Kaunitz, were both sympathetic to the movement, as was Catherine II of Russia, whose policies, while dosed liberally with enlightened rhetoric, had a Cameralist flavour. From mid-century, the French Physiocratic school of economic thinkers, headed by Quesnay, Mirabeau, Le Mercier de la Rivière, and Dupont de Nemours, provided the impetus for a new generation of reformers. They preached the virtues of free trade, notably in grain, as a route to agricultural improvement and called for representative assemblies of property-holders to oversee local administration.

Concern with public welfare found an echo in another reforming current—that provided by the Church. In Prussia, the Lutheran Pietist movement, which preached the virtues of education, self-improvement, and Christian social responsibility, had a profound affect on Frederick William I. Despite the immense intellectual gulf separating the king from his son, he would have had no difficulty in recognizing himself as the 'first servant of the state'. It was the purpose of that service that divided them. Frederick William believed that, by constantly striving to strengthen and improve the administration of his realm, he was doing God's work. Frederick II rejected Christianity at an early age, and yet he found an alternative creed in state service. He was not alone and the Herculean efforts of Peter I to transform Russia had as their leitmotif service to the state—a duty that was both compulsory and for life. It was Joseph II, however, who revealed just how far a conscientious monarch could go in the pursuit of this particular Holy Grail. He wrote: 'everything exists for the state; this word contains everything, so all who live in it should come together to promote its interests.' Nor was he reluctant to put his principles into practice. This curious monarch was forever touring his immense domains, cajoling officials, and promulgating laws, all in an ultimately fruitless attempt to create a unified state out of a dynastic accident. By working himself into an early grave, he gave a particularly poignant example of how far proprietary notions of kingship had receded. Yet Joseph and Frederick were exceptional characters and in the smaller states of Europe patrimonial attitudes continued to flourish undisturbed. The rulers of Baden, Hesse-Cassel, or Mainz came closest to fulfilling the ideals of paternalistic rule and it was here that such ideas survived the longest.

The Catholic Church was another source of reforming energy. Foremost amongst the ecclesiastical innovators was the Italian cleric Ludovico Antonio Muratori. In his *Manual for Princes* of 1749 he argued that politics and morality were inseparable and that rulers could not escape their obligation to ensure the well-being of the subject. What stopped this from being a pious platitude was his accompanying insistence that the objective could be achieved by reform. In a second work, *On a Well Ordered Devotion*, Muratori called for a simpler less baroque piety purged of the pilgrimages, saints' days, and festivals of post-tridentine Catholicism. His ideas fed into another reforming stream within Catholic thought, Jansenism. Few would now dispute that Jansenism, originally an austere Augustinian movement, was one of the most significant intellectual influences of the age. Its disciples called for a less baroque worship that would elevate the role of the parish priest and encourage the laity to read the scriptures and participate actively in works of charity. The contribution of Jansenists can be detected in most of the major religious reform programmes implemented after 1750, and their ascendancy was underlined by the suppression of their great enemies, the Jesuits, in 1773. In France, however, Jansenists suffered rigorous persecution, provoking opposition that did as much harm to Church and State as the worst jibes of the *philosophes*.

Enlightened absolutism should, therefore, be seen as a process whereby European monarchies responded to a changing conception of government. Rulers increasingly described themselves as the first servant of the state, rather than as its proprietor, and through the teachings of a broad range of religious and secular thinkers they came to accept an obligation to promote public welfare. As they did so, the notion of government as a science, requiring the application of reason and method, took hold. Policies were to be selected because they worked, even if that meant poaching them from rivals and then tailoring them to suit local conditions. The optimistic belief that man and his institutions could be improved gave an unprecedented impetus to reform, with the state seeking to regulate the lives of the public in a more systematic fashion than ever before.

As the relationship between the sovereign and the state was redefined, so too was that between the state and the subject. Traditionally rulers granted collective rights or privileges to corporate bodies, not individuals, but in the course of the eighteenth century the potentially revolutionary idea that men had universal rights began to affect government thinking. Nothing illustrates this phenomenon better than the issue of religious toleration. Frederick II once exclaimed that, 'since the peaceful practice of one's religion is an integral part of what man perceives as his happiness, I shall never deviate from my firm resolve to protect the rights and liberties of every religion. The disputes of clerics are in no way the concern of princes.' Here the philosopher king came close to echoing Montesquieu, who in his *Persian Letters* had written: 'It is no use to say that it is not in the king's interest to allow more than one religion in the state. Even if every religion in the world gathered together there it would not do him any harm, because every single one of them commands obedience and preaches respect for authority.' There is no reason to doubt Frederick II's sincerity, although his convictions did dovetail nicely with Prussian state interests. The acquisition of Silesia in 1740 had brought a substantial Catholic minority into an overwhelmingly Lutheran kingdom. By making toleration official policy, to the extent of encouraging the construction of a Catholic cathedral in Berlin, the king sent an unequivocal message of reassurance to his new subjects. At mid-century his attitude remained exceptional. During the 1750s French Huguenots suffered the last great wave of state-sponsored persecution, and Jansenists within the Gallican Church fared little better. Catholics in Britain and the Dutch Republic were subject to legal discrimination, and, when the outraged Maria Theresa discovered a community of Protestants living in Upper Austria, she exiled them to remote Transylvania.

Yet, if religious persecution remained a feature of the period, it was more fitful and less intense than during the age of reformation. As the eighteenth century progressed, governments became convinced of the benefits offered by a more relaxed stance towards individual belief. The notorious Calas case of 1762 marked a closing chapter in the history of the official persecution of French Protestants, and one of the last free acts of Louis XVI in 1788 was to restore civil status to Calvinists denied since the revocation of the Edict of Nantes in 1685. These gains were consolidated during the Revolution and they were extended to other minorities, notably the Jews. Events in France were preceded by Joseph II's relaxation of the harsh restrictions on the civil liberties of the Jewish population. Similar examples can be found from Portugal, where Pombal abolished the distinction between old and new Christians, to Russia, where Catherine II pursued a policy of *de facto* religious toleration distinguished by her self-appointed right to interfere in the organization of the many faiths within her polyglot empire.

The spread of enlightened ideas had undoubtedly helped the campaign for toleration, as had the more utilitarian notion that states' could ill-afford to lose valuable subjects. Yet it is also possible to identify a religious motive for reform. Jansenists believed that an end to persecution would smooth the path of conversion for Protestants and Jews. Joseph II was probably familiar with this argument and it helps to explain his disappointment when freedom of worship heralded the first serious upsurge in Protestantism seen in his domains since the early seventeenth century. What the issue of toleration highlights is the curious phenomenon whereby *philosophes* and devout Christians could be pulling in the same direction, but for completely different reasons. Joseph II reduced the number of religious houses belonging to the contemplative orders. Yet there was more to the story than just an enlightened monarch pursuing a policy of secularization. He employed the revenue taken from the Church to fund charitable and educational works, notably the *Armeninstitut* system of workhouses for the poor and unemployed. The emperor was no less committed to the creation of a numerous and disciplined clergy, engaged in what he perceived to be the useful occupations of education and health care. The revolutionary Constituent Assembly made even more dramatic changes to the structure of the French Church, confiscating church lands and imposing the Civil Constitution of the Clergy in June 1790. Once again it is possible to detect the influence of Jansenism through the presence of two leading draftsmen of the Civil Constitution, abbés Grégoire and Camus. In France these changes led to schism because, with Louis XVI estranged from the Revolution, the Constituent lacked the authority necessary to impose its measures on the Pope and the aristocratic episcopate.

The gradual acceptance of religious pluralism was accompanied by a willingness to allow freedom of expression. Amongst the more precocious in this domain were Britain, where censorship effectively lapsed after 1695, the Dutch Republic, and Poland. In the latter case the very feebleness of the state ensured that the great enlightened tracts were rapidly available. Elsewhere censorship was increasingly brought under state control and before 1789 this was accompanied by a more liberal attitude towards what could legitimately be published. A brief spell in the Bastille was a rite of passage for the French *philosophes*, but from *mid-century* the chief censor, Lamoignon de Malesherbes, helped foster a more relaxed climate. Censorship did not, however, collapse completely until the pre-revolutionary crisis of 1788–9. A free press was one of the key articles of the Declaration of the Rights of Man, but it could not survive the Terror and was not firmly established in France before 1871. Despite his own philosophical temperament, Frederick II was not keen that his subjects share his passion for intellectual speculation. As Lessing wryly observed, freedom of expression consisted of the right to be as rude about religion as one liked. Joseph II went furthest and abolished prior censorship altogether, even permitting criticisms of his own actions. He was nevertheless capable of arbitrary interventions, notably his decision to ban performances of Beaumarchais's *Figaro*.

The eighteenth century thus saw some movement towards recognition of individual rights and it marked a crucial step in the direction of the modern liberal state. The same forces were at work in the world of the law. Europeans were not born equal and, depending on their social status, were subject to different legal tribunals and punishments. Significant advances were made in the area of judicial reform with a flurry of legal codes appearing after 1760, notably Grand Duke Leopold's Tuscan law code of 1786, the Prussian General Legal Code of 1794, and the Code Napoleon of 1804. These were important landmarks in the long battle to standardize the labyrinthine world of the law. It was, however, the French Revolution that went furthest towards enshrining the principle of legal equality in the Declaration of the Rights of Man, together with other civil liberties such as freedom of conscience and expression and protection from arbitrary arrest. This liberal and individualistic definition of citizens' rights culminated with the abolition of nobility in 1790.

The emerging concept of the citizen was accompanied by the growing belief that the state had an obligation to promote public welfare. Nowhere was this more clearly demonstrated than in the field of education. The need for specialist military training and for a pool of trained administrators prompted monarchs to establish academies for the noble élites. In his remorseless attempt to modernize Russia, Peter I established schools of engineering, artillery, and navigation, while in 1721 Frederick-William I merged the academies of Berlin, Kolberg, and Magdeburg into a single cadet school. Encouraged by Madame de Pompadour, Louis XV founded the École Militaire in 1751, and Maria Theresa established the Theresianum and the Oriental academy to educate future administrators and diplomats.

In 1773 the dissolution of the Jesuits, who had dominated educational provision since the sixteenth century, created a short-term crisis and a long-term opportunity for Catholic Europe. Government commissions sprang up to address the problem of replacing schools and teachers and of reforming the universities. The results were mixed. In Poland the great magnates plundered Jesuit property, handicapping the efforts of Stanislas Poniatowski's cash-starved national education commission. Despite these and many other setbacks, the enlightened monarch used his personal fortune to establish the Knights school in 1765. Aimed at educating patriotic young officers for the army and state administration, it had produced nearly 1,000 graduates by the final partition. The dissolution of the Jesuits also gave impetus to reformers in Charles III's Spain, where secondary schools, such as the Madrid seminary of the nobility, were created to educate the *hidalgos*. Nothing revealed Pombal's desire to modernize Portuguese institutions more clearly than his ambitious restructuring of the University of Coimbra, where he introduced a revised curriculum in the hope of forming a new élite of state servants.

There was even progress in the provision of primary education, which, on paper at least, had been compulsory in Prussia since the reign of Frederick William I. Similar schemes were implemented in Austria and Bohemia and in many of the smaller states of the Holy Roman Empire, including the ecclesiastical principalities of Cologne, Mainz, and Trier. The Cameralist ideal of a kingdom filled with

productive subjects had undoubtedly inspired some of these measures, but we should not forget that both Protestant and Catholic
reformers were conscious of the need for improved literacy to facili-
tate the propagation of the faith. Secular rulers were, however, becoming increasingly reluctant to allow the Church free rein in the field of
education. They viewed the problem in utilitarian terms and were
anxious to encourage instruction that would produce efficient state
servants and prosperous peasants. It was not until the second half of
the nineteenth century that governments turned the dream of
universal education into a reality, but they were building on the
foundations laid a century before.

Many other new fields of state activity can be identified, notably
those touching upon public health and hygiene. Decrees were passed
transferring cemeteries outside city walls to reduce the risk of disease,
streets were paved and cleaned, and lighting was introduced to
increase public safety. Governments everywhere exhibited certain
bureaucratic tendencies, not least a fascination for the compilation of
statistics mapping economic output, population, and wealth. They
were conscious of the benefits to be gained from centralized administration and a more egalitarian fiscal system. Some even made an
effort to tackle the scourge of poverty. Joseph II's confiscation of
monastic property was directed, in part, towards funding workhouses
for the unemployed and there was a renewed interest in similar
schemes in pre-revolutionary France. Yet the problem of poverty was
too vast for eighteenth-century governments, given their limited
access to human and material resources. Many of the projects of the
enlightened absolutists would never reach fruition for this reason,
because they did not possess the sophisticated modern bureaucracies
required to implement universal schemes of social welfare. Instead,
state servants continued to be recruited and promoted on the basis of
social caste, patronage, or bribery and their official duties were too
often perceived as a route to personal enrichment and family
advancement. The reformers of the age of enlightenment can, therefore, be likened to great adventurers claiming vast tracts of
competence for the state, which would later be colonized by the
professional bureaucrats of the nineteenth and twentieth centuries.

Finally, when examining the activities of the enlightened absolutists, it is clear that these were reforms imposed from above. If certain
amongst them were prepared to concede that there was an original

contract between the sovereign and his subjects, it was not one that permitted subsequent discussion of the terms. The great exception was Leopold, grand duke of Tuscany. He was heavily influenced by the Physiocrats, who advocated provincial assemblies composed of the propertied élites to oversee local administration. The Grand Duke went further and actually drafted a Tuscan constitution that would have limited his own powers to the benefit of a national assembly. Neither the local élites nor his brother, Joseph II, were impressed and the project came to naught. Yet Leopold was a ruler who understood the logical outcome of theories of sovereignty based on a contract between monarch and subject. He informed his sister, Maria Christina, 'that every country needs a fundamental law, a contract between the people and the sovereign which limits the authority and power of the latter; when the sovereign breaks the contract he renounces his office, which is only given to him on this condition and that [the people] is no longer obliged to obey him'. Fortunately for Leopold and for the majority of his fellow monarchs, the people were largely unaware of these inalienable rights and, perhaps more importantly, were resolutely attached to the status quo. When the French revolutionary wave broke on the rest of Europe, it would do so in vain, not least because of the efforts of reformers over the preceding century.

Corporate politics

The absence of a national parliament in France after 1614 led subsequent historians to invent the concept of absolutism, which was, at one time or another, applied to nearly every other state in Europe. A powerful monarch ruling by divine right seemingly left little scope for politics beyond the high political world of the court. Such an approach is misleading. To appreciate the complexity of politics in the absolute monarchies it is necessary to reflect on their corporate nature. At their coronations, monarchs such as Charles III, Louis XV, or Maria Theresa swore to uphold the privileges of the provinces, towns, and corporations of their kingdoms. Any attempt to undermine those rights was liable to provoke opposition and it was only after a revolt that monarchs felt justified in abolishing them. In more peaceful times, the sovereign was expected to act as a guarantor of privilege and to arbitrate disputes between different corps. Classic examples of corporate politics were the almost endless quarrels between ecclesiastical and royal courts, or the disputes involving, amongst others, provincial estates, royal officials, municipal councils, and guilds. To modern eyes some of the disputes appear almost infantile. During the regency in France a fearsome argument developed between the *ducs et pairs* and the presidents of the Parlement of Paris about who had the right to wear a bonnet. Disagreements were common about such diverse matters as the order of processions, the colour and cut of clothing, forms of address, not to mention the no less thorny judicial or administrative issues that could pit one corps against another. There was nothing unusual about groups of elegantly clad gentleman scuffling unceremoniously in order to place themselves at the head of a procession or to bag the best pews for a church service. The great Condé, governor of Burgundy, once recounted his difficulties in opening a session of the provincial estates due to a precedence dispute involving the local military commander and the first president of the Parlement about who should walk at his side. Condé initially feigned gout to avoid a scandal, but, realizing that this was not a permanent solution, he decided to allow one of the protagonists to walk in front of him and the other behind so that neither should give way to the other.

In this incident Condé was acting as the representative of the king and his action was subject to royal confirmation. The monarch was the referee of disputes, and one of the qualities that distinguished effective rulers from the rest was an ability to act tactfully when confronted by disputatious subjects. But what did these quarrels mean to the participants themselves? Arguments about ceremonial precedence, like those affecting professional competence, were about power. If a corps allowed a rival to poach part of its authority, then it risked a decline in its rank and prestige. Nothing could be more dangerous, not only would face be lost, but also its position in the hierarchy would be eroded and in the future the government might feel justified in ignoring its rights. Early modern corporations were, therefore, in a permanent state of readiness to repulse attacks on their privileges, no matter how slight a threat might at first appear. When we consider the number of individuals that belonged to corps in France or the Holy Roman Empire, it becomes apparent that far more people were engaged in corporate politics than was once assumed. A town councillor, churchwarden, or a member of a craft guild was no less determined to defend his honour than a great cleric or magistrate.

European monarchs prided themselves on being the fount of justice in their kingdoms, and, as corporate privileges were legal rights, the principal means of protecting them was an appeal to the sovereign. Once in conflict rival corps would present the ruler with proofs demonstrating the justice of their cause. As even the most conscientious monarch might flinch at the prospect of wading through these rather boring texts, it was necessary to employ other strategies simultaneously. As always, access to the monarch was vital. For a great institution like the Church, pressure could easily be exerted via a royal confessor, a court sermon, or an ecclesiastical deputation. Less significant corps were, on the other hand, obliged to rely on intermediaries. These power brokers were influential figures such as provincial governors, sympathetic royal officials, churchmen, or court aristocrats who would speak to the monarch or his ministers on behalf of others. What they received in return was the potentially useful obligation of those they had aided, confirmation of their own rank, and gifts that could take any form from cash payments to presents of wine or regional delicacies. Here it is possible to glimpse the distinguishing characteristics of politics in the absolute monarchies, which was still shaped by personal relationships, corporate identities, and ties of clientage. More recognizably, bureaucratic channels for conflict resolution did exist, but any corps that put all of its eggs into that particular basket was liable to face disappointment. As for the monarch, adjudicating in favour of one corps rather than another was rarely a straightforward task, and a clear-cut decision risked alienating powerful interests, which accounts for so many precedence and jurisdictional disputes being left deliberately unresolved. The competing bodies were left in a state of mutual resentment, allowing the prince to remain above the fray and to indulge in the ancient pastime of divide and rule.

When the sovereign came into conflict with a corporate body, the situation became rapidly more complicated. Eighteenth-century Europe presents no better illustration of this phenomenon than the disputes between French monarchs and their parlements. These great law courts were responsible for registering laws issued by the king, and they could petition him with remonstrances if they found objections. As venal officeholders, the noble judges who sat in the parlements did not represent any constituents and they were not averse to protecting their own privileges. Yet, in the absence of the Estates General the parlements assumed greater significance. Montesquieu, himself once a member of the Parlement of Bordeaux, praised their role as intermediary powers that limited royal authority, thus ensuring that France was a monarchy and not a despotism. These sentiments were shared by educated opinion, giving the parlements great authority when they questioned royal taxation or criticized administrative abuse. It was for this reason that Louis XV was so unpopular when he allowed his chancellor, Maupeou, to remodel the judicial system in 1771. Although some of his reforms were laudable, they were combined with strict curbs on the powers of the parlements, convincing many that the hour of despotism had struck. Louis XVI was, therefore, partially justified in re-establishing the old judicial system on his accession in 1774.

The parlements were integrated into the world of high politics because of their ability to criticize and delay legislation. References abound to the *parti* of such and such a minister, or, during the reign of Louis XVI, to the ministerial or the queen's party. There was also a very active Jansenist party, which campaigned throughout the reign of Louis XV against its ecclesiastical opponents, especially the Jesuits. These were not political parties in the sense of the Whigs or Tories, or Hats and Caps. Instead they were relatively loose factional groups, which, with the possible exception of the Jansenists, had no ideological basis.

When in conflict with the crown, the parlements employed all of the tactics associated with high politics, but during the reign of Louis XV they revived constitutional arguments last heard during the civil wars of the sixteenth and seventeenth centuries. Their attack was based upon the contention that the Parlement of Paris, to which the others were supposedly affiliated, was the real national parliament of France, not the Estates General. Using a mixture of historical wishful thinking and antiquarianism, the judges argued that the Parlement was descended from the early medieval assemblies of Frankish warriors that had once met on the Champ de Mars to discuss public affairs with the king. The judges claimed similar rights, declaring that no royal edict could become law until it had been freely verified and registered by themselves. None of these theories were new, but what made them potentially dangerous for the crown was the willingness of the parlements to publish their ideas in remonstrances. These texts were avidly consumed by an attentive public that followed the struggles between the king and his judges closely. As a result, the crown was obliged to counter-attack with its own version of French constitutional theory, most notably Louis XV's flagellation speech of 1766, which combined a harsh condemnation of the parlements with a bold restatement of the principles of divine-right patrimonial monarchy. The failure of French kings to respond with anything more potent was an important cause of the Revolution.

Representative politics

At the dawn of the eighteenth century absolute monarchy was at its zenith and an informed observer could have been forgiven for assuming that representative institutions would soon be confined to the dustbin of history. No Estates General had met in France since 1614, the Swedish Riksdag had been humbled by Karl XII, and a victorious Philip V was able to dispense with the Cortes of Catalonia and of Aragon after his victory in the War of the Spanish Succession. Over the next century there was no great revival of national parliaments, but their potential value did become steadily more apparent. This was due, in large measure, to the great success story of the eighteenth century, Britain. Its spectacular victories against the French in the colonial struggle in North America and India, when combined with its commercial prosperity, caused serious reflection on the continent and especially amongst the disgruntled subjects of Louis XV. Despite the setback of the War of American Independence, the British quickly disproved the siren voices predicting their fall, and by the nineteenth century their military and industrial power and political stability made their constitutional monarchy the envy of Europe.

The British Parliament had no direct equivalent elsewhere, although the Polish Sejm and Hungarian Diet did possess points in common. The Sejm had an upper chamber, the senate, composed of the great ecclesiastical, military, and royal officials, all of whom were appointed for life, and a lower chamber of envoys elected by noble dietines. Alongside the right to elect their king, the *szlachta* had more firmly established political rights—their golden liberties—than any other contemporary nobility. The Sejm possessed full legislative powers, and the crown could issue laws only with its consent. As the British model demonstrated, this need not have posed an obstacle to good government. Unfortunately for Poland, the *szlachta* had an obsessive, almost paranoid fear of royal absolutism. In 1652 these misgivings had given birth to the constitutional absurdity of the *liberum veto*, a procedural device whereby a dissenting member of the assembly could block legislation. Once exercised, the veto not only stopped the offending law, but also broke the Sejm, invalidating the entire legislative programme. It was a recipe for anarchy and, with Poland's neighbours forever anxious to keep the Commonwealth weak, there was never a shortage of bribes to ensure that the veto was liberally applied. The Sejms of 1701–2, 1729, 1730, and 1732, to name just a few, were all scuppered in this fashion and the Polish constitution ensured that the government was paralysed. To add insult to injury, the *szlachta* had also preserved the constitutional right of confederation, a euphemism for legitimate revolt, whenever the king displeased them. The confederation of Bar (1768–72) raised against the reforming initiatives of Stanislas Poniatowski illustrated the continuing vitality of the principle and provided Russia, Prussia, and Austria with the pretext needed to launch the first partition.

The national parliaments of Britain, Sweden, and Poland had profited from monarchical weakness or the consequences of civil war or military defeat and had preserved the crucial principle that revenue could not be raised without consent. The Estates of Württemberg, on the other hand, were able to capitalize upon the peculiar constitution of the Holy Roman Empire, which allowed them to appeal successfully to the Aulic Council against the absolutist ambitions of their duke. Not that political life in these countries should always be interpreted in terms of conflict. National parliaments or provincial estates could not only share the burden of administration, but also create a climate of confidence invaluable when it came to raising taxes and loans. If the right of consent to taxation was the jewel in the parliamentary crown, other gems shone no less brightly. All legislation issued by the crown in Sweden and Poland required consent and the monarch could neither declare war nor sign a peace treaty without parliamentary approval. Remarkably the estates of Brabant raised an army to oppose the policies and troops of Joseph II, but provincial estates could not usually meddle in such weighty matters. They did, however, enjoy considerable latitude when it came to issues of taxation and administration in the local context.

The powers of national parliaments were impressive, but did they actually represent the interests of anything more than a narrow élite of aristocrats or property-owners? A quick glance at those who participated in the electoral process suggests that they did. It has been estimated that there were potentially 150,000 politically active *szlachta* in Poland. Even if not all could attend monarchical elections, they were able to vote for envoys in local dietines. In Britain the electorate was far from democratic, with the most generous estimates indicating no more than 350,000 electors in 1800. During the eighthteenth century approximately one-fifth of the seats in the House of Commons were nominated by patrons and as many more were controlled in their interest. Yet in towns such as Bristol, Leicester, Norwich, or London the majority of resident male householders had the vote and control was beyond the capacities of individual patrons. The Swedish Riksdag, on the other hand, was an assembly of four estates, and each chamber had different regulations regarding entrance. Every noble family had the right to representation and a gathering of 1,000 members was not unknown. The same pattern could be observed in the meetings of the provincial estates of Brittany, where hundreds of nobles flocked to the biennial assemblies, usually to oppose the king while dining at his expense. Clerical representatives in Sweden were elected by diocese, on occasions by secret ballot, although in most estates local bishops and the heads of religious houses were present. The deputies of the Swedish towns were elected on a suffrage that had almost as many inconsistencies as the British, but in France, Louis XIV had killed off any serious urban representation in the remaining provincial estates by making the position of mayor hereditary in 1692. Taken as a whole, the Swedish political system was probably the most representative in Europe before the Jacobins introduced universal manhood suffrage in 1792. Such was the divisive nature of revolutionary politics that, as the opportunity to vote expanded, the desire to do so decreased.

When we turn our attention to election campaigns, it is apparent that a broad segment of society was drawn into the attendant drama. Eighteenth-century British politics was traditionally depicted in terms of corruption and patronage. That image has now been revised and the richness of political debate is more fully appreciated. Voters expected a degree of respect and attention and where this was lacking it might create the conditions for a contest. Fortunes were expended on winning seats, with the sum of £100,000 spent on the Shrewsbury election of 1790 alone. Yet this did not mean that all seats were bought, and if they had been offered cash for votes many electors would have felt deeply insulted. Instead they expected to be treated as honourable men whose relationship with the candidate was based on friendship and mutual respect. Any hospitality or favours bestowed were interpreted as giving concrete expression to those ties of amity.

Descriptions of eighteenth-century election campaigns do, however, conjure up images of modern practice. One tired candidate wrote: 'for several days . . . I had to talk politics from morning till night with this rabble, admire their discourse, appear dazzled by their wit and, what is more, I continually had to embrace their filthy, verminous persons.' Another declared: 'I am half dead already what with drinking, smoking and walking the streets at all hours.' They could clearly have exchanged horror stories about their time on the stump, but what is remarkable is that our two candidates were nearly 1,000 miles apart. The first, Stanislaw Poniatowski, future king of Poland, was standing for election to the chamber of envoys, while the other, John Chetwynd, was seeking the favour of the electorate of Preston. Neither could take their support for granted and they were obliged to pamper voters with drink, bed, and board while these often protracted elections took place.

Nor was canvassing for votes simply a matter of plunging randomly into a crowd. During the eighteenth century most British constituencies came under the sway of election agents, whose job it was to protect the interest of their patrons. Election committees were established with the task of rounding up voters and organizing their travel, subsistence, and entertainment. For voters and society at large, elections were meant to be fun—a form of carnival where otherwise inconsequential individuals could feel important and where even those unable to vote could share the pageantry and merriment of the occasion. In contested British elections, for example, it was customary for rival candidates or their patrons to stage elaborate entrances on the day voting began. Charles Caesar entered Hertford with a retinue of 600 in 1715, while Lord Sheffield was met in his carriage

two miles from Bristol in 1790 and escorted into the city by his supporters. Rival candidates sought to display their strength by adorning
the streets and their supporters with banners and rosettes. When a
result was declared, bonfires, dancing, and the inevitable heavy drinking was part of a communal ritual that clearly involved a much wider
cross section of society than is apparent from electoral lists. Those
who cheered a candidate, sported his colours, or heckled an opponent
might not have counted for much in the grand scheme of things, but
their involvement should not be ignored.

In contested elections, local issues were usually decisive. Voters
expected their MP and his patron to look after their interests, finding
employment, spending lavishly in the constituency, and offering
material assistance in times of calamity. If a seat changed hands, or a
challenge was mounted in a previously uncontested borough, then a
sense of neglect amongst the constituents was the probable cause.
The Earl of Hardwicke received warning of impending trouble when
he was informed that his electoral agent in Cambridgeshire had been
'about with a bottle in one hand and a guinea in the other, and will
part with neither'. Again the Polish system provides an interesting
parallel. In 1761 Michael Czartoryski complained 'that virtually
everyone who does anything at all satisfactorily for the common good
expects a personal sign of gratitude and reward from me'. His moan-
ing was disingenuous. Like all great patrons he owed his authority to
an ability to dispense bounty and to access levers of power beyond
the limits of voters or clients.

Elections were generally parochial affairs, but there were some
issues that could strike a national chord. In Britain religion was
undoubtedly the most sensitive, and both the Jewish Naturalization
Bill of 1753 and the Catholic Relief Act of 1778 unleashed a national
tide of bigotry. Opposition to the American War of Independence
was equally controversial, rallying support across constituency
boundaries, as did resistance to taxation, notably the Excise Bill of
1733 and the Cider Tax of 1763. On these highly charged issues British
MPs would occasionally receive instructions from their constituencies ordering them to vote in a particular fashion. By the end of the
century, however, the principle that an MP was the representative not
the delegate of his electors was firmly established. France had a similar debate in 1789 and many deputies were sent to the Estates General
with detailed instructions, especially in relation to the vexed question

of whether voting should be by order or head. That crisis was resolved by the revolutionary decision of the Third Estate to declare itself the National Assembly, and thereafter its members acted as the representatives of the sovereign nation. In Poland, on the other hand, deputies to the chamber of envoys were technically delegates, obliged to report back to the dietines within one month of the closure of the Sejm. Although these rules were not rigorously enforced, they provide further evidence of the political power of the *szlachta*.

Members of national parliaments were drawn from a narrow social circle. Sons of peers and members of the gentry dominated the House of Commons, although there was a significant smattering of representatives from the armed forces and professions. Amongst the Polish envoys there was also a high proportion of magnates' sons, who like their British counterparts were frequently expected to cut their teeth in the lower chamber before rising to the senate. These were not professional politicians and they sought election to satisfy a host of traditional motives, and protecting family interest, rank, and honour was as important as personal ambition or party affinity. It was only very slowly that the concept of politics as a career began to take shape, and the hordes of young lawyers who infested successive French revolutionary assemblies gave a sharp indication of future trends. Finally, the careers of Tom Paine, Joseph Priestley, Maximilien Robespierre, Saint Just, and John Wilkes, while individually very different, had in common a vocational approach to politics that marked them out from the gentleman amateur.

As the emphasis on local issues and patronage suggests, parliamentary governments were not controlled by political parties. When they used the term *partia*, Poles were thinking of the great magnate families and their followers, which were clan networks, loose associations based on kinship and clientage, fighting over the spoils of their enfeebled state. Much the same can be said of the French, Saxon, or Russian parties, which, as their names suggest, were funded by foreign governments in the usually vain hope of influencing the outcome of royal elections. At first glance, the Swedish political parties, the Hats and the Caps, seem scarcely more sophisticated, as they too were in foreign pay. Closer inspection does, however, reveal features reminiscent of modern organizations. Carl Gyllenborg was the inspiration behind the emergence of the Hats, leading a remarkable campaign against the ministry of Arvid Horn. In 1734 he founded

Stockholm's first political club, initiated a polemical campaign—including the production of a satirical play, *Den Svenska Sprätt-höken*—and toured the provinces buying up proxy votes for the election of 1738. When the new deputies arrived in Stockholm, they were greeted with lists telling them how to vote in the elections to the Riksdag's crucial committees. It was a textbook parliamentary *coup* and it laid the basis for nearly twenty years of Hat political ascendancy.

Both the Hats and the Caps were élitist groups with no mass membership and without the deep roots in Swedish society required to survive the royalist *coup* of 1772. British historians, on the other hand, are now more sympathetic to the idea that the Whigs and the Tories had a distinct identity and that terms such as a 'Tory vote' or 'Whig party' are not anachronistic. They were not, however, the tightly controlled parties of the modern age and a successful ministry needed to manage Parliament. There was no finer exponent of this art than Robert Walpole, whose critics railed against his 'little sordid genius for tricks and cunning, which founds all its success on corruption, stock jobbing and other iniquitous arts'. In an age before party bureaucracies, government whips, and spin doctors, patronage was the key to the control of Parliament and Walpole was the master craftsman.

Politics and the people

One of the most far-reaching consequences of the economic growth of the eighteenth century was the emergence of a more affluent, educated, and politically conscious public. Such diverse regions as Scotland, Sweden, northern France, Belgium, and the Dutch Republic could boast of almost universal male literacy, and, with the exception of Russia, much of the rest of the continent was rapidly catching up. Not surprisingly, the market for political news dispensed in the form of newspapers, books, and periodicals experienced a corresponding boom. Britain was to the fore in this regard, with an estimated annual sale of 2.5 million newspapers in 1713, a figure that had grown to 12.6 million by 1775. Both regional and national newspapers carried political information and commentary, including reports on events in

Parliament, the military and diplomatic affairs of Europe, and *causes célèbres* such as the John Wilkes saga. In the Holy Roman Empire newspapers were also a feature of daily life, with no fewer than 200 in circulation by 1789 with an estimated readership of three million. The Dutch Republic also possessed a healthy demand for political literature. Lively periodicals such as the Republican *Nederlandsche Jaerboehen* or the weeklies the *Post* and the *Kruyer* were published nationally with print runs of several thousands. Some of these periodicals, notably the *Gazette de Leyde* and the *Gazette d'Amsterdam*, circulated well beyond their national boundaries, and were especially popular in France. Louis XVI's ministers abandoned any hopes of blocking their spread and instead began to leak information in the hope of obtaining favourable coverage. The indigenous French press was less vibrant and official organs such as the *Gazette de France* were little more than court circulars. For more exciting commentary on religious and parlementary matters, the principal alternative was the clandestine *Nouvelles ecclésiastiques*. The Jansenist *Nouvelles* was one of the most remarkable publishing phenomena of the eighteenth century. It appeared continuously from 1728 until 1803, providing information and reports on the affairs of Church and State.

Newspapers and periodicals were only part of an explosion of printed works that flooded European towns. None of these items was cheap, not even newspapers in Britain, and they were beyond the pockets of ordinary working men or artisans. Yet there is every reason to believe that their actual readership was much higher than their print runs suggest. Across Europe, the eighteenth century witnessed a proliferation of reading rooms, coffee shops, public houses, learned academies, Masonic lodges, and clubs where those searching political nourishment could gather to read the news or to discuss current affairs. The *Liverpool General Advertiser* summed up the situation judiciously in 1791, declaring that, 'without newspapers, our coffee houses, ale-houses and barbers' shops would undergo a change next to depopulation; and our countrycottagers, the curate, the exciseman and the blacksmith would lose the self-satisfaction of being as wise as William Pitt'. When royal censorship collapsed in 1788, the French were no less enthusiastic, and it has been estimated that in 1789 alone 100 newspapers were established.

The intrusiveness of politics into daily life was not simply confined to the printed page. If a poster of Che Guevara was *de rigueur* for radical students in the 1960s and 1970s, their predecessors at Oxford during the 1750s could cock a snook at authority by buying a cheap print of the Young Pretender. During his many campaigns, John Wilkes pioneered a variety of techniques. His infamous issue Number 45 of the *North Briton* became a propaganda symbol, appearing in every form from graffiti chalked on walls to elaborately decorated snuff boxes. Josiah Wedgewood demonstrated his sharp commercial eye by producing memorabilia celebrating Wilkes's struggle, and when Dutch politics flared into life in the 1780s the canny entrepreneur catered for all shades of the political spectrum. Proud Orangists could purchase lockets featuring the stadholder and his family, while patriots had the choice of snuff boxes, tobacco pouches, and glassware. One piece featured a dog cocking his leg against an orange tree alongside the charming motto 'Honi soit qui mal y p——'. The French Revolution created a vast market for political ephemera, although symbols such as trees of liberty and phrygian caps tapped into deeper currents of popular culture. As in British elections, there was a carnival air to much popular involvement in politics. During the struggles of the Dutch orangists and their patriot opponents, both sides bedecked themselves in their respective colours of orange and black and held processions and banquets that drew in broad segments of the population. Similar scenes were enacted in pre-revolutionary France. When the Parlement of Dijon celebrated a victory in 1763, the whole town closed for two weeks of banquets, heavy drinking, dancing, and fireworks. Elsewhere songs, ditties, and broadsheets all carried comments and criticisms about rulers and their policies and helped to inform the people.

Reading about politics or collecting memorabilia was one thing, taking an active part was more problematic. For those excluded from the formal political process, the traditional remedy was the petition. The history of British radical and parliamentary reform movements was closely associated with petitioning, which would reach its apogee with the massive and ultimately fruitless campaigns of the Chartists. The 1780s witnessed a craze for petitions in the Dutch Republic, where thousands pledged their allegiance in this fashion. The same tactics were so popular with the ordinary working men of Paris that the Constituent Assembly temporarily banned them in May 1791. Petitions were, of course, about more than just appending a signature. They required organization, public meetings, and discussion, all of which created opportunities for political argument and participation. A more sophisticated form of activism, encompassing both élites and ordinary people, was provided by the special interest groups that emerged in the course of the century. Commercial and mercantile interests such as the West Indian sugar-planters, or the goldsmiths company, worked assiduously to influence the British Parliament. More striking was the Society for the Abolition of the Slave Trade, which marked the birth of the modern single-issue pressure group. The struggle against slavery touched a humanitarian and moral chord in British society, bringing together parliamentarians, such as William Wilberforce, with the thousands of ordinary Britons who signed petitions and boycotted West Indian sugar.

Whether they liked it or not, governments were aware that politics was an affair of the people and they were particularly anxious to know what their subjects thought of their conduct. Despite his reforming zeal, Joseph II employed an army of spies, and in Russia the secret police, the preobrazhenskii prikaz, were justifiably feared. The French finance minister, Orry, was more constructive, delib-erately spreading rumours about impending tax increases with the aim of testing public opinion. His colleagues were generally less imaginative, preferring to plant spies throughout Paris to report on the conversations and mood of the people. When a deranged servant, Robert-François Damiens, tried to assassinate Louis XV in 1757, the government was horrified to discover that others were uttering no less diabolical threats. An awareness that long before 1789 French people were insulting their king has tempted some historians to write of the desacralization of the monarchy under Louis XV. This is prob-ably going too far. Disgruntled subjects had almost certainly been calling their monarch a 'Jean Foutre' (stupid bugger) for generations, and any trawl through police or judicial files will produce evidence of popular displeasure. Mocking rulers and social betters with earthy insults, placards, songs, and ditties was a feature of early modern society and the volume of complaint waxed and waned with public prosperity.

Expressions of popular anger were carefully monitored, because both governments and propertied élites feared the violence of the politic-ally excluded. The Gordon riots of 1780 saw London subjected to a week of rioting with massive destruction of property, and events in

France a decade later offered confirmation, if it was needed, of the danger popular disturbances could pose. For governments and élites alike, any assembly or demonstration was liable to be labelled the work of the mob, when in reality crowds rarely acted in an anarchic way. Amongst the most common causes of demonstrations were bread riots brought on by economic hardship or natural disaster. With the staple diet threatened, women were to the fore in attacking bakers and forcing them to sell at an 'honest price'. The authorities might occasionally make an example of the ringleaders, but they were generally lenient in the face of such unrest. For the urban poor and even respectable tradesmen, hunger was never far away and during the French Revolution the Parisian sans-culottes had a national maximum for prices as one of their principal political goals.

Violence could also be directed against unpopular policies. In 1750, Paris was wracked by the curious child riots, as angry parents protested against police, who were abusing their right to round up vagrants for transportation by picking up innocent children and then demanding a ransom for their safe return. A number of minor officials were lynched and the police chief narrowly escaped a similar fate before his house was sacked. The policy was changed. Madrid experienced its own taste of popular violence in March 1766, when for four days the city was in the hands of thousands of demonstrators protesting about government reforms and the price of bread. Charles III was obliged to flee from his capital and suffered the humiliation of having to negotiate with the rioters. Debate still rages about whether the uprising was spontaneous or the result of plotting by discontented grandees. The aristocratic opponents of Charles III's reforms probably did encourage the revolt and similar examples of popular fury being aroused for conservative ends are not hard to find. The Gordon riots were caused, in part, by manipulation of popular prejudice and the stadholders in the Dutch Republic also capitalized on the orangist sentiments of the urban masses. They had provided the muscle behind William IV's rise to power in 1747 and they helped to consolidate his successor after the suppression of the patriots in 1787. For the French revolutionaries, the power of the popular uprising proved to be a double-edged sword. The revolt of Paris in July 1789 saved the Revolution from a royalist *coup*. Yet the same dynamic was exploited by competing factions making political stability elusive, leading at its most extreme to the horrors of the September massacres. It was left to

Napoleon to put the genie of direct political action back into the bottle with his 'whiff of grapeshot'.

If governments were wary of popular involvement in politics, they rarely condescended to consider the rights of women. The age of enlightenment did little to alter the fundamental misogyny of European societies and wherever possible women were excluded from active participation on the grounds that they were physically and intellectually the inferiors of men. The French Revolution thus produced the Declaration of the Rights of Man and English radicals agitated for universal manhood suffrage. Male advocates of womens' rights were few, and bold French women such as Olympe de Gouges, author of the Declaration of the Rights of Women, and Claire Lacombe and Pauline Leon, founders of the Société de Citoyennes Républicaines Révolutionnaires, were all arrested. It might have afforded some compensation to be persecuted for their 'political crimes', but they failed to rally much support from their sisters. We should, however, be wary of assuming that women avoided involvement in politics because men told them to do so. No account of high politics during the period could claim to be exhaustive without acknowledging the pivotal role of women as power brokers and patrons. Similarly women, through the medium of the salon, helped to develop a forum for political discussion and a vehicle for the political ambitions of others. Nor was the expanding field of journalism untouched. The *Journal des dames*, a French periodical published between 1759 and 1778, was used by its editors, Mme de Beaumer and Mme de Maisonneuve, to promote womens' rights and to comment upon the political issues of the day. Finally it was the women of Paris, exercising their ancient right to petition the king for cheap bread, who sparked the crisis of October 1789 that deprived Louis XVI of his political and physical liberty.

Radicals and republicans

The emergence of a politically conscious public coincides rather neatly with the turbulent decades at the end of the eighteenth century, which saw revolts and revolutions from North America to Belgium. The War of American Independence was a source of inspiration for many Europeans. They idealized the struggle of a citizen army against the overmighty British and marvelled at the establishment of a republic with a written constitution. The French Revolution followed close on its heels and revolts and movements of political reform spread across the continent, inspiring later historians to write of an Atlantic revolution. Current thinking downplays that theory and stresses instead the importance of national traditions in determining political behaviour. Common features were nevertheless present, not least through the impact of the various forms of political literature and sociability referred to above.

Britain remained remarkably stable in the aftermath of defeat in America. Continuing economic prosperity was a vital factor, but stability was primarily the result of a political system that, despite the power of the ruling oligarchy, allowed for the expression of much broader social and economic interests. There was a revival of radicalism in the late eighteenth century, with renewed agitation for parliamentary reform to be founded upon the principles of manhood suffrage, annual elections, and the ending of property qualifications for MPs. Thomas Hardy, Tom Paine, Richard Price, Joseph Priestly, and their fellow radicals castigated corruption, oligarchy, and even the monarchy itself, with many welcoming both the Revolution in France and Jacobin republicanism. British radicalism had deep and complex roots reaching back to the commonwealthman ideology of James Harrington, Thomas Gordan, and John Toland as well as to the Tory critics of the Whig ascendancy of the 1730s and 1740s. Not surprisingly, therefore, the radical movement was as fissiparous as its intellectual heritage was diverse and it never coalesced around a common leader, platform, or ideology. Nor was it capable of mobilizing popular support on the scale required to force change or threaten revolution. A frightened government suspended habeas corpus, sent would-be Jacobins, such as Thomas Muir and Joseph Gerrald, to Botany Bay, and passed repressive legislation, including the Treasonable and Seditious Practices Act (1795). Yet it was taking a sledgehammer to crack a nut, because, given the opportunity, the broad mass of the population revealed itself to be enthusiastically loyalist. Popular conservatism was a more substantial and reliable constituency than anything its radical opponents could muster.

If the American War of Independence failed to make the fortunes of British radicals, it did have serious repercussions in the Dutch

Republic. Despite fighting alongside the colonists and their French allies, the Dutch suffered humiliating defeats at the hands of the British fleet. These reverses crowned a century of relative decline in the economic and international strength of the republic and triggered not only a reaction against the orangists, but also the corruption of the regents. Leading patriotic writers such as Baron van der Capellen and Rutger van Schimmelpenninck called for reform of the republican system in the name of the people. Van der Capellen translated Richard Price's *Observations on Civil Liberty*, which drew in turn on Locke, and it is possible to identify the work of, among others, Rousseau in patriot literature. As in America, the citizens' militia was an integral part of a patriot ideology that extolled the right of a free people to bear arms in defence of liberty. Thousands flocked to join the militias, although they were impotent when confronted by the Prussian troops sent to uphold the stadholder in 1787. Clearly the legacy of classical republicanism was never far from the thoughts of the patriots, and Cicero's vision of a moral republic was combined with a partisan reading of the history of the revolt against Spain in a vain search for the magic formula required to reinvigorate the country's institutions and reverse its alarming decline.

Dutch patriot dreams of a national renaissance were echoed with even greater urgency in Poland. Under the enlightened rule of Stanislas Poniatowski, painstakingly slow progress was made in weaning the *szlachta* off their blind attachment to their golden liberties. The King was instrumental in creating the opportunity for reform, and he was helped by the impact of the Polish Enlightenment and by wounded national pride. The result was Europe's first written constitution in May 1791, promulgated by the unique four year Sejm (1788–92) which cut through the Gordian knot of Polish politics by abolishing the *liberum veto* and by establishing biennial parliaments to be filled with representative deputies. Article three of eleven declared that 'all government in human societies originates in the will of the nation', which revealed one of the constitution's principal weaknesses. Although the reforms were warmly welcomed throughout the Commonwealth, there was no attempt to grapple with the problem of serfdom. The nation was not, therefore, a universal concept and it continued to exclude the majority of Poles. The ideas of reformers such as Stanislaw Staszic and Jan Ferdynand Nax, who dreamed of a citizens' army, could not be put into practice, not even when the second and third partitions destroyed the hopes and aspirations of May 1791.

Not for the last time, Poland fell victim to the geopolitical realities of being sandwiched between the great eastern powers of Austria, Prussia, and Russia. Attempts at revolt or reform met a similar fate in Belgium, Corsica, the Dutch Republic, and the prince-bishopric of Liège, to name but a few, and only in a great power like France could revolution flower without immediate risk of foreign interference. Victory in the American War of Independence brought debts and disappointment for the government of Louis XVI, but it did inspire ambitious young aristocrats like the Marquis de Lafayette, who had experienced the struggle against the British at first hand. Together with his friend Thomas Jefferson, Lafayette helped draft the Declaration of the Rights of Man, which enshrined much of the enlightened doctrine of individual liberties that symbolized the hopes of 1789. What made the declaration revolutionary was the inclusion of the principle that sovereignty lay not with the king, but the nation. It was in the name of the sovereign people that the Constituent Assembly tore down the corporatist, privileged, and parochial infrastructure of the *Ancien Régime*, replacing it with a new France inhabited by equal citizens with uniform laws and institutions. The Constituent was, in many ways, implementing the programme of the enlightened absolutists that the French monarchs had been either unwilling or incapable of directing. It does not, therefore, come as a surprise to learn that Joseph II was initially enthusiastic about events in France, and a king of his stamp might have led the process of social and administrative reform to his own advantage. Unfortunately, Louis XVI failed to comprehend the scale of change that was needed. Instead he offered a hopeless mixture of half measures, equivocation, and outright hostility that destroyed any hopes of creating the broad consensus needed to prevent the Revolution from careering in a radical direction. The King's attitude, made manifest by his abortive flight to Varennes in June 1791, provided the opportunity for a nascent republican movement to emerge from the shadows. It was, however, the French decision to go to war in the spring of 1792 that triggered the crisis leading to the overthrow of the monarchy and helped to foster a climate conducive to Terror.

By the end of 1793, a revolution that had promised freedom and civil liberty was waging a bloody civil war against many of its own citizens, who now lived under a reign of Terror that Camille Desmoulins memorably compared to that of Nero. While Robespierre and his allies on the Committee of Public Safety sought to forge the republic of virtue, thousands were executed and hundreds of thousands more arrested on trumped-up charges or mere suspicion. Thermidor finally checked the carnage, and the subsequent Director-ial regime was confronted with a hostile Jacobin left and a vengeful monarchist right and the perplexing problem of how to reconcile the seemingly incompatible aims of liberty and equality with order. In this task it largely failed, and, as many had long feared, the Revolution eventually brought forth its Caesar. Yet Napoleon was more than just a military despot. His great achievement was to project himself as a man of the Revolution, its very embodiment, who would protect the gains of 1789 while providing France with internal stability and external glory on a scale unseen since the age of Louis XIV. An emperor astute enough to 'listen' to the voice of the people through referenda, Napoleon has been much emulated, but rarely equalled by authoritarian rulers ever since.

The outbreak of Revolution in France coincided with the revolt of neighbouring Belgium against the rule of Joseph II. Here the trad-itional nature of politics was very much in evidence. In his enthusi-asm for a centralized state, the Emperor trampled over the privileges and religious sensibilities of a deeply conservative population. The result was a revolt in the name of provincial liberties couched in identical language to the Act of Abjuration pronounced against Philip II in 1581! Similar sentiments ensured that the Belgians would be no less indomitable when confronted by the religious and administrative reforms imported by the French in 1792. As the crowned heads of Europe slammed down the shutters on the age of reform, they would have been wise to reflect on the Belgian experience. Political reaction, while perfectly understandable in the circumstances, was ultimately unnecessary. The vast majority of the European population was fundamentally conservative and immune to the advocates of revolution. In Spain, southern Italy, much of Germany, and even Britain, the masses revealed a deep affection for throne and altar that was an invaluable resource in the battles against revolutionary and Napoleonic France. It would be the ace in the pack for European governments as they faced the challenge of liberals, radicals, and would-be revolutionaries in the century to come.

Conclusion

Louis XIV was famously credited with the phrase 'l'état c'est moi'. Although almost certainly apocryphal, the expression appeared apt, because few could conceive of the interests of the state or its subjects in separation from those of the king. In the course of the eighteenth century that particular trinity was exploded, with the people or nation coming to stand in opposition to the king while the state sailed merrily on independent of both. In France the consequences of that process were particularly violent, but elsewhere the role of the state was redefined in a less traumatic fashion. Divine-right and patrimonial theories gave way before the principle that government should work in the interests of public welfare and significant advances were made in promoting economic development, education, and legal reform. Yet these were reforms imposed from above. The challenge for European rulers as they entered the nineteenth century was increasingly from the belief that sovereignty lay with people. Much of the political history of Europe after 1800 would be about the struggle to put that theory into practice.

2

Orders and classes: eighteenth-century society under pressure

Christof Dipper

The society of old-regime Europe was undermined by three forces: demographic growth, capitalism, and the centralizing state. Every social group was affected by the surge in population, the development of the cash economy exposed ever increasing numbers of people to market forces, while the state challenged the claim of the traditional social orders to be autonomous by transforming them into subordinate if privileged élites. In this chapter, attention will be paid first to this process of destabilization. The less spectacular but more stable conditions will be left to later, the hinge between change and continuity being formed by the section on poverty, for it was poverty that formed the hinge between orders and classes.

The stages of demographic expansion

Accounts of population movements in the past usually begin with a reference to the unreliability of the data. In what is known as the 'pre-statistical period', it is indeed the case that virtually all preconditions for statistical accuracy are lacking, even if they are more deficient for some regions than for others. In this regard, there is a clear north–south split in Europe in the eighteenth century (and in the previous century too), due partly to the greater degree of control sought by rulers and churches north of the Alps, and partly to the absence of catastrophic wars in several remote corners of the continent.

However, uncertainty about statistics and global figures is found less damaging than in the past because historians are less interested in general overviews and columns of figures than in the causes and conditions of the developments that lay behind the changes. So they prefer to look at individual communities, or even households and families, which they seek to 'reconstitute', relying mainly on parish records. The data generated by this exercise reveal the mechanisms underlying demographic change: birth rates, marriage patterns, and mortality.

If we now turn our attention to Europe as a whole, despite this warning, we see at once that the eighteenth century does not present a unified picture. On the contrary, it was not until c.1740 that the population deficit that had opened up since the beginning of the Thirty Years War (1618) was at last made good. One scholar—Jan de Vries—estimates that Europe's population increased by 16 per cent between 1700 and 1750 and by another 30 per cent by the end of the century; Bairoch's projections suggest 15 per cent and 23 per cent respectively.

In the 1740s, with a quicker rate of growth everywhere, a new demographic wave rolled in. It cascaded over regions that still enjoyed some agrarian slack as well as those that had none. This was a fundamentally new phenomenon, and those living in the core zones of central Europe and in England especially were forced to look for alternative sources of livelihood. Population pressure was felt most acutely in the countryside. The regions affected least were Spain, central and northern Italy, the Alpine territories of the Habsburg Monarchy, Bavaria, Lorraine, north-west Germany, Denmark, Norway, and Scotland. Before we examine the reasons for this growth, which was detected by such acute contemporary observers as Süssmilch, Quesnay, and Malthus, we need to bear in mind that sexual behaviour patterns and consequently population movements were determined mainly by economic factors. The objective was to strike a balance between food production and consumers. As procreation was much more difficult to control than it is today and as death escaped human control almost altogether, society fell back on marriage as a regulator. The fewer children that were needed, the later daughters were allowed to marry. Marriage was treated as a privilege. For this agrarian society, which lived in constant fear of overpopulation, historians have reconstituted what they call 'the European marriage pattern', by which, first, a substantial proportion of the population (between 20 and 60 per cent of adults) was excluded from marriage altogether and, secondly, a relatively advanced age of marriage (between 24 and 29) was imposed on women. In Slavonic regions and in the Balkans, however, this pattern was never established.

In many parts of Europe, the population wave that began in the 1740s took place at a time when the population was 'complete' by traditional standards. It was the emergence of new forms of agricultural income and other still unresearched developments that first eroded and then in the next century invalidated the 'European marriage pattern'. The most striking deviation from this pattern was shown by England, for there the age of marriage for women fell continuously and a growing proportion of the population engaged in matrimony. On the continent the same sort of result was achieved by different conditions, less closely linked with behaviour management. Here it seems that it was a series of good harvests in the 1730s that supplied the trigger, for the increased supply of food ensured that twenty-five years later there would be more people of marriageable age. In both cases, however, a chain reaction began that led to an unprecedented acceleration in demographic growth. The result was that the price of food increased at an ever-accelerating rate from the 1770s. That made attractive the production of cereals on land previously used for other purposes and so more land was brought into cultivation. At the same time, the more numerous workforce allowed the cultivation of crops that were more labour intensive but more nourishing than wheat or rye. The main beneficiaries were potatoes and other root crops which began to appear on an ever-increasing number of household menus. These crops had the additional advantage of increasing nitrogen in the soil, thus reducing the need to let land lie fallow and making crop rotations possible.

If these innovations kept dearth at bay during normal years, food remained scarce, indeed became increasingly scarce, as the rise in prices showed. Even if one excludes the major famines occasioned by adverse weather conditions (1706–12, 1724–8, 1739–41, 1766–77), the most important indicator—the price of grain—increased appreciably during the second half of the century in the course of the three price rises (1755–7, 1766–8, 1770+). In the Alpine regions of the Habsburg Monarchy, it increased by 40 per cent, in Denmark by 50 per cent, in the densely populated north and east of France, the Lower Rhine, and central Germany by two-thirds, while in Britain and northern Italy it actually doubled. As wages could not keep pace, a creeping process of impoverishment ensued, accelerating progressively to become the generally recognized pauperism of the nineteenth century. Population patterns and economic performance had separated: they were destined never to be reunited.

This surge in population meant that in 1800 in Europe (excluding Russia, Poland, and the Balkans) there were between forty and fifty million more people than 100 years earlier. Three generations had brought more children into the world and—what was more important—had raised them to adulthood. As we have seen, the elasticity of the economy was limited, indeed had very little slack even when the increase began, with the result that many of the newcomers were pushed beyond the margins of organized society. Unlike in the post-industrial world, social organization changed as a direct result of demographic growth. In concrete terms this meant nothing less than that the underclass multiplied. There are various estimates of the size of this very heterogeneous group, but they all suggest a figure of about 50 per cent for 1800. By far the largest proportion lived in the countryside, which was where the population increase had begun.

The dissolution of the society of orders

By the end of the eighteenth century, society had travelled a long way down the road that led towards the formation of a proletariat, much further indeed than historians used to believe or contemporaries liked to think. The latter interpreted changing family strategies, growing land hunger and changing patterns of consumption as symptoms of a social crisis, reacting with stubborn defences of the traditional social structure. Their conception of civil society rested on a perfect correspondence of authority, social status, and moral order, which meant that social change had to be opposed.

Even today we still associate the concept of the traditional 'society of orders' with an image of immobility. Indeed, all contemporaries reflecting on the ideal form of social order in some way—theologians, philosophers, jurists, and so on—would have preferred to be dealing with a static society. But the view that had prevailed since the Middle Ages that society was divided into three orders or Estates (clergy, nobility, commoners) no longer corresponded to reality. Developed within Aristotelian and scholastic discourse, this model represented both an ethical and a political prescription, an attempt that began in the late Middle Ages to hold the line against change.

In reality, society changed without ceasing during the early modern period, but not always at the same rate. In the eighteenth century the tempo accelerated, especially during the second half. The most important cause was the unprecedented rise in the population, thanks to greater employment opportunities provided by economic developments. The second cause was the advance of the cash economy. Ownership of money and the importance attached to money increased in two stages during the early modern period, first during the 'long sixteenth century' and once again in the eighteenth century. Together with the commercialization of the commodity world, they also brought a creeping devaluation of traditional ethics, the end of the moral stigma attached to luxury in the 1770s is a clear sign of this process. At the same time, the enhanced significance of money opened up new possibilities of social mobility. Well-to-do commoners used their money to acquire public office and landed property, which in turn paved the way for ennoblement. This also cost money, indeed some monarchs such as Louis XIV or Maria Theresa introduced a regular tariff which allowed both sides to calculate the benefits of noble status. The lower orders drawn into the cash economy also adopted a new lifestyle: sermons, moral homilies, and official publications are full of complaints about the early marriages and 'excessive' consumption indulged in by those who worked at a craft at home.

This dynamic necessarily involved a shift in the relations between various social groups. Opinions varied, but most saw the intrusion of market forces as a threat to be countered. It is not so very different today. As the effect of money was to devalue tradition, it was seen as unlawful and was resisted accordingly. *'Pecunia nervus rerum'* (money is the sinew of things) has been a well-known saying since Cicero, but for centuries it was applied only to money as a means of payment, as a means of exchange. But now, speaking metaphorically, money came to be seen to have the power to direct economy and society, and that was something different—namely, the beginning of modern capitalism.

Not surprisingly, this process coincided with the boom that began around 1760. Contrary to what is often written, it was not confined to the coal and cotton districts of the Midlands and the north of England. There were also sectoral shifts no less dynamic and impressive in Bohemia, Moravia, Silesia, Saxony, and the Zürich region, on the Lower Rhine, in Flanders and in northern France. In all these regions there was sustained growth despite demographic expansion and so societies avoided the Malthusian trap.

The boom affected branches of the economy that lay outside the mercantilist or cameralist economic order: in other words, the manufacture of standardized goods on a putting-out basis designed for social strata with low purchasing power. The sale of these mass goods was facilitated by such measures as the liberalizing of long-distance trade and a more effective international payments system. It was here that a 'market culture' found a point of entry, and it was from here that it spread ever further. This was possible because in the meantime almost everywhere in Europe it was the market that came to determine the price levels of commercial goods. The principle was extended increasingly to the most important foodstuff—grain— because at a time of intensifying urbanization and commercialization there was a correspondingly marked increase in the number of people who had to buy what they ate. That in turn led to agricultural specialization and the erosion of the traditional corporative structure. This was particularly important, because it was agriculture that continued to sustain a large majority of the population for the next hundred years or so.

The opportunities enjoyed by contemporaries to respond to these challenges naturally varied greatly. That is so obvious as to be banal. Less banal is the observation that the distribution of advantages and disadvantages was not specific to a group or social order but that all groups both benefited and suffered. Even less banal is the question of how these advantages and disadvantages were handled, for it is a question that allows deep insights into the structure of authority and society.

Estate-owners

Let us begin with the well-off. In the eighteenth century it was possible to earn enormous sums of money in commerce and banking, thanks to high profit margins (and correspondingly high risks), but the epitome of wealth and prestige was still associated with the ownership of land. The physiocrats' use of the simple phrase *classe propriétaire* (land-owning class) is indicative, because it enabled them to avoid the question of social rank. Indeed, just a glance at Europe reveals that in many places not only monarchs, clergy, and nobles but also commoners had obtained land and a lifestyle to go with it. It was this that injected a dynamism that we shall now consider.

The proportion of landowners without noble titles was greatest in England, thanks to its special social composition. Next came France and then, some way behind, Italy and the Austrian Netherlands. Between the Rhine and the Elbe this was too modern a phenomenon to be found to any large extent, although east of the Elbe, in Saxony, Brandenburg, Pomerania, and east Prussia, the dominance of the large self-contained estate *(Gutswirtschaft)* did allow rich commoners to acquire landed property, usually employing noble frontmen to make the purchase.

The existence of an 'agrarian bourgeoisie' testifies to dynamism in this sector, to the development of a market in land and a rise in rents. Rising rent levels in turn unleashed further dynamics. In England the 'enclosures' reached a first peak between 1755 and 1780 and despite high costs showed considerable profits. Speculation in land could be found all over Europe. In general we can say that the price of estates tripled between the first third of the eighteenth century and the revolutionary wars. That encouraged speculation, financed often by borrowing that ruined many purchasers if there was an interruption in the upward trend of prices or if interest rates rose. All in all, the market in land became mobile, especially west of the Rhine and along waterways and coasts. Landed property still conferred most prestige but the nobility and clergy had lost their monopoly.

Who were the new men, where did they get the money for their estate purchases, and why did landed property bestow so much prestige?

Given the current state of research, questions such as these can hardly be answered for the whole continent and for the whole century. However, the relatively well-researched sales of *biens nationaux* during the revolutionary period do allow a flash of light to fall on the admission of new social groups to the rural élite. Noble purchasers did acquire a number of lots, not many but expensive ones, thus proving their above-average capital resources. But the most heavily involved were manufacturers and merchants, senior officials, tax collectors, and tenant farmers.

This snap-shot can be applied to the land market in previous decades only with reservations. The different conditions prevailing for the purchase and sale of land in the pre-revolutionary era disadvantaged everyone who did not have a rural presence already. So those mainly involved were well-off tenant farmers and grain-dealers, tax collectors and lawyers, brewers and publicans; many of them combined more than one of these functions in a single person. For this reason, there is little evidence of tensions between noble landowners and non-noble new purchasers. They had usually been long connected by business interests and had also engaged in social intercourse through associations such as Masonic lodges. In other words, everyone knew each other and the ways of the rural world, spoke the same language, and accorded each other the necessary respect. It was important that the traditional hierarchy remained intact and that the nobility did not get the impression that they and their old estates were exposed to an attack by the middle class.

Nor did old and new landowners differ much when it came to cultivation. It is a myth that the new owners were looking for a quick return on capital and so proved to be the better husbandmen or the more ruthless exploiters. There is little evidence of the patriarchal relationship between noble and peasant that aristocratic apologists made so much of after 1789. All over Europe land registers were revised with a view to enforcing legal titles, attempts were made to increase services and dues, and claims to common land were intensified, while applications for reductions in the event of natural catastrophes, fires, or harvest failures were refused. In some places even new forms of seigneurial dues were imposed: in Luxembourg, for example, the tithe was imposed on the potato crop. As the cash nexus became increasingly important, seigneurial dues for the élites came to mean just a way of stabilizing or increasing income. So rates rose appreciably right across Europe. When the 'great fear' erupted in many parts of France in 1789, the peasants who revolted made no distinction between noble and commoner lords. That is a clear indication of what was really going on. The demands of the insurgents were directed towards the abolition of seigneurial dues and liberation from 'profiteers' and not against the nobility. Such was the extent to which the landowning class in France was unified—in terms of perception from below at least. In other countries the potential for conflict may have been less, but not the differences between landowners.

Especially during the second half of the century, ownership of land promised security for invested capital, rising income, and high prestige. The last-named of these was certainly the most important. No matter how much the market had expanded access to ownership, land was not merely an object for investment and speculation. All over Europe it came with certain rights attached, whether they were seigneurial or communal. The Revolution did nothing to shake the status of land, it just opened up access a bit further. So in drawing up a balance we are confronted by the paradoxical fact that the developing market in land was used to expand participation in the prestige of the traditional landowning élites. The social climbers thrust their way into the noble preserve not to destroy it but to make it their own. It was Napoleon who drew the obvious conclusion.

Tenants

Much older by far than the market in land was the market in the leasing of estates. It had created the agrarian middle class that we have already met as purchasers. Leasing naturally reacted with special sensitivity to rising and falling prices, for the agreements were usually made for three, six, or at most nine years. So rent levels increased in tandem with the land market. In the agrarian sector it was undoubtedly the tenants who were best placed to deal with the changes. They had always had to deal with the market, and their position allowed them to pass the growing pressure on to those below them.

It was the tenant farmers who were responsible for agricultural progress. That was in the nature of things, for the tenant farmers were obliged to feed neither the family of the landowner nor their own family directly from their produce. Rent was paid in cash, while obligations in kind virtually disappeared and that allowed adaptation to changing needs. The change stemmed from the growing division of labour in society and to the growing interconnection of previously isolated regions that accompanied it. The extension of the rotation of crops and the cultivation of forage crops in England, the transition to an improved three-field system on the continent, the greater attention paid to the breeding of cattle and sheep (the latter being Spain's contribution to agricultural productivity), the move to rice and conversion of land into permanent pasture in the Po valley, and finally the introduction of maize to Italy and southern and south-western France—all these were first introduced to agriculture on rented land. A growing number of travel reports, manuals, and academic treatises made the tenant farmer the point of reference for the agricultural future of Europe. That increased their prestige and so their social position rose. By the end of the century they could no longer be counted among the peasantry, adapting their lifestyle as much as possible to resemble that of their landlords. But what distinguished them most from the rest of the rural population was the nature of their dwellings and the care they devoted to the education of their children—especially, of course, to their sons.

Peasants

For the sake of simplicity we shall distinguish between those groups that owned land and those that did not, or, to be more precise, between those who made a positive contribution to the market for foodstuffs and those whose labour secured a bare subsistence for their families. Let us call the first group peasants and the second rural labourers, although aware that in reality hybrid forms predominated in many places.

The most important characteristic common to the peasants of continental Europe was that they did not dispose freely of the product of their labour, nor indeed were they able to produce freely. Only in Britain can one find a process of energetic modernization of the agricultural conditions of production, by which is meant a move to individual responsibility for the calculation of returns and market conditions. And for that reason it was also only in Britain that the corresponding theory could be developed that property rested on labour—as Locke did in his *Second Treatise on Government* (1689). A hundred years later on the continent this axiom of natural law would acquire some significance in the defeudalization process. For the time being there, the peasant was regarded, first as being tied to the little universe of the village and its communally organized agricultural system, and, secondly, where the seigneurial regime still persisted, as being the subject of a landlord or estate lord with his authority to regulate and control many aspects of his life. The unbalanced power relationship between the two parties prevented any true negotiation in most cases, so that both *de facto* and *de jure* peasant services—in kind but above all in the form of dues—rested not on a free contract but on coercion. So the burdens imposed on the operation were determined by the legal situation, by the needs and capacities of the landlord, not by the principle of cost-effectiveness. The same applies to various forms of share cropping that predominated in most wine-growing regions, generally in central and southern France and almost everywhere in Italy, for here too the contracts did not allow any opportunity for individual management.

But even this complex picture does not reveal the whole story about the peasants' conditions or their ability to adapt to changing conditions. They had a whole variety of lords with differing and often conflicting interests. The rulers viewed peasants primarily as tax-payers and their sons as soldiers. The institutional landowners, first and foremost the Church but also communities, charitable institutions, and universities, took the very long view and so often limited their exploitation—the old regime's adage 'living is good under the episcopal crozier' was not a fiction. In clear contrast to these groups, which for the most part enjoyed other sources of income, there were the noble or middle-class landlords who lived mainly from what they could extract from their peasants. So the burdens were correspond-ingly high. Where business management considerations meant that seigneurial exploitation could be pushed no higher and where direct farming promised higher profits, the landlords were all too keen to resort to simple expropriation (*Bauernlegen*) and to turn their peas-ants without further ado into indentured labourers. It was no acci-dent that such cases proliferated after the middle of the century, although the origins of the bifurcation between the agrarian systems east and west of the Elbe go further back. Only in Prussia did *raison d'état* prompt rulers to intervene to afford the peasants protection, in the first instance on the royal domains and then with less success on the noble estates. Around 1800 this led to considerable tension in the more developed regions of the Prussian monarchy, as the lords tried to share in the prospering economy by raising dues and services, while for the same reason the peasants refused to perform their services. The royal courts' attempt to impose binding obligations on both sides failed to satisfy either party. The time had come for the abolition of the seigneurial regime.

This identifies the second force that, for all the disadvantages of the seigneurial system, gave the peasants some room for manœuvre: rising prices, or, in other words, the market. Where limits to seigneurial exploitation either existed or could be imposed, and where transport conditions allowed a response to growing demands, there were new opportunities for peasant undertakings. Deficient sources make it difficult to establish with any precision who made use of these opportunities. Nevertheless, one example can illuminate the connection: in the region around Berlin in 1805 peasants needed to sell only about half as much grain to pay their taxes as they had done forty years earlier. As seigneurial dues did not keep pace with the increase in prices (mainly as a result of state intervention) and as grain cultivation increased by between a third and four-fifths, the net profits of holdings between 20 and 70 hectares enjoyed extraordinary growth. No wonder that the owners of these farms began to have their servants call them 'Mister', a practice that also began to be usual for the urban middle class at about the same time. This intensification of the market also brought the countryside into closer contact with the urban community, as can be seen from intermarriages and the increasing practice of these rich peasants of setting up their sons as craftsmen in the towns.

Rural labourers

Families with little or no land could only dream of this sort of thing. It was over them that the flood of population growth had washed with the most devastating effect. Across Europe the population rose by not less than forty to fifty million, and by far the largest number belonged to the lower orders. And it was in the second half of the century that their numbers grew fastest. It was not only gross population figures that determined their status or their opportunities, however. Also important were inheritance laws, urban density, and the incidence of rural manufacturing. Between the Atlantic and the Elbe, around the Mediterranean, in Poland and in Russia, there was hardly a family without some land, be it ever so small, thanks to partible inheritance. That was important for survival, for whoever could call even a snippet of land his own could also claim a share of the communal forest, grazing land, and also arable land where it existed. It is not yet possible to speak of rural labourers in the nineteenth-century sense and indeed the concept was not yet established. Most were day labourers, tenants and micro-landowners all rolled into one and sufficiently in control of their own lives to be able to marry when they liked. So it was no wonder that these regions were the most densely populated in Europe.

Things were different where one of the children inherited the lion's share. Sharp social divisions were the result. Part of the offspring lived celibate lives on the parental farm or sometimes on a neighbouring farm where there were insufficient children, or worked as labourers on the lord's domain. Inheritance of a few parcels of land might allow marriage but not self-subsistence. Nor did communal land offer an adequate substitute. This pattern produced thinly populated regions, so that the labour force on the farms and estates did not suffice when the fields were being tilled or harvested or when the grain was being threshed in winter. These seasonal peaks provided a bare living for those who relied on supplementary earnings. It is easy to imagine what effects a change to pastoral farming or the introduction of machinery had for these groups. While these changes did not make a major impact until the end of the nineteenth century, there had been a move towards the specialized production of milk and meat more than a century earlier along the coasts of the North Sea and Baltic and in the Po valley, and that brought a substantial reduction in the demand for labour. That this development occurred at a time when even regions with slack to take up were experiencing a first population surge did not make life any easier for the lower strata.

As always, those with no property and those with little property had to adapt to changing circumstances. What they wanted most was to become proper peasants, but the reserves of land were just not big enough. Public money allowed the draining and cultivation of some of the last great bogs, and here and there a few new farms were won from the North Sea with the help of dykes, but all that affected only a few tens of thousands of families. In the central regions of Europe the frontier of settlement had been pushed to climatic limits centuries earlier and the perseverance of the 'little ice age' into the eighteenth century did not allow any higher regions to be cultivated. So other possibilities had to be considered.

In theory it is clear that most of these possibilities had to be found outside agriculture. Whether they really were is a different matter, but it was here that the most striking changes to European society in the eighteenth century occurred. A growing number of people moved out of the agrarian sector and sought their living increasingly from wage-labouring, generally recognized as the most important designator of a class-based society.

The growing oversupply of labour in agriculture directed more and more people to manufacturing activities, especially those suited to smallholders with their low technical qualifications, lack of capital and limited liberty. The list of what was available is short: transport by sea and land; retailing by peddling or shopkeeping; and— incomparably the largest sector—manufacturing. The last-named stretched from textile production—spinning, weaving, lacemaking, stocking-knitting, etc.—to timber-working—carving, turning, weaving, button-making, charcoal-burning, potash-making, etc.—to specialized industries that were confined to certain regions, such as silkworm breeding, mining, glass-blowing, iron smelting, and metalworking. These examples could be multiplied. In the eighteenth century hundreds of thousands worked at the spinner's wheel and the weaver's loom, producing goods for others, and tens of thousands migrated from place to place as seasonal workers, getting in the harvest, felling trees to meet the rapidly growing demand for wood, sweeping chimneys or building houses, peddling lemons, mousetraps, and popular literature. For future developments, it was important that many of these activities could be undertaken independently. But the further removed the market, the greater the need for intermediaries. This brought merchants into play and with them many of the symptoms that accompany modern commercial capitalism.

The surplus rural population's attempts to supplement its income necessarily involved participation in a market of local or greater extent in which money alone regulated exchange. So not only in its upper echelons was the rural world increasingly penetrated by the cash nexus that eroded the traditional social order and its value-system. Even so, money in the hands of the lower orders performed a different function. The more they were separated from agriculture and therefore the less they needed for the purchase or rent of land, the more they spent on consumer goods. What the possessing classes criticized as 'reckless expenditure' on the part of their inferiors was, from an economic point of view, a contribution to the market society and even more importantly was also a contribution to the formation of a market culture. The increase in the circulation of money thus propelled the economy of the late eighteenth century irrevocably in quite a new direction.

This reveals something of the great variety of function performed by this social group. For agriculture it was important that the lower orders formed a labour reservoir that could service peak demands and also that through their renting of land and purchasing of food or raw materials (flax, wool, dyestuffs), they supplemented the perennially modest cash reserves of the peasants. They performed a similar service for the manufacturing sector. They bought its products, mainly standardized items of mass production, and provided the necessary labour force. Although their individual purchasing power was extremely small, taken as a whole they created a perceptibly growing demand for a new type of commodity: cheap mass-produced goods. Because the inflexible craft industries of the towns could not make an adequate response, the only solution was the putting-out system, a form of enterprise that united town and country.

In this way, the late eighteenth century witnessed an economic differentiation of Europe as a result of social forces. Some of the more concentrated manufacturing regions had already lost the ability to supply themselves with food from their own resources. The spatial division of labour that this introduced could be accommodated only by the development of a market for agricultural produce and appropriate transport services, both of which were given an additional impulse as a result.

The rapid increase in secondary occupations benefited all sectors, the agrarian no less than the manufacturing and also the tertiary sector that is so often neglected. Landless or virtually landless families seeking their livelihood in two or three of these sectors unintentionally cushioned these sectors' economic risks. As these people led what was technically an independent existence, they had no other choice but to exploit themselves—that is they had to work for little or no money to try to close the gap between income and expenditure caused by the rising price of food, the falling price of manufactured goods, or the reduced demand for labour services. So entrepreneurs, especially those engaged in putting-out, were less affected by recessions and thus by an important potential obstacle.

The interconnections we have discussed show that it was especially in the countryside that important preconditions had been prepared for the transformation of the economic order into a new kind of system. They are a reminder of the rural and agrarian origins of modern capitalism, as Marx stressed. They were rediscovered by scholars in the 1970s and tied into the concept of proto-industrialization to form a complex system combining demography, social structure, domestic industry, and agriculture, as Sheilagh Ogilvie has shown in her chapter in this volume. One of the most important discoveries has been that the possibility of risk reduction and the free availability of labour were much more important for potential entrepreneurs at the end of the eighteenth century and the beginning of the next than the supply of capital to which historians so long gave prominence. It was rural society above all that provided both conditions, and it bears repeating that it was rural society that made a crucial if often underestimated contribution to the development of the industrial system. Industrialization did not come about because of the spectacular series of inventions—Arkwright's water frame, Hargreaves's spinning jenny, Crompton's mule, or Watts's steam engine—and it was not confined to a few counties in the English Midlands.

Industrial workers

These last sections have taken us imperceptibly into the industrial sector, and intentionally so, for the notion that there were three clearly divided sectors in the eighteenth century is an anachronism. On the other hand, it would be wrong to ignore the sectoral divisions. But at first let us stay with what they had in common. Two things strike one immediately. For the world of manufacturing, mining, and metalworking, most labourers came from the immediate environs. They came from the countryside, where many still owned a plot of land and still had relations, indeed in eastern Europe the workers were still serfs. In other words, rural labourers and industrial workers at this time were often the same people, so the link to the land was still intensive and the country's natural rhythms extended into the towns. When the harvest began, many manufacturing enterprises had to close because a large part of their labour force went missing for weeks on end.

The second common characteristic was closely connected with the first and was no less important in determining experience, behaviour, and opportunity: it was the miserable, indeed the declining rates of pay. Economists and historians regard a reduction in real wages as one of the distinguishing features of the modern period. In reality this thesis applies only to those paid in cash, and they without doubt constituted a tiny minority. What is meant is that the scissors between the cost of living and rewards from labouring opened wider and wider. Strictly speaking, in a society of orders that was ruled out, for here everyone received his due, which varied of course from one social group to another because so did needs. Traditionally, society should guarantee what was essential for human existence, and the due allocation of goods in accordance with social status was one of its main responsibilities. That represented the general expectation and to that extent the social order was accepted as just. So nothing indicates the erosion of this order better than the fact that a growing section of society no longer did receive 'his due'—namely all those who were paid in cash. There was no room for wage labour in the traditional society of self-sufficient economies and that was why it was wage labourers who were the first to leave it. The hypothesis of falling real wages in the modern period really amounts to nothing more than the observation that demographic pressure in pre-industrial conditions allowed the numbers of those on the margins to grow and thus exert constant downward pressure on wage rates. No other social group was more drastically or more directly affected by social change than those who would later be categorized as workers.

How can a fall in wages be reconciled with an expansion of manufacturing production? The apparent contradiction disappears if three things are borne in mind. First, it must be remembered that in this context it is exclusively a question of standardized mass production, first and foremost yarn and cloth. By the late eighteenth century, technological improvements and inventions were promoting a significant increase in productivity. That led to a drastic fall in prices, at certain times faster than the average fall in wages. Secondly, demand increased not only as a result of this differential in the development of wages and prices but also quite simply because the population grew. The forty or fifty million additional Europeans not only had to be fed they also had to be clothed and provided with a roof over their heads. Housing was skimped on most, and so the first slums appeared. On the other hand, nourishment was a relatively inelastic need and consumed a correspondingly high proportion of a person's income, normally at least two-thirds. There was not much left for clothing, but fortunately one way out of the impasse was provided by the change in fashion, which provided cotton or cotton-mixed fabrics that were cheaper than traditional woollens, albeit less durable. Thirdly, a small percentage of the mass-produced goods were exported from Europe to overseas.

The workers engaged in manufacturing produced all manner of goods, from coal to paper, wallpaper, glass, metal, and above all, textiles (at every stage from weaving to finishing). They acquired the skills they needed in an informal manner from entrepreneurs, foremen or their seniors. The lower the level of skill required, the higher the proportion of women and children involved. In textile manufacturing they often constituted more than 50 per cent of the workforce and the wage rates were correspondingly low. This indicates one of the three kinds of hierarchy that characterized this working environment—the gender specific. The two others were formed by age and training. The young were just starting out, were paid less, and were subjected to a rigorous discipline, with fines and beating part of daily life. And, of course the young were also mobile. From all sides came laments about wilful absenteeism: as the factory-owners complained, the workers just dropped their tools and disappeared 'whenever they felt like it'. The reliability of the employees stood in direct ratio to their age, at least so long as there was no recession. The third hierarchy was determined by training. At the head of these large enterprises or early forms of factories stood the specialists. They were seldom members of craft guilds, for few skills that were needed here could be acquired in handicraft. They learned their profession on the job, were correspondingly mature and commanded the skills necessary to produce properly smelted metal, high-quality paper, cleanly printed wallpaper and fabrics, smoothly polished mirrors. They were often from another country or at least another region, as specialized knowledge was not available everywhere: Bohemian glass-makers, Walloon casters, Saxon porcelain manufacturers, silk-weavers from

Lyons, mechanics from the Jura, not forgetting the English foremen. This often put considerable strain on the tolerance of other religions and lifestyles.

Hierarchies are revealed by status and wages. The growing differentiation of the latter in the eighteenth century showed that the structure was changing. Depending on the type of manufacturing involved, the rates paid to beginners or the young could be anywhere from four to sixteen times lower than those paid to labour élites. Clearly demand far outstripped supply at the top, which is not surprising in view of the period of prosperity that began around 1740. In absolute terms, the highest earners were to be found in the mines, in mirror factories, and the arsenals. Their wages were high because so much was paid in kind. In addition to cash, the specialists also received board and lodging, including heating and light, which ensured a perceptible increase in wages after 1770 when prices began to rise steeply. But these were the exceptions. If the fall in real wages mentioned above cannot be calculated exactly—only French historians are prepared to venture an estimate, suggesting a fall of between 25 and 40 per cent in the four decades before the Revolution—it is certain that it did happen all over the continent and continued until the 'hungry forties' of the following century. British workers too perceived this period as a time of crisis, although recent research has suggested that real wages either stagnated or even grew slightly during the closing decades of the eighteenth century, which may be explained as a result of a fall in the price of manufactured goods due to industrialization.

The world of work in the manufacturing sector was different in every respect from the conditions that prevailed in agriculture or handicraft, for here work was always a group activity. The size of the manufacturing enterprises usually varied between five and twenty employees, although there were some with over a hundred. Workers were exposed to conditions that were usually unhealthy and to frequent bouts of unemployment. As manufacturing produced mainly for consumers whose purchasing power depended on the harvest, a rise in the price of food robbed most concerns of their demand. A calendar year embraced barely 270 working days—and that figure may have been appreciably smaller in Catholic regions thanks to the numerous religious festivals until the 1770s when there was a general move by the secular authorities to reduce their number.

Both workers in manufacturing and families engaged in proto-industrial activity in the countryside used specific defence mechanisms when trying to deal with their insecure and changing conditions—general poverty and fluctuating wage levels but also possession of money even when young. The keepers of the traditional code of morals reviled them as 'prodigal' or 'immoral'. Their behaviour was attacked as evidence of a decline in morals, especially their wanton refusal to take precautions against a rainy day. They were accused of living riotously in good times, and then relying on poor relief during recessions; of marrying young, often without the blessing of the Church, and of abandoning their children, of laziness and absenteeism, of unruly behaviour, 'indecent' language and a lack of respect for their elders and betters. There were also complaints about their violence. Fighting was common in the working quarters, mainly directed against rivals in business and love, but also against foremen and the authorities. The latter responded partly by the billeting of troops or in England the calling out of the militia and partly by transferring judicial powers to landlords and factory-owners, who thus exercised a quasi-feudal control over their labour force.

The moral guardians had identified the symptoms accurately but not the causes. Just as modern society itself was still in its early stages, so modern social science had not yet progressed beyond the very first stages. Moral verdicts were a substitute for social criticism. The latter could be found occasionally, as in the work of the Abbé Raynal or Diderot, himself from modest origins, and the English radicals. The usual answer, however, was repression, and only in England did the Methodists adopt a perspective more attuned to reality and develop programmes for the improvement of workers' morals and living conditions through Sunday schools, temperance societies, spinning instruction for girls, soup kitchens, and so on. In England practical charity was accepted as an obligation by some members of the élite.

The workers themselves did hardly anything to improve their condition. Richly various, divided by several different hierarchies, pursuing all manner of trades and living widely scattered, they had nothing in common but their wretched position. At best it can be said that the crisis of the 1770s led to labour unrest in the newer branches such as paper and mirror-manufacturing, which required high levels of skill and were therefore not far removed from handicraft modes of behaviour. For the rest, it was the conflict pattern of the rural world from which most of the workers stemmed that determined their behaviour: spontaneous strikes, violence, and short-term objectives (what later critics were to call 'immediatism'). These outbreaks achieved very little in material terms and only encouraged the authorities to equate 'labouring classes' with 'dangerous classes', a stereotype that was to have a long life.

High finance

It is the thesis of this chapter that there were many more elements of class formation to be found at the bottom of society than at the top. It was easier at the top to ward off the intrusion of the market, yet it was the top that benefited most from change. To put it another way: at the bottom the vagaries of the market affected sheer existence, while at the top it was mainly a matter for speculation. At the bottom, one is controlled by capitalism, at the top one helps to create it; at the bottom, capitalism is fate, at the top it is a profession.

Since time out of mind, trade in goods had been conducted on three levels. At the base there was the mass of peddlers, hawkers, hucksters, at best shopkeepers. This sector was characterized by simple goods, low customer purchasing power, manifold regulation, and a high degree of specialization. Where transactions were conducted using money, it was irregular, inflation-prone copper currency that was used. The next level comprised the long-distance, competitive world of the merchants. This was an urban world, likewise highly specialized, using silver money (and recently gold too in Britain and France) but also credit in many different forms and controlled by the authorities. At the summit there was a small group—high finance. This provided the links between countries and continents, was specialized in terms of neither nationality nor religion, lived from the commission business, was financed by credit, insured against maritime loss, and serviced transactions mainly by credit.

Like rural society, commerce in the eighteenth century was largely a constituent part of the society of orders, so that new and dynamic forces had to operate outside it. While tradesmen and merchants were organised as corporations, the most fundamental retailing level of peddlers, hawkers, and village shopkeepers (still a rarity in this period) had to get along without this collective security. For them this would have been a matter of regret, while for the upper echelons the lack of control was welcome. Although the latter still called themselves 'merchants', they no longer dealt in goods but in money. As contemporary commercial manuals never tired of complaining, they were free from all guild ties and all state regulation. The money market was perhaps the only truly free zone in the eighteenth century.

What governed admission to this world of high finance, which in the course of the eighteenth century generated for Europe—and especially Britain—a growing world trade and extraordinary prosperity? Essential qualifications were professional training and capital. The training came from a long apprenticeship, often served overseas, and the integration in a network that exchanged information quickly and confidentially; the capital usually came from inherited wealth. Interlopers at this level were as rare as total business failures, for the network bound firms and individuals together. Great trading companies, usually furnished with privileges, had run overseas commerce since the beginning of the seventeenth century, although towards its end joint-stock companies became more important, at least in the more developed centres of north-western Europe. In terms of commercial and financial techniques, the contribution of the eighteenth century was barely perceptible: the circulation of banknotes, for example, did not really get established on the continent. Moreover, in the course of the century only three stock exchanges were founded, and they were typical latecomers—La Rochelle in 1761, Berlin in the same year, and Vienna ten years after that.

The estimate of national income conducted by Colquhoun in 1803 reveals the unprecedented dynamism of English merchants and bankers. Although peers were of course still at the top of his league table, their share of national income appears to have stagnated during the previous hundred years. But the share of wholesale trade and finance had increased seven times, not only because this group was more numerous but also because its members were much richer. Intermarriage with the aristocracy also provided clear evidence of social climbing.

For the continent no such calculations are possible. Nor is the position of bankers within the social hierarchy simple to describe. Take, for example, the Rothschilds, still obliged to live in a Frankfurt ghetto despite all their riches. On the other hand, in many Free Cities of the Holy Roman Empire such as Frankfurt, Cologne, and

Hamburg, and also in other European equivalents such as Geneva, Antwerp, and Genoa, there were bankers who sat on town councils, a clear indication of their high status. In the monarchies of the old regime, however, they occupied only a subordinate position. Examples of financiers acquiring princely status such as the Fuggers and the Welsers in the sixteenth century were not repeated in the eighteenth. This was perhaps the price that had to be paid for operating outside the society of orders, where the interdependence of rank, prestige, influence and property was held to be part of the natural order and was defended as such with all means until the Revolution.

Within the world of high finance on the continent there was a clear hierarchy. The top group was formed by the 'Protestant bankers' consisting of Calvinist Genevans and Huguenot *émigrés*. Located in the London–Cadiz–Geneva triangle, they dominated west European markets, especially the French. The Huguenots had earned their capital from overseas trade, the Genevans from the silk trade and the clock-making industry, and for that reason, their links to manufacturing enterprises remained remarkably close. But since they had started dealing with the French state, they had moved their operations to Paris and concentrated on state loans and tax farming. Their close connections with the political world was never better personified than by Jacques Necker, the long-standing banker of Louis XV and the finance minister of Louis XVI.

In central Europe, most banking concerns were characterized by a combination of financial transactions, commission business, and manufacturing. The Vienna banking house of Fries financed the cotton manufacturing of Lower Austria, Schaafhausen and Herstatt of Cologne financed the Rhenish metal industry, Eichhorn of Breslau and Barons Stromer and Tucher of Nuremberg financed the Bohemian textile industry. But here too the lion's share of business consisted in state credits, for the simple reason that the demand was greater and the risks were less. If every prince of the Holy Roman Empire had a 'court Jew' to supply credit, the major loans were provided by consortia in which only a few Jewish bankers participated, with the legendary Rothschilds to the fore.

During the wars of the French Revolution and Napoleon, the traditional society of orders collapsed, while the world of high finance, which had been separate from it to a certain extent, had to undergo an intense crisis of adaptation. All the continental banking houses engaged in overseas commerce went bankrupt, mainly as a result of Napoleon's continental blockade. Quick profits could be won from switching to supplying armies, but most bankers preferred the classical business of providing state loans, for this was safer than ever, following the stabilization of currencies at the turn of the century. Bankers in Liverpool, Bristol, and above all, London enjoyed two decades free from continental competition during which they could extend their global presence and help their government to finance the war. Just how much could be earned in this way is shown by the increase of the British national debt from £228,000,000 in 1793 to no less than £876,000,000 in 1816. Napoleon thus made a powerful contribution to the hegemony of London banking.

Jews

If one looks at the European social order, as we have done, mainly from the perspective of what was progressive and led to the development of classes, then we should pay attention to a group normally left out of social history on the grounds that numerically it was only a small minority. Of all the social groups examined so far, the Jews had by far the most class characteristics, indeed one could say that the Jewish minority consisted entirely of classes, because Jews' opportunities in life depended almost exclusively on their opportunities for earning a living. The latter were not a matter of choice but were extremely regulated. To put it bluntly: continental Jews were hemmed in by every form of restriction that could be imagined by state avarice and Christian prejudice, designed to keep them as a necessary but unpopular marginal group disqualified from normal society—that is, the society of orders. But, within the tight boundaries imposed by the regulation of domicile and profession, the market ruled without restriction, and so we are justified in speaking of a Jewish class society.

In the eighteenth century, this class society was confronted by two dramatic and closely related events: proletarianization and emancipation. Proletarianization was partly due to the restrictions on property acquisition, civil rights, and domicile that limited Jews' occupations. It was also partly due to the economic pressure exerted by demographic increase, deriving in turn both from a surplus of births, as with the Christian majority, and also from immigration from the

East. Finally, it was also partly due to the decline of the urban economy, which was also a general characteristic of the age.

If one disregards the Ottoman Empire, the great mass of Jews
lived in the Polish–Lithuanian Commonwealth, where relatively
favourable economic opportunities were interrupted periodically by
local and even nationwide pogroms. It was the latter that unleashed
waves of emigration to central Europe. In this region, stretching
from Bohemia to Alsace, the interest taken in Jews by both absolutist states and self-governing city republics was almost exclusively
fiscal. Any ability other than that to pay taxes was of no interest.
The political consequences of this concern had led to a tripartite
division of the Jewish minority. At the top stood a small élite,
amounting to some 2 per cent and consisting mainly of court Jews
and princes' agents, who led a lifestyle that barely distinguished
them from the upper ranks of officials and the court nobility. Four
times larger was the group of so-called protected Jews who paid
very high special dues for their toleration and could usually pass
this status on to only one of their children. In the towns they
earned their living through petty credit transactions, in various
kinds of dealing and sometimes as medical practitioners, and in the
countryside through cattle-dealing and allied trades, which also
often involved money lending. In the eighteenth century, however,
nine out of ten Jews did not enjoy this protected status and wan-
dered from one community to the next, seeking to eke out their
peddling by begging. These 'beggar Jews' became a social problem
of the first order, for they could not pursue a settled existence and
lived constantly on the margins of legality. This prompted the absolutist state to intervene repeatedly with fresh regulations and pro-
hibitions, all of which were aimed at deporting the problem. So the
second half of the eighteenth century was full of complaints about
the Jewish minority and about the majority within that minority—
the beggar Jews.

There really was a Jewish question and the need to deal with it
became ever more pressing. The solutions proposed towards the end
of the eighteenth century could not have been more various. Some
Jewish spokesmen called for nothing less than collective equality,
while others demanded complete acculturation: the abandoning of
Yiddish, professional restructuring, and the acceptance of a middle-
class code of values.

In the eighteenth century, this problem could not be solved. So far as Alsace and the German territories occupied by France after 1794 were concerned, the emancipatory legislation of the French Revolution caused a breach between the minority of urban Jews, who were in favour of emancipation, and most rural Jews, who remained attached to their traditions. It was a breach that Napoleon used as a pretext for the reversal of the whole emancipation process. In the Holy Roman Empire, the first measures taken by enlightened princes to promote emancipation unleashed local conflicts. Neither the people of the villages nor the guilds of the towns were prepared to share their inadequate and dwindling resources with those hitherto excluded. But nor did the nineteenth century find a solution acceptable to both sides. Outside central Europe, Jewish life was confined to a few towns. Even where Jews continued to live in ghettos, as in Italy, their trade was distinguished by acquired riches and international connections. Consequently, the emancipation imposed by French conquerors after 1794 did not encounter the same obstacles as in Germany.

Apparently unspectacular was the development in England, where Jews had been settling again from the mid-seventeenth century onwards, at first only in London. Immigration was not impeded by any serious legal obstacles. More important was the geographical insularity that inhibited the flow of beggar Jews from central and eastern Europe. Even so, the number of English Jews increased by ten times in the course of the eighteenth century, an increase that prompted repeated criticism and attempts to halt immigration. Agitation reached a climax in 1753, when rioting against the naturalization law, encouraged by the Anglican Church, prompted the government to back down. However, this setback did not alter the Jews' freedom of movement or—within certain limits—their choice of profession. It has rightly been pointed out that Sephardic Jews in England were seeking complete equality at a time when their co-religionists on the continent were still attacking any of their number who made even the smallest move towards cultural assimilation with Gentile society. But it should also not be forgotten that Anglicans did not view the Jews as their worst enemies and treated less leniently all kinds of Christian dissenters, especially the 'Papists'. On the continent, on the other hand, Christian minorities used to be treated more generously than the Jews.

Poverty and poor relief

Poverty developed in a dramatic fashion in the eighteenth century. The increase in population and the rise in the price of food by 60 per cent and more led to a considerable increase in hardship in almost all parts of Europe during the closing decades. Among the most obvious consequences was crime. More and more often, the unemployed, beggars, and vagrants joined to form gangs that terrorized whole regions. From the 1770s onwards, travelling became hazardous in southern France, Lombardy, and the Neapolitan hinterland, as in the central uplands of Germany between the Hunsrück and the Bohemian Forest after the outbreak of the revolutionary wars.

Poverty *per se* was nothing new, of course. It was its nature that changed in the course of the eighteenth century. Poverty was no longer primarily the result of the unholy trinity of famine, plague, and war, which anyway made little discrimination between rich and poor. In their place came a new phenomenon: the permanent under-nourishment of a significant portion of both the rural and the urban population. The undernourished can contract marriages and pro-duce children and thus perpetuate their misery. This was exactly what happened in the eighteenth century and it was something new that poverty proved self-generating. Also new was the fact that the poor could work hard and continuously yet still suffer hardship. While traditionally the poor were widows or orphans, invalids or lunatics, handicapped or pilgrims, very young or very old, mainly female and almost always single town-dwellers, the new variety of poverty had a different configuration. The new poor were mainly rural, male, and in the best years of their life.

European society was not ready for this phenomenon. Tradition-ally, ecclesiastical and municipal institutions had been sufficient to attend to the poor, albeit only after a fashion, by means of alms-houses, foundations, and confraternities. Those who were categorized as 'idle' because they were of an age to work for a living, now began to be locked up in 'workhouses' or 'places of correction'. Progress had been limited in this direction, however, because of the high cost. Cheaper options employed were conscription into the armed forces, deportation, branding, and other brutal measures. But the 'great confinement' of the poor is a myth, not least because it is now clear that most poverty was to be found in the countryside, where such institutions were not to be found.

Contemporaries reacted with incomprehension. They continued to see poverty as a moral issue and so continued to call on the authorities to punish, on the propertied to do more for the poor, and on the poor to work harder and to save more. Only in Britain had the symptoms been understood and the economic causes of rural poverty discovered. Gilbert's Act of 1782 obliged those responsible to provide workhouses for those who could not help themselves. That was a first step. A more important second stride was taken by Justices of the Peace in Berkshire in 1795 when they responded to the impossibility of finding work for a living wage by pegging a family's level of support to the price of bread and the number of mouths to be fed. 'The Speenhamland system', as it became known, was soon adopted by many communities in southern and eastern England. In 1796 the 'workhouse test' was abandoned. One unintended consequence was that farmers now reduced wages, so that the burden on the poor rate rose to heights that had not been anticipated.

The British chose a different path because a more modern society allowed a sharper insight into the economic nexus. Adam Smith's advocacy of a high wages policy underlined this, as did the appearance of the neologism 'labouring poor'. The latter shows that this new kind of poverty had been conceptualized by the second half of the eighteenth century. The pragmatic character of the concept protected it against becoming part of an ideology. That was what happened on the continent as a consequence of the French Revolution, with the result that the social and political situation was described in ideological terms. So words such as the French *prolétaire* or the German *Proletarier* were used not just to describe what existed at present but to agitate for future action. The new kind of poverty was in the process of acquiring a revolutionary quality.

Social forces making for continuity

The time has come to address what in the eighteenth century generally counted as the social norm: the society of orders. Even social climbers did not call it into question, rather they sought to share in the advantages enjoyed by their social superiors. These advantages were defended with corresponding vehemence, and less by the pen than by action. It was a state of affairs that was experienced rather than conceptualized and so was taken for granted.

When it came to the defence of the status quo, only two social groups counted: the nobility and the burghers of the towns (in terms of the social hierarchy the clergy should be counted with one or other of these groups). The burghers did not include all urban residents, only those who were tied into the corporation and participated in the running of the town's affairs. It was they and the nobility who had at their disposal instruments of power to assert their interests and so were seen as the main enemy by those who advocated a new society organized on the basis of individual rights. So it is on them that we shall concentrate.

At once, however, we encounter two major problems of perspective. Our image of these two groups has been considerably distorted by what is inevitably our post-evolutionary perspective. Together with the closely related Catholic clergy, they were among the main victims of the Revolution, and, because the Revolution won, it is seen to be right. That means that attention is focused on signs of decay rather than simple continuity. Just because the latter is unspectacular, it leaves less tangible evidence. The revelation of what was ordinary can reveal much of what the age thought of itself but is often distorted. This is something to be borne in mind when pre-revolutionary society—itself a problematic formulation—is analysed.

The nobility

The unity of the nobility was an ideological construction of the French Revolution. In old regime France there was the *noblesse d'épée* and the *noblesse de robe*; in Spain the grandees and the *hidalgos*; in Italy the patriciate, the feudal nobility, and more recently the service nobility; in the Holy Roman Empire, there were nobles subject only to the Emperor and nobles subject to the princes. Even in Britain a distinction was made between the peers of the realm and the gentry. Legally speaking all these groups were quite separate and no one in the eighteenth century thought of breaking down the barriers between them. They were separated by law, marriage, income, lifestyle, and proximity to the throne. With all that said, in what follows we may permit ourselves to treat the nobility as a whole because what interests us here is how it tried to maintain its status. There is no space to deal with the numerous variations and we must concentrate on what the members of the nobility had in common.

The nobility sought to secure its existence in three ways: by family systems, by marriage strategies, and by privileges. In the first two cases it was in control of its own destiny and nothing changed in the course of the eighteenth century that might be described as weakness or even loss. So far as privileges were concerned, however, the nobility had to deal with the state, the very essence of innovation, and here things did change—and not to the advantage of the nobility.

In old-regime society every social group had developed its own family system. While the nobility's age of marriage and number of children varied and so reveal little that is specific, in other spheres of activity peculiarities do appear. In the first place, there is the high proportion of children who never married. Of course, care was taken to ensure the family's survival, but the number of marriages was restricted, to keep the property intact. This was a calculation fraught with uncertainties, which explains the high—and sharply rising—number of families dying out in the course of the century. Secondly, there is the lack of emotion in relations between husband and wife and between parents and children. Instead there was a rigorous hierarchy of the eldest in any generation. As correspondence and journals reveal, 'fear' was a concept to be used in a favourable sense when human relations were being discussed. Decision-making on the fate of a child belonged exclusively to the father, and there was no appeal: incarceration was not ruled out, expulsion from the ancestral home was frequent. Thirdly, there was a concern for keeping the family pride going, indeed for every generation ancestor worship was a central concern. All members of the family were expected to have precise knowledge of the ancestors who looked down on them from portraits, were immortalized on gravestones and were recorded in family trees. Without a pedigree authenticated by fellow nobles, true nobility was unthinkable—a problem that could cause acute embarrassment to the recently ennobled or the progeny of *mésalliances*. Periodic testing of claims to nobility sorted out the chaff from the wheat.

That raises the question of marriage strategies. Love played no part. A good dowry was, of course, desirable, but it was equality of rank that was decisive. *Mésalliances* were a form of social suicide, while morganatic marriages were confined to sovereigns or their greatest magnates and even they could not save their issue from being treated as outsiders. Consequently, the marriage of the heir was a central concern when a family planned its future. The more exclusive a family became, the smaller the number of eligible partners. One feature of the great noble families of Europe was their international flavour, as was also revealed—at least during the first half of the century—by the international careers of men such as Prince Eugene of Savoy (who signed his name using the trilingual form 'Eugenio von Savoie'). At the other end of the scale was the provincial noble. He secured a niche for himself by marrying into a regional network. Here all the families were related to each other. So external competition was excluded and internal problems could be regulated by agreement.

Finally, there were privileges. In the first place they made the noble a separate legal order. The noble conception of honour not only produced a specific concept of criminal behaviour but also demanded special procedures. Duelling, the right to trial by one's peers, and exemption from demeaning forms of punishment were all taken for granted by nobles across Europe in the late eighteenth century, even if they were subjected to growing criticism by enlightened thinkers, including nobles. A second bundle of privileges applied to the sphere of lordship, which was of two kinds. There was the authority exercised over land and people, involving the receipt of dues and tithes, the dispensing of justice, and in some places the control of serfs; and there was the authority exercised through participation in government by membership of a national or regional assembly. Although noble apologists never tired of stressing that this was a question not of privilege but of right, in reality it came to look the other way round by the eighteenth century. Many monarchs had succeeded long ago in freeing themselves from the control of noble assemblies, the keyword 'absolutism' must serve here as a summary of a complex development. More recently, that is during the second half of the century, rulers had moved on to place limits on the nobles' powers over their subjects. This encroachment on the central core of the nobles' self-image unleashed resistance, even revolt, as was demonstrated by the Belgians and Hungarians immediately before the outbreak of the Revolution in France. Their ruler, Joseph II, had trampled on the nobility's most fundamental political axioms by opposing to their ideal of a feudal relationship based on loyalty, faith, and respect for tradition the modern alternative of an institutional state of monarch, bureaucrats, and subjects. But the nobles could not sustain their ideal in the eighteenth century and their decline from being an Estate that participated in power to being just a privileged élite was inexorable.

A third bundle of privileges was also subject to inexorable change in the eighteenth century: service. Since time immemorial the nobility had thought of itself as the servant of the monarch. For the grandees it was an expensive honour; for the lesser nobility it was in part their livelihood, especially in Russia and the Holy Roman Empire. Since the late seventeenth century, however, government increasingly meant administration, except perhaps in Russia and Britain. But the nobility showed little enthusiasm for acquiring the necessary specialist skills or for adapting its lifestyle to accommodate a bureaucratic career. Nobility involved a way of life, not the exercise of a profession bound by rules and regulations.

If service changed in the course of the century to become work, it was a different matter in the armed services. The type of warfare pursued during the seventeenth and eighteenth centuries required an army whose officers could combine without difficulty a noble way of life with military service. *Mutatis mutandis*, the same applied to service at court. Here too it was a question not of work but of honour. The court was organized ceremonially not bureaucratically and attendance did not carry with it the connotation of a full-time job. So, when a noble formed a mental picture of his passage through life, service at court played a central role.

Attempts to protect their world against incursions by middle-class *parvenus* or new nobles could succeed only where the nobles could organize themselves as an autonomous unit or where they enjoyed the support of the sovereign. That situation applied above all in the Holy Roman Empire, but even there it did not apply to the state apparatus. German sovereigns were also noticeably restrained in their creation of new nobles. In France, on the other hand, where around a quarter of landed property was in middle-class hands by this time, the line could not be held and a regular tariff for the sale of noble status had been established. In 1789 between 40 and 50 per cent of the nobility belonged to the *noblesse nouvelle*, with at most three to five generations behind them and enjoyed a correspondingly low status.

Although England had enjoyed relatively high social mobility since the Civil War, its peerage was normally recruited from the gentry. True climbers starting with nothing found it much more difficult, although the high offices of state did offer a route to the top as an alternative to the ownership of land. Even so, throughout the old regime it remained exceptional for personal achievement to join wealth as a means of crossing social barriers. Only the top lawyers of the central law courts of the Holy Roman Empire could entertain realistic hopes of making the breakthrough. That was demonstrated by the narrow aperture limiting access to the highest reaches of society: expert knowledge, high political office, or even outstanding achievement in office were by no means enough. The surest route to noble status led through the expanding market in land, and that remained the case until the third quarter of the nineteenth century, when a combination of agrarian depression and maturing industrialization began to restructure European society in quite a new way.

Conflict lines varied across Europe at the end of the eighteenth century. In the centre, between Stockholm and Florence, the line ran between the nobility and the expanding state. In France and Naples it ran between the nobility and the Third Estate. Revolutionaries were to be found sitting on thrones as well as in the National Assembly. For the nobles, the identity of the revolutionary was unimportant, indeed it might even be said that they saw Joseph II as more dangerous than the Abbé Sieyès. The latter certainly found more people who thought like him among the nobility than the former did, for it was more attractive to merge in a new élite than to submit oneself to an absolute monarch. From this perspective, the Revolution was fighting the wrong enemy, although de Tocqueville was later to point out that the real victor was not the bourgeoisie but the state. In the end therefore, conflict lines coincided: the nobility and modern institutions were like fire and water.

If Montesquieu's script had been followed, neither conflict line would have existed. But the old regime's favourite political theorist took Britain as his model, and there the state remained weak and relations between nobility and Third Estate amicable. In the Russian Empire there was no Third Estate, for here the reforms of Peter the Great had made the nobility the sole support of the state, and it performed the role played further west by the bureaucracy. In short, while on the continent the nobility had to fight for its autonomy and even its existence, on either periphery nobility and state were so closely bound together that the Revolution could be defeated and the nobility rescued.

Townspeople

No less than the nobility, the bourgeoisie is an ideological construct dating from the French Revolution. Since 1848 the latter has been described as a 'bourgeois revolution' and the bourgeoisie has been associated with progress. Yet the 'bourgeois society' of the nineteenth century had little in common with the urban societies of the eighteenth. It would be better to use the word 'townspeople', especially as the concept of bourgeois varied from country to country under the old regime and referred to very different phenomena. Indeed, it was unknown in Italy, where one spoke of 'patriciate' and 'people', or in Britain, where 'gentry' and 'middle-class' were used. In France it was only the urban oligarchy that referred to itself as *bourgeois*, while in central Europe its equivalent (*Bürgerschaft*) applied to all full members of an urban community.

Much more unified was the guild structure of the old regime. Its system of rules was the essence of what the old regime understood by the urban order. By a combination of privileges and compulsions, it limited the market for products and labour and shaped the way of life of its members in accordance with its own concept of honour. In central Europe the guilds also governed the cities, for only their members could be full citizens, a requirement that *inter alia* obliged academics to join guilds and excluded Jews, for the guilds maintained their Christian character until the nineteenth century. The Holy Roman Empire was, therefore, the epitome of guild control, although that should not be taken to mean that the guilds also flourished in a material sense. On the contrary, the guilds there found themselves running a diminishing asset and their formal success was bought at a cost of pauperization. That, in turn, brought political decline.

Life was no less restricted in towns run by oligarchies standing above the guilds. That was particularly the case in northern and central Italy, the great urban centre of medieval Europe. Here the rural areas too were in the hands of the towns and the patriciate ruled unchallenged. In these conditions, modern political institutions could develop in name only and the prince was in effect only the first of the patricians. The *bonne bourgeoisie* of France had looked after themselves differently but no worse. They formed the hinge between crown and towns, administering royal justice and collecting taxes (although the higher offices were held by *noblesse de robe*) and running municipal government with the king's permission. So they turned themselves into the only social group that was indispensable and so even survived into the twentieth century. Conditions in Britain were different again. Here the towns were ruled by patriciates composed of landowners and business people whose political influence in the House of Commons was ensured by the fact that the boroughs had four times as many members as the counties. In this way any conflict of interest between national and local politics was excluded and, thanks to the élites' decision to opt for the market, that meant that guild privileges could not be defended.

The fact that urban society was divided along legal and political lines did not alter its position as part of the society of orders. Both patricians and guildmen sought to defend their position and, like the nobles, they tried to do so both by self-regulation and by privileges. The former involved a combination of marriage strategies, enforcing business practices in accordance with moral and legal norms, and promoting a moral code opposed to the market and competition. The objective was, of course, to hold at bay all interlopers, so their behaviour acquired an increasingly defensive character. So did their privileges, which in the course of the eighteenth century were appreciably reduced by the central authorities. Both in political and economic terms, the European city had reached its nadir.

Despite—or perhaps because of—that decline, the urban status quo has been defended with even greater obstinacy than that of other groups. Where the guilds could still run their own affairs autonomously, they did not depart one jot from the traditional system. No attempt was made to adapt the organization of labour, retailing methods, production techniques, or the use of raw materials to changing circumstances. That was especially the case in Germany, where the imperial law designed to reform the guilds of 1731 was ignored, except in Prussia. Less successful were their colleagues in Tuscany and Lombardy, where the Habsburg administration banned the guilds in the 1770s. In France a similar attempt by Turgot was foiled by the resistance of the parlements, municipalities, and guildmen, so that it was left to the revolutionaries to enforce freedom of trades in 1791.

More successful were the attempts by the journeymen to defend their own special culture, thanks to their widespread and long-standing organization. They survived the revolutionary era and saved key aspects—control of their own funds and the compulsion to move from place to place—for the nineteenth century. This then fed into the labour movements that derived from initiatives undertaken by journeymen and skilled workers and for long were characterized by modes of thought and behaviour reminiscent of the guilds.

The determination of the guildmen to defend their autonomy was demonstrated not least by the urban riots with political objectives that multiplied towards the end of the eighteenth century. In this case it was masters or journeymen who reacted with violence against any threat to their autonomy. If their protests were directed against the municipal authorities, they usually proved successful in extracting concessions. Many a sovereign also sensibly chose the path of com-promise. Louis XVI was badly advised when he chose to ignore the mass discontent of the petty bourgeoisie in 1789. As central authority began to crumble, they rose in revolt across France and wrested self-government for their communities.

The bourgeois or patrician oligarchies found it easier to defend their privileges. They were able to maintain their social exclusiveness, their code of honour, and the great majority kept their rentier men-tality even when defeated politically. In the Habsburg territories of Italy their autonomy fell victim to reforming absolutism; in France, where they had got too close to central government (municipal offices were venal after 1692), they were swept away by the revolt of the Third Estate; in central Europe they went down to the 'princes' revolution' that followed the destruction of the Holy Roman Empire. However, by that time it had become clear that monarchs would content themselves with just the abolition of autonomy, and that meant the urban élites did not fall too deep. The new order was based on a division of powers between a royal commissar and a new muni-cipal authority elected on the basis of a census, with the result that most of the old families reappeared.

It would be wrong, therefore, to conclude that the losses we have described meant that the groups that previously dominated the towns had now collapsed: on the contrary. As with the nobility, the modern state was concerned only to suppress all claims to autonomy and to enlarge the number of full citizens and did not show any real enthusiasm for promoting liberty and the market. So the bourgeois–patrician élites continued to run European cities deep into the nineteenth century—into the twentieth century indeed in some places—and this middle-class alliance made an important contribution to the stability of a polarizing society.

The image of society

At the end of this chapter the reader will naturally ask how eighteenth-century society can be labelled. It is an old question, but that does not mean that a satisfactory answer has yet been found. To conclude that at the turn of the nineteenth century Europe was moving from a society based on orders to a society based on classes is not just banal but also too vague, for the 'society of orders' and the 'class society' are ideal types. Reality prefers mongrels. Other possible solutions are also unhelpful. The concept of a 'modern society' is so formal that it can be made to mean anything, according to individual taste; the 'early modern bourgeois society' favoured recently by some German scholars has not yet been defined adequately; and it has been suggested already that to speak of 'bourgeois society' or 'civil society' is to use an ideological construction that tells us more about the person using it than the phenomenon it purports to describe. So let us ask instead about the social ideas and expectations of contemporaries.

The society of orders had its defenders throughout the eighteenth century and beyond. It was simply there, hallowed by tradition and supported by theory, ever since the application of Aristotle's doctrine of *societas civilis* had been made. In essence this consisted of a political theory articulated by Montesquieu with special cogency: there can be freedom only when the sovereignty of the ruler is limited, and for that the clergy, nobility, and urban oligarchies are needed. Of course this ignored all the new trends in the economy and society that the eighteenth century witnessed. Once the market had begun to transform society, however, the problem of innovation had to be addressed. So contemporaries had to choose whether to accept or to resist. Approval was especially audible in Britain where Locke was extraordinarily influential. Locke saw his country divided into two classes: the rich and the poor. He regarded that as natural, as something required by the economy and that politics had to deal with. Locke's analysis was superior to traditional theory, because it was both more incisive and opposed to revolutionary change. He took society as it was, requiring only from the sovereign that he should grant the right of political participation to all those whom the market had helped to acquire property. This theory of propertied individualism was then supported and popularized by Scottish moral philosophers from Hutcheson to Adam Smith and was then broadcast to the continent in various versions from the 1770s. The new United States of America even seemed to prove that a society could be founded without poverty but with liberty. In France the physiocrats propagated the model of a society of landowners, while natural-law theorists in Germany and utilitarians in Italy drafted reforms appropriate for their own societies. Nor did it remain just theory. It was put into practice in France by the alliance of the liberal nobility with the Third Estate in their vote against 'feudalism' on 4–5 August 1789. The constitution of 1791 formally sanctioned a process that reached its completion with Napoleon's society of *notables*.

Few approved of this course of development, either in theory or in practice. It seemed to them that the market demanded too many sacrifices and they could find no moral justification for either poverty or mass political participation. So they sought a third way between the society of order and the market economy. They were guided by an ideal of an *heureuse médiocrité* that would allow a standard of living that was materially modest but socially and morally justified. To establish such a society would require state intervention to return the market to the simple function of exchanging goods. For them justice was more important than liberty.

Yet social development passed over the bourgeois society of the 'middling sort'. That was not the fault of politics, for between 1789 and 1814 an attempt was made west of the Rhine and south of the Alps to abolish the seigneurial structure and to replace it with the rule of the *notables*. But the social dynamic was unimpressed and everywhere social development showed the same characteristics, for the market forces established themselves in the same measure as population continued to increase. As Jacob Burkhardt remarked, against these two powers there was no defence. That was the bitter experience of all those who lived between 1750 and 1850.

3

The European economy in the eighteenth century

Sheilagh Ogilvie

A clear view of the economy in the eighteenth century is hard to get, with the Industrial Revolution in the way. Looking back, it is tempting to see the whole century as preparing the ground for factories and machines. Looking forward, the century is often portrayed as the graveyard of the traditional 'moral economy' of self-subsistent peasant farms and guild workshops. The eighteenth century is a sort of border zone, alternately claimed by both pre-modern and modern camps, in which all signposts point to the Industrial Revolution.

A cool look at the timing already shows the cracks in this easy identification of the eighteenth century with either industry or revolution. Only one country industrialized in the eighteenth century: Britain, after about 1760, and then only gradually, in a few exceptional regions and branches of industry. Parts of Belgium and Switzerland, and a few enclaves in France and German-speaking central Europe, saw the beginnings of industrialization around 1800. But industrial take-off in France as a whole is dated to 1815–30, in Germany and Austria-Hungary to 1830–50, in Italy, Spain, Scandinavia, and the Dutch Netherlands only to the period after 1850 or even 1870. Most areas of eastern and east central Europe, as well as many regions of Germany, particularly in the east and south, did not industrialize until after 1880.

In short, reports of the death of the pre-industrial economy before 1800 have been greatly exaggerated. In the closing years of the eighteenth century, most of Europe was touched by factory industrialization only indirectly. Even in Britain, economic and political commentators at the end of the eighteenth century appeared all but unaware of it. In 1776 Adam Smith wrote that 'The capital employed in agriculture . . . puts into motion a greater quantity of productive labour than any equal capital employed in manufactures . . . [and] adds a much greater value to the annual produce of the land and labour of the country, to the real wealth and revenue of its inhabitants.' So astute an observer as Thomas Malthus was, as late as 1799, basing his influential economic and demographic theories on the functioning of a pre-industrial agrarian economy, in which food supply was the single crucial economic variable.

For the eighteenth century, Smith and Malthus were right. Agriculture, not industry, led the economy. Its performance determined the success of industry and trade, and influenced every aspect of society, politics, and culture. Peasant women and men toiling incessantly in fields and barns were so mundane as to be almost invisible; but in eighteenth-century Europe, just as in the twentieth-century Third World, the choice between stagnation and growth lay in their calloused hands. Between 1700 and 1800, agriculture saw much greater changes than industry, so much so that this century is often regarded as that of the 'agricultural revolution'. But this revolution, like the industrial one, was concentrated in certain European economies, although in slightly more of them than England, as we shall see. In other parts of Europe, farm techniques and agrarian institutions were hardly different in 1800 than they had been in 1700—or even in 1500. How the 'agricultural revolution' was encouraged in some European societies, and suppressed in others, is the story told in the first section of this chapter.

Industry, too, changed slowly in most European economies between 1700 and 1800. Manufacturing was widespread in Europe long before the first factories. Craft workshops made a rich variety of goods for local consumption, and 'proto-industries' churned out mass exports for more distant markets. Industries expanded, contracted, and relocated throughout the eighteenth century, and on the whole there were more of them at the end than at the beginning. But change was gradual, not explosive. Techniques, products, and institutions changed imperceptibly, if at all. While the first mech-anized factories were built in some European regions after 1760, hand techniques and guild organizations predominated in most others long past 1800. What caused some areas of Europe to develop cen-tralized, mechanized, and competitive manufacturing in the second half of the eighteenth century, while others sustained the dispersed, manual, and corporative traditions that had characterized industry since the Middle Ages, is the question explored in the second section of this chapter.

In trade, as in industry, the historical spotlight has dwelt on what is visible and seems prophetic. Long-distance shipments by wealthy merchants to exotic destinations have attracted most interest, not so much because they were typical of trade in the eighteenth century, but because colonies and global markets became important in the nineteenth and twentieth. But in 1800 overseas trade, although it had grown since 1700, was still a trickle compared to the flood of com-merce among European regions or between towns and their rural hinterlands. Qualitatively, too, the greatest changes occurred not in overseas shipments but in repetitive exchanges of mundane goods over modest distances. In certain parts of Europe, transport improved, permanent shops replaced periodic fairs, peddling and shopkeeping proliferated, and cheap consumer goods were brought within the budgets of labourers and servant girls. Where these cheap and interesting new goods were available, people began to spend more time doing income-earning work and less in leisure, so they could purchase the new consumer items. In other parts of Europe, however, this 'consumer revolution' had hardly begun by the end of the eighteenth century: obstacles to commerce still kept the price of non-local goods so high that only the rich could afford them. The third section of this chapter tells the story of how and why trade became so much more efficient in some European economies between 1700 and 1800, but not in others.

The eighteenth century is usually portrayed as a century of 'revolu-tion': industrial, agricultural, commercial, and, of course, political. But this was a century of economic divergence more than of any common European experience. The so-called revolutions touched only a few societies and regions, while others remained inviolate. Even in those economies that did change, this change had its roots further back in history, while in those that did not, stagnation also had earlier roots. The key question is what these roots were. Why did pre-industrial economies vary so greatly, and why did they part company even more decisively during the eighteenth century?

The answer lies in the social and political framework within which people made economic decisions. Over the centuries, European societies had developed an array of economic institutions that regulated the allocation of resources: sometimes to ensure their efficient use, more often to control their distribution. Four of these institutions still dominated most European economies in the eighteenth century: the seigneurial system (with wide-ranging powers for landlords), the village community, the privileged town, and the occupational corporation or guild. Markets could work only within the framework of these non-market rules. Governments could regulate the economy only by cooperating with these traditional institutions, or trying to break them down. But, although these institutions existed everywhere in eighteenth-century Europe, their practical powers varied widely. As we shall see, agriculture, industry, and trade followed separate paths in different parts of Europe. This was because landlords, villages, towns, and guilds regulated people's economic decisions differently in different societies. We cannot understand the eighteenth-century economic 'revolutions' until we realize that societies constrained economies as much as economies revolutionized society.

Agriculture

Nowhere was this social framework more crucial than in agriculture, the most important sector of the eighteenth-century economy. Agriculture had a dual importance: for people's survival at the time, and for economic growth in the future. In 1700 agriculture employed four-fifths of all workers in the most highly developed economies such as the Netherlands and England, and more in the less developed east and south of the continent. Agriculture also took up most of the land in the economy. Industrial uses for land were few, since most manufacturing was done in people's houses. Trade and services, which nowadays consume so much land in highways, railways, shopping malls, and housing estates, used almost no land in the eighteenth century: roads were minimal, railways non-existent, permanent markets rare, and cities small by modern standards. London, Paris, and Naples were by far the largest cities, yet London's population was only 575,000 in 1700 and 900,000 in 1800; Paris stagnated at 500,000 inhabitants for the whole century; Naples had less than 220,000 people in 1700, rising to about 425,000 by 1800. Capital, too, went mainly into agriculture. Farmers' savings were sucked away into repairing buildings, clearing woods, draining marshes, and buying animals. Servants, labourers, cottagers, and even rural weavers saved up to buy farms. Even townsmen often invested the profits of crafts or commerce in land, which in most eighteenth-century economies still offered the best balance between risk and return.

So agriculture consumed most inputs (labour, land, and capital) in the eighteenth-century economy, and this was because it produced the most valuable output: food. As the French royal military engineer Vauban observed in 1707, 'The true wealth of a country lies in plentiful food supplies.' By this he meant not just economic but political wealth. In the seventeenth century, the tiny United Provinces had stood firm against the might of Spain, and one reason was the productivity of its market-oriented farmers compared to Spain's exploited peasants. In the eighteenth century, armies were much larger, and princes demanded granaries to match.

But the average European farming family in 1700 produced only 20–30 per cent more food than it ate itself. This was barely enough to keep society on an even keel. Landlords, churches, and princes extorted most of the surplus in rents, tithes, and taxes. National harvests fluctuated on average 25 per cent from year to year. Regional harvests fluctuated even more, which meant that everybody lived on a knife edge: ordinary people because they might not eat this spring, princes because their unfed armies might mutiny, or their peasants stage a tax revolt. In 1700 European farmers produced just enough to feed most of the population most of the time, plus a surplus divided between forced payments to a tiny stratum of unproductive aristocrats and rulers, and voluntary exchange with a small group of specialized manufacturers and traders. In bad years, it was manufacturing and trade that suffered first: as late as 1850, even in so advanced a north-west European economy as France, a bad harvest always led to a crisis in industry.

For industry or commerce to grow, inputs and outputs had to be released from farming. This is why agriculture was the key to economic development—a lesson from European history belatedly recognized in recent decades by modern developing economies. Farmers had to produce enough to buy off rulers and priests, insure society against the ever-present risk of harvest failure, and feed more non-farming artisans and traders. And they had to produce this extra food (and more industrial raw materials, too) at the same time as releasing labour, capital, and land for industrial or commercial uses. Early industry and commerce required little land and only small capital investments, but needed large amounts of labour. This labour could move into industry only if it was released from agriculture, and the only way an eighteenth-century economy could afford that was if larger food surpluses became available—either imported from other countries, or produced at home. Imports were scarce: transport costs were high, and even the richest farming regions produced only small surpluses. Only 1 per cent of European grain output was traded internationally in 1700. The Low Countries imported 13–14 per cent of their grain as early as 1600, but they contained only 3 per cent of Europe's population. By contrast, Britain imported a mere 3 per cent of its wheat as late as 1811–30, Germany only 10 per cent of its entire food supply in 1890. This meant food surpluses had to be produced at home. To have an industrial revolution, you first needed an agricultural revolution.

This was the key economic change of the eighteenth century. The Low Countries, the 'miracle economy' of pre-industrial Europe, had already started to revolutionize their farming before 1600. England, the other early starter, followed suit around 1680. In France after 1750, in Switzerland after 1780, and in Denmark and many west German territories after 1790, traditional farming methods were abandoned, agricultural yields rose dramatically, and the landscape and economies of Europe were transformed. The results can be seen in European yield ratios: how much grain you harvested compared to how much you sowed. As Table 3.1 shows, yield ratios were pitifully stable between 1500 and 1820 in most parts of Europe. Only in the Low Countries and England, despite a soil and climate not naturally suited to grain-farming, did yield ratios already lie at a high level before 1600, and improve noticeably from 1650 on. Even the rich soils and beneficent climate of France and the Mediterranean yielded less than seven seeds harvested for each seed sown around 1500. By 1800 this average had hardly improved, with the gains from the agricultural

Table 3.1 Average grain yields in different parts of Europe, 1500–1820 (seed harvested as multiple of seed sown)

Period	North-west corner (England, the Low Countries)	Mediterranean (France, Spain, Italy)	Central and Nordic (Germany, Switzerland, Scandinavia)	Eastern (Russia, Poland, Czechoslovakia, Hungary)
1500–49	7.4	6.7	4.0	3.9
1550–99	7.3	n.a.	4.4	4.3
1600–49	6.7	n.a.	4.5	4.0
1650–99	9.3	6.2	4.1	3.8
1700–49	n.a.	6.3	4.1	3.5
1750–99	10.1	7.0	5.1	4.7
1800–20	11.1	6.2	5.4	n.a.

Notes: Ratios are averaged over the three main arable crops (wheat, rye, and barley).
n.a. = not available.
Source: Peter Kriedte, *Peasants, Landlords and Merchant Capitalists: Europe and the World Economy, 1500–1800* (Leamington Spa, 1983; German orig., Göttingen, 1980), 22.

revolution in central and northern France offset by falling yields around the Mediterranean. On the poorer soils of central Europe, yield ratios hovered around 4 between 1500 and 1750, and only gradually rose past 5 between 1750 and 1800. In eastern Europe, despite a rich endowment of prime arable soils, yield ratios actually fell from 4.3 in 1550 to 3.5 in 1750. This was the era of 'refeudalization', when the institutional powers of the great east European feudal landlords enormously increased. Only in the later eighteenth century, as a few of the worst seigneurial constraints began to be reformed (for example, the gradual reduction in serfs' *Robot* (forced-labour) services in the Czech Lands after 1771), did east European yields gradually turn upwards.

As the slow and divergent growth in grain yields illustrates, the agricultural revolution was neither inevitable nor universal. As late as 1787, the English agricultural traveller Arthur Young was astonished to find many regions of France still dominated by 'the common barbarous course' of the three-field system. He was only slightly exaggerating when he concluded that 'agriculture in such a kingdom is on the same footing as in the tenth century. If those lands were then tilled at all, they were in all probability as well tilled as at present.' In Austria, Italy, Sweden, and many east German territories, the agricultural revolution did not even begin before 1820, in Russia and Spain not before 1860. Just as in the present-day Third World, technical knowledge, population pressure, and the example of other economies was not enough: for agricultural development, the social framework had to change.

The technical problem for eighteenth-century agriculture was simple. Cereals are the most efficient source of food energy, but growing them depletes the soil. Unless nutrients can be restored, harvests fall year after year. There were three solutions to this problem: fertilizing, rotating crops, and resting the land. Each was costly. Chemical fertilizers were unavailable, for eighteenth-century scientists knew too little about plant physiology to devise the right chemical composition. Until German and French chemists made that breakthrough after 1850, organic wastes were the only source of fertilizer. The cheapest was manure. Farmers seldom raised animals purely as food sources, since in 1700 one meat or milk calorie took eight grain calories to produce. Stock were valued mainly as walking manure carts. Other fertilizers—ash, turf, flax waste, pigeon dung, human night soil—either contained fewer nutrients or had to be expensively transported. Animals were the cheapest source of fertilizer, but they were still a major cost: they needed pasture, and that took land away from food crops.

Lacking enough manure to grow cereals continuously, farmers rotated fields through different uses. The most common rotation involved planting a cereal crop (wheat or rye) the first year, a porridge or pancake crop (barley, oats, or millet) the second, and leaving the field uncropped (fallow) the third. The other common rotation alternated a cereal with fallow over a two-year cycle. These rotations had drawbacks, too. The porridge crop was less valuable than the cereal, and fallowing meant that at any one time one-third to one-half of all arable land was producing nothing. Manuring, rotating crops, and fallowing did replenish the soil, but at the cost of reducing crop cultivation.

The agricultural revolution freed farmers from this trap for the first time in history. The 'new husbandry', as it was called in England, replaced the two- and three-field systems with new crop rotations that replenished the soil faster and removed less land from cultivation. The new rotations involved four main innovations. First, they included new crops such as legumes that actually returned nutrients to the soil. Secondly, they included high-energy (and nutrient-returning) fodder crops such as turnips and clover or, as in 'convertible husbandry', a pasture phase for arable fields, so more manure-producing animals could be raised on much less permanent pasture. Thirdly, the new crop sequences were devised so that each year's crop removed different chemicals from a different soil layer, extending the arable lifespan of the field. Fourthly, thanks to the first three innovations, fallow could be reduced or abolished altogether, so all land was producing all the time.

Escaping from the vicious trade-off between soil depletion and idle arable land was the key. But other innovations helped as well. The spread of non-traditional crops such as potatoes, maize, and buckwheat increased food energy per unit of land. The potato had been known since 1536, but it spread widely in Europe only after 1756 when grain prices began to rise steadily; by 1800, potatoes occupied 15 per cent of the arable land in East Flanders, in Ireland dangerously more. Industrial crops such as flax and dye-plants (madder, woad, and weld), and other cash crops such as coleseed, hops, and tobacco, increased revenue per hectare, enabling more people to live from the earnings of smaller plots. Selective breeding produced bigger cattle, sheep, and pigs. Oxen, which could plough only 0.4 hectares a day, gave way to horses, which ploughed 0.5–0.6. Iron ploughs engineered to reduce soil resistance replaced clumsy wooden ones, increasing ploughing productivity to 0.8 hectares a day by 1800. (This was still much less than the 5 hectares a day achieved around 1850 with the steam plough.) In backward regions, the plough replaced the hoe. Everywhere, the scythe replaced the sickle. The seed-drill replaced broadcast sowing. But these were all peripheral: the new crop rotations were the core change.

The puzzle is not why these innovations were introduced, but why they had not been introduced much earlier. It was not a lack of technical knowledge, education, or the requisite mentality. The basic techniques had been laid out clearly in the agronomic handbooks of Ancient Rome. Precocious estates and regions had used them for centuries, and they were widely adopted in the Low Countries by 1600 and England by 1690. The parts of Europe where they first spread were not those, such as Scandinavia or the German Lutheran territories, where school attendance or literacy rates were highest. Nor were the new practices first imposed on ignorant and reluctant peasants by an educated and forward-looking élite: they spread initially on small family farms in Flanders and Brabant, and among modest tenant farmers in Norfolk, Suffolk, and Essex. Local studies suggest that, long before the agricultural revolution, small-scale cultivators throughout Europe carefully balanced costs and revenues, responded sensitively to changes in prices, and were keenly interested in increasing profits. The barriers to agricultural innovation were not in people's minds.

Nor was the problem a lack of demand. It is sometimes argued that the Dutch and British agricultural revolutions were kicked off by early population growth and urbanization, which the rest of Europe experienced only in the eighteenth or nineteenth century. Tables 3.2

Table 3.2 Population of different parts of Europe, 1700–1800

	1700		1750		1800	
	Millions of people	% of European total	Millions of people	% of European total	Millions of people	% of European total
North and west	*16.0*	*19.7*	*18.3*	*19.4*	*26.1*	*21.3*
Scandinavia	2.9	3.6	3.6	3.8	5.0	4.1
England and Wales	5.4	6.6	6.1	6.5	9.2	7.5
Scotland	1.0	1.2	1.3	1.4	1.6	1.3
Ireland	2.8	3.4	3.2	3.4	5.3	4.3
Netherlands	1.9	2.3	1.9	2.0	2.1	1.7
Belgium	2.0	2.5	2.2	2.3	2.9	2.4
Central	*35.2*	*43.2*	*40.0*	*42.5*	*53.2*	*43.4*
Germany	15.0	18.4	17.0	18.0	24.5	20.0
France	19.0	23.3	21.7	23.0	27.0	22.0
Switzerland	1.2	1.5	1.3	1.4	1.7	1.4
Mediterranean	*22.8*	*28.0*	*26.5*	*28.1*	*31.2*	*25.4*
Northern Italy	5.7	7.0	6.5	6.9	7.2	5.9
Central Italy	2.8	3.4	3.1	3.3	3.6	2.9
Southern Italy	4.8	5.9	5.7	6.1	7.0	5.7
Spain	7.5	9.2	8.9	9.4	10.5	8.6
Portugal	2.0	2.5	2.3	2.4	2.9	2.4
Eastern	*7.4*	*9.1*	*9.4*	*10.0*	*12.2*	*9.9*
Austria-Bohemia	4.6	5.7	5.7	6.1	7.9	6.4
Poland	2.8	3.4	3.7	3.9	4.3	3.5
Europe	*81.4*	*100.0*	*94.2*	*100.0*	*122.7*	*100.0*

Source: Jan de Vries, *European Urbanization, 1500–1800* (Cambridge, Mass., 1984), 36.

and 3.3 suggest this argument is back to front: population size and cities grew in the Netherlands and England because agriculture grew to feed them, not vice versa. Parts of Italy, Iberia, and even southern Germany had been as highly urbanized as the Netherlands in the late sixteenth century, but stagnated after 1590 because the cities there, instead of offering high enough food prices to induce the surrounding farmers to invest in the new husbandry, used political force to compel farmers to sell their output in the cities. As Table 3.3 shows, England was much less urbanized than average in 1500 and 1600, pulled level with the rest of Europe around 1700, and surpassed it only between 1700 and 1750. The early onset of agricultural

Table 3.3 Urbanization in different parts of Europe, 1600–1800
(% of population living in cities of at least 10,000 inhabitants)

	1600	1650	1700	1750	1800
North and west	*8.2*	*10.9*	*13.1*	*13.6*	*14.9*
Scandinavia	1.4	2.4	4.0	4.6	4.6
England and Wales	5.8	8.8	13.3	16.7	20.3
Scotland	3.0	3.5	5.3	9.2	17.3
Ireland	0.0	0.9	3.4	5.0	7.0
Netherlands	24.3	31.7	33.6	30.5	28.8
Belgium	18.8	20.8	23.9	19.6	18.9
Central	*5.0*	*6.0*	*7.1*	*7.5*	*7.1*
Germany	4.1	4.4	4.8	5.6	5.5
France	5.9	7.2	9.2	9.1	8.8
Switzerland	2.5	2.2	3.3	4.6	3.7
Mediterranean	*13.7*	*12.5*	*11.7*	*11.8*	*12.9*
Northern Italy	16.6	14.3	13.6	14.2	14.3
Central Italy	12.5	14.2	14.3	14.5	13.6
Southern Italy	14.9	13.5	12.2	13.8	15.3
Spain	11.4	9.5	9.0	8.6	11.1
Portugal	14.1	16.6	11.5	9.1	8.7
Eastern	*1.4*	*1.7*	*2.6*	*3.5*	*4.2*
Austria-Bohemia	2.1	2.4	3.9	5.2	5.2
Poland	0.4	0.7	0.5	1.0	2.5
Europe	*7.6*	*8.3*	*9.2*	*9.5*	*10.0*
British Isles	4.2	6.5	9.4	12.3	15.6
Low Countries	21.5	26.1	28.6	24.7	23.0
Rest of northern Europe	4.3	5.0	6.1	6.5	6.4

Source: Jan de Vries, *European Urbanization, 1500–1800* (Cambridge, Mass., 1984), 39.

innovation there cannot be ascribed to above-average urban demand. Eighteenth-century Prussian and Polish estates experienced an intense demand pull from cities in the Low Countries, but satisfied it by extorting more forced labour from serfs, not by introducing more productive techniques. Most European economies saw fast population growth in the eighteenth century, as Table 3.2 illustrates, but only some introduced agricultural innovations. The others saw living standards fall and paupers multiply. In short, as the examples of twentieth-century Africa and India also demonstrate, population growth and urbanization are neither necessary nor sufficient conditions for agricultural development.

New techniques provided ways of increasing agricultural productivity. Growing demand provided an incentive to do so. But whether people responded to that incentive required something extra: the emergence of social arrangements that did not prevent farmers from changing their practices or—better yet—encouraged them to do so. In the eighteenth century, such social institutions, hitherto found only in the Low Countries and England, began to emerge in the vast majority of west European regions. The new crop rotations, which formed the core of the agricultural revolution, required land, labour, and capital to be used in new ways, and cereal and pastoral surpluses to be exchanged flexibly and freely for goods that the newly specialized farms no longer produced themselves. The social rules governing markets in land, labour, capital, food, and manufactures in each European society decided whether this could happen.

For farmers to introduce new rotations and crops, land had to be used differently. But rulers, priests, landlords, and communities had for centuries regulated how land could be used—whether to ensure its efficient use, or to control who shared the farmer's harvest. Princes, clerics, and feudal lords often levied taxes, tithes, and rents as shares of certain crops. If new crops unspecified in old charters were untaxable, powerful interests resisted their introduction. In Württemberg, for example, as late as the 1820s peasants were still being forbidden to introduce new fodder crops, because the Church wanted them to cultivate traditional cereals that were tithed, and the prince wanted them to grow the sour and unprofitable local wine grapes that paid excise. Landlords also jealously guarded their right to dispossess peasants at will (as in 'refeudalized' eastern Europe) or to repossess farms on the death of the tenant (as with the *mainmorte* rights increasingly enforced by eighteenth-century French seigneurs). Such insecure tenures discouraged cultivators from investing in soil improvements since, as one seventeenth-century English writer put it, 'a man doth sande for himself, lyme for his sonne, and marle for his grandchild'.

Another problem was that, traditionally, most farmland was open to communal use: the pasture and fallow at all times, and the stubble in the interval between harvest and planting. For a farmer to experiment with the new crops and rotations, these common pastures and open fields needed to be enclosed (in late-twentieth-century terms, 'privatized', with each farmer in the village given a share to use individually). But noble privilege often blocked this. In Spain until the nineteenth century a small group of nobles enjoyed *Mesta* privileges, permitting them to herd thousands of transhumant (seasonally migrant) sheep across communal and private land. Not only did they use their legislative influence to oppose enclosure, but the damage their herds inflicted on the fields reduced incentives for peasants to improve the land, contributing, as one English traveller wrote in 1786–7, to 'the want of cultivation in the interior provinces of Spain'. In Silesia, as late as 1821, when asked why they did not use new rotations that cultivated the fallow, peasants replied that they were 'not allowed to . . . the lord has the right of grazing sheep, and as long as there is stubble grazing, we have to let the fallow lie'. It was where landlords enjoyed few legal privileges (as in Britain and the Low Countries) or lost them through popular revolt or state action (as in revolutionary France and parts of western Germany in the eighteenth century) that land could be used in the new ways required by the agricultural revolution.

Village communities also blocked changes in land use. To operate the traditional two- and three-field systems, villages had often evolved complex rules: compulsory crop-sequencing, extensive communal pastures, common grazing rights on private stubble, and collective coordination of different phases of agricultural work. Where such communal regulation was strong, it was difficult for individual farmers to experiment with new crops or new rotations, especially when these involved converting arable land to pastoral uses. Where only the larger farmers possessed legal title to common pastures and open fields, but cottagers customarily used them for pasture and gleaning, opposition from the land-poor majority could block enclosure. Strong communities could also forbid land sales to outsiders, as in many areas of western Germany; this hindered land from passing into the possession of those who might have the capital or the knowledge to introduce new techniques. It was therefore no coincidence that the new husbandry was first introduced in Flanders and England, where community institutions were comparatively weak. Only in the later eighteenth century were communal powers loosened in some regions of France, Switzerland, Denmark, and western Germany, so that farmers could experiment with using land in new ways, an essential precursor to identifying which new rotations and crops might suit local conditions. Even in England, understandable opposition from cottagers with use rights over common pastures and open fields, but no property rights to entitle them to a share during enclosure, meant that it took the entire eighteenth century and innumerable individual Acts of Parliament to enclose the land in each village so it could be included in new rotation systems. In most areas of Europe, this process had hardly begun by 1800. As late as the 1790s, communal resistance to the new husbandry in France was still so strong that the Marquise de Marbeuf was brought before a revolutionary tribunal for having taken land away from cereal-growing to sow the new fodder crops, and was sentenced to death for this 'unpatriotic' act.

The new agricultural techniques also required changes in the use of labour. As the French agricultural writer Montlinot wrote of Flemish farmers in 1776, 'if their soil is productive, it is because its gifts are bought by a degree of labour and manuring unthought of in other lands'. Not only did the new crops and rotations require more intensive digging, ploughing, fertilizing, and weeding, but higher grain and milk yields created more work in harvesting, threshing, butter-churning, and cheese-making. Peasants needed to use their own family's labour more intensively and to employ plentiful and flexible supplies of servants and day labourers. But traditional agrarian institutions often blocked efficient labour use. In eastern Europe, eastern Germany, Italy, Iberia, and parts of Scandinavia, between 1600 and 1800 the process of 'refeudalization' strengthened landlords' legal rights to compel peasants to perform forced labour on the demesne (the part of the estate farmed directly by the landlord for his own profit). Even in comparatively progressive Hanover, as late as 1820 landlords used forced labour from *Leibeigenen* (serfs) because it was costless, although, as the English traveller Hodgskin remarked, 'If the landlord had to hire labourers, he might have his work tolerably well performed, but it is now shamefully performed, because the people who have it to do have no interest whatever in doing it well and no other wish but to perform as little as possible within the prescribed time.'

Even though the new husbandry did not involve machines, it did require some capital. Enclosure of pastures and open fields required fences, hedges, and ditches. New crops required seed purchases. Soil improvement required extra fertilizer, sand, lime, and marl. Heavier harvests required more draught animals. Workers had to be supported during the transition to new techniques. Changing farming practice always requires at least small investments, as shown by the current focus on agricultural 'micro-credit' in modern developing economies. Dutch and English agriculture efficiently tapped the few sources of capital in eighteenth-century Europe. In the Netherlands, capital-rich townsmen invested directly in land and lent funds to farmers through the country's advanced credit markets, in which interest rates stood at 3 per cent in 1750, the lowest in Europe. In England, landlords had to make their estates pay, since they enjoyed few of the seigneurial privileges of their French or east European counterparts. This gave them strong incentives to lend their tenants capital for farm improvements, or even borrow themselves for this purpose in England's developing financial markets, where in 1715 interest rates stood at 5 per cent. Grain merchants extended credit to farmers, and incidentally smoothed price fluctuations, by speculating on the outcome of the harvest, as Daniel Defoe described in 1727: 'Corn-Factors in the Country ride about among the Farmers, and buy the Corn, even in the Barn before it is thresh'd, nay, sometimes they buy it in the Field standing, not only before it is reap'd but before it is ripe.'

Elsewhere in Europe, these credit conduits to agriculture developed more slowly. Much of the available capital in the economy was accumulated by rulers through taxes, state loans, and sales of monopolies and offices, then squandered on war or court display. Another substantial portion was levied as rents (or arbitrary confiscations) by noble landlords, and then spent on royal offices, monopolies, or conspicuous consumption. As late as 1781, the German traveller Freiherr von Stein voiced deep pessimism about economic growth in Poland because 'the wealth of the nation is in the hands of the aristocracy, which wastes it in an unreasonable manner, and uses it for frivolities'; a 10 per cent interest rate had to be paid on capital. As the travel writer William Coxe remarked in 1792 of Russian peasants, 'with regard to any capital which they may have acquired by their industry, it may be seized, and there can be no redress'. In many economies—France, Spain, Italy, and many German territories—even commercial and industrial profits tended to flow into landed estates, noble status (conferring tax freedom), bureaucratic office, or legal monopolies over certain lines of business. In societies where the greatest returns and least risk lay in purchasing land or royal favour, it is not surprising that risky economic projects such as *improvement* of the land or (as we shall see shortly) industrial and commercial ventures were starved of capital. Part of the delay in introducing the new agricultural techniques outside the Netherlands and England before 1750 resulted from the difficulty of saving or borrowing the requisite capital.

Farmers not only needed markets where they could get the inputs of land, labour, and capital required by the new agricultural techniques. They also needed markets where they could sell their output profitably, and buy goods they no longer produced themselves. But many of the same institutions that blocked efficient use of land, labour, and capital also blocked exchanges of food, raw materials, and industrial goods. Rulers and town governments in Spain, France, and the Italian and German city states often enforced so-called staples, legal rights of prior purchase that they used to force farmers in the surrounding countryside to sell their output in towns at lower-than-market prices. As in twentieth-century Africa and China, where similar price ceilings have been widespread, the aim was to prevent urban food riots, but the result was to discourage peasants from producing surpluses or investing in new techniques. This was one of the reasons the highly urbanized regions of northern Italy and southern Germany failed to stimulate an agricultural revolution around 1600, in contrast to the Dutch and Flemish cities, which had to pay farmers market prices. In Spain, price ceilings (and other institutional disadvantages) drove peasants off the land, and by 1797 there were almost 1,000 deserted villages in rural Castile; grain had to be imported to alleviate famine.

Towns were not the only barrier to farmers' profiting from investing in the new husbandry. Seigneurial tolls (internal customs barriers) blocked the development of a national grain market in France until 1789, discouraging farmers and worsening famines. In Bohemia, Poland, and many east German territories, the great land-lords forced peasants to sell them grain at fixed (low) prices. The landlords exported the grain to western Europe or used it to brew their own beer on the demesne farm, which they then forced the peasants to buy back from them at fixed (high) prices. In such condi-tions, peasants could not gain enough profit from grain surpluses for it to be worthwhile investing in new techniques—even if other insti-tutional obstacles had permitted.

Circumvention of urban and seigneurial privileges in markets for foodstuffs had wiped out famine in the Low Countries and England by the early eighteenth century. In France, Germany, and eastern Europe, by contrast, it recurred long past 1800. Partly this was because market prices motivated farmers to invest in increasing output, and to sell their surpluses rather than consuming extra food themselves. But it was also because, as modern development economists have shown, famine is seldom caused by sheer lack of food. In the eight-eenth century, as in the twentieth, it was caused by a failure of 'entitlements', economists' jargon for people's ability to buy cheap non-local food when local harvests fail. In eighteenth-century Europe, even when the harvest failed in one region, food was usually available somewhere. Integrated grain markets, free of urban or sei-gneurial privileges, could move food swiftly from regions of plenty to those of scarcity. Prices might be high, but at least the grain got there, the emerging welfare system could supplement the incomes of the local poor, and fewer people starved.

The eighteenth century, therefore, saw a breakthrough that had never been made before. Not just in a few favoured regions such as the Low Countries (where only 3 per cent of Europeans were lucky enough to live), but throughout western and central Europe, people broke out of the productivity trap that had stifled economic growth for millennia. At last, farmers escaped from the vicious trade-off between soil exhaustion and leaving land idle. At last, ordinary people could buy off nobles, priests, and princes and still have something left over to buy non-necessities: extra clothing, better tools, comfort-able furnishings, clocks, toys, books. This in turn gave work to craftsmen, shopkeepers, peddlers, and merchants. Between 1700 and 1800, the farming revolution freed people and resources from the brutal struggle against starvation, and they moved into industry and trade.

This did not happen everywhere. Escaping the agricultural productivity trap did not need just technical know-how or consumer demand. Land, labour, and capital had to be used differently, and farmers had to be able to sell profitably to customers and find cheap supplies of goods they no longer made at home. In the twentieth century, we take this for granted, but getting there was not easy. Age-old social arrangements had to be got round or broken down, and often they were staunchly defended by privileged groups. The Low Countries and England were lucky: they emerged from the medieval period with landlords that had economic weight but few legal powers, village communities that were only loosely organized, and town privileges that were poorly enforced. In the chinks of Dutch, Flemish, and English society, new ways of farming and selling food sprang up and grew vigorously in the sixteenth and seventeenth centuries, before any institution or interest group could organize stopping them. But in most other parts of Europe, landlords, towns and communities were still very strong in 1700. It took almost the whole eighteenth century to break down the social obstacles to releasing even a share of the immense productive forces locked up in the rural economy. Even the vaunted abolition of seigneurial privileges in France during the Revolution, and in Prussia and many other German territories after their defeat by Napoleon in 1807, left many restrictive practices intact. Not until traditional institutional privileges were fully broken down—by popular revolution, military defeat, or long and grinding social conflict—could farmers break out of the old productivity trap that had blocked the growth of the whole economy for thousands of years. The process had begun in the Netherlands in the sixteenth century, and lasted into the nineteenth century in the far east and south of the continent. But in most of Europe the decisive steps were taken in the eighteenth century.

Industry

In industry, unlike agriculture, there was no known body of techniques that could galvanize productivity once the obstacles had been swept away. The industrial equivalent of the new husbandry did not appear until the 1760s and 1770s, when British entrepreneurs began to combine new mechanical devices with new ways of harnessing energy, opening up a Pandora's box of threatening alternatives to every existing industrial practice. But before these inventions could be widely implemented, people had to experiment with them in a business setting, and that did not happen until the 1780s or 1790s. For most of the eighteenth century, there was no single path to industrial success. Even the most efficient industries had only small cost advantages over less efficient competitors, and such advantages were quickly pared away by the high cost of trading goods over any distance. Industry, even more than agriculture, varied enormously from one European region to the next, and many quite inefficient industries survived because they faced no effective competition.

With agriculture still employing an estimated 80 per cent of the labour force, the European economy in 1700 was still overwhelmingly agricultural. But even the most purely agricultural economy needed some industry: food had to be processed, clothing manufactured, tools made, shelter built. In eighteenth-century Europe, these needs were satisfied in three ways. First, households manufactured things for their own use, in between farming and other tasks. Women in particular were expected to make a wide range of products that families now buy from specialized industries. Women habitually baked bread, churned butter, brewed beer, sewed clothes, knitted stockings, spun yarn, and even sometimes milled flour and wove cloth. Families built and repaired their own houses and barns, mended their own tools and harness, sometimes smithed iron and tanned leather. Without the training or tools of the specialist, households did these things slowly and poorly, but where people could not use their time to earn more income, this was the cheapest option.

The second way industrial needs were satisfied was through the work of craftsman, who specialized in making specific products and sold them to local customers. In most European societies craftsmen were still in principle supposed to be restricted to the towns, which claimed a monopoly over all industrial work. But the eighteenth century has been described as an age of 'ruralization' or 'territorialization' of crafts. In some societies, this process had begun much earlier, with a trickle of craftsmen already moving into the countrysides of the Netherlands, England, and southern Germany before 1500. But in the eighteenth century, despite loud protests from the privileged urban guilds, the trickle became a flood. In Brandenburg-Prussia, even in the later eighteenth century, the Hohenzollern rulers were still trying to ban craftsmen from practising outside the towns for fear they would evade the excise tax. But this was an exception, and, although it kept rural crafts in check, it did not stamp them out wholly.

The third source of industrial goods was what have been called 'proto-industries'. Historians distinguish these from traditional crafts mainly on the grounds that they exported to distant markets instead of (or as well as) selling to local customers. Their broader customer base enabled them to cluster densely, creating distinctive *Gewerbelandschaften* (industrial landscapes) where a large share of the labour force participated in a single industry: usually weaving or spinning, but sometimes metalworking, glass-making, or, as in the Erzgebirge of Saxony, carving wooden toys. Often, these export-oriented proto-industries were located in the countryside, where farming families did industrial work during the less busy seasons of the agricultural year, or where women and children span and wove while men did the farm work. In parts of the Low Countries, southern Germany, and southern England, proto-industries had already begun to emerge in the late Middle Ages. But the eighteenth century was their heyday, with export-oriented industrial landscapes emerging from Russia to Ireland and from Scandinavia to Ottoman Bulgaria.

The boundaries between these three forms of industry— household manufacturing, local crafts, and proto-industries—were very fluid. Consumers shifted back and forth, depending on which offered the cheapest and best access to manufactured goods. This has prompted some historians to speculate that the growth of one of the three, at the expense of the others, was what caused the Industrial Revolution. In 1972, for instance, a historian of Flanders, Franklin Mendels, advanced a 'theory of proto-industrialization', in which he argued that the eighteenth century saw the export-oriented proto-industries taking over from the local-oriented crafts. From his study of linen production in eighteenth-century Flanders, Mendels argued that the growth of proto-industries created the population growth, the pool of industrial labour, the accumulation of capital and entrepreneurship, the foreign markets, and the institutional changes necessary for factory industrialization.

The theory of proto-industrialization has, since it was first proposed, generated volumes of excellent research on pre-factory industries. The upshot, however, has been to dismiss the original hypotheses almost completely. Historians have cast doubt on the idea that fast population growth was actually favourable for industrialization. Even if it was favourable, population grew fast during the eighteenth century in some agricultural regions as well, and it grew slowly in some proto-industrial ones. The early factories after 1760 seldom employed former proto-industrial producers, who often demonstratively refused to work in them, and even smashed the machines. The first factory workers were usually recruited from more easily disciplined groups such as paupers, labourers, women, and children. Finance and entrepreneurship for the early factories came from a wide range of sources; some were proto-industrial, but many more were agricultural, commercial, and even political. Foreign markets were easily won and lost: the markets captured in the earlier eighteenth century by Silesian and Westphalian linen proto-industries were as easily recaptured after 1770 by English cotton factories. Finally, proto-industries did not break down traditional institutions. We now know that the unregulated market transactions Mendels observed in Flanders were an extraordinary exception, paralleled only in England and a few other unusual institutional enclaves. In the rest of eighteenth-century Europe, proto-industry (like agriculture) was regulated by traditional institutions: guilds, merchant organizations, privileged towns, village communities, feudal landlords. The spate of research on proto-industrialization has shown that industrial development was affected much more strongly by institutional variations than by the presence (or absence) of proto-industry.

There is better evidence to support a second theory of how changes in pre-factory industry may have prepared the way for the factory. This is the idea of the 'industrious revolution', proposed in the late 1980s by a historian of the Netherlands, Jan de Vries. De Vries stressed a different set of changes in eighteenth-century industry: not the move from crafts to proto-industries, but the move from household manufacturing to market-oriented crafts and proto-industries. During the eighteenth century, de Vries argues, Europeans began to use their time differently—in a sense, more 'industriously'. They began to allocate less time to leisure and 'household production' (producing things for their own use within the family), and more to 'market production' (producing things to sell on the market to get income, which they then used to buy the things they no longer produced themselves). They did this not just in industry, but in agriculture as well, and de Vries argues that this big change in behaviour had far-reaching implications. It brought more human time into productive use, and it created more consumer demand, both of them essential for factory industrialization.

The jury is still out on the 'industrious revolution', but studies of consumption patterns using probate inventories and commercial records bear out at least part of this story. During the eighteenth century, people in some parts of Europe did indeed begin to buy more industrial goods from specialists and make fewer themselves. Studies of time allocation are more difficult, but the few that exist suggest that people were working longer hours, taking fewer holidays, and working more for wages and less for subsistence. The shift from household-oriented to market-oriented industrial work, however, did not happen to the same extent everywhere. The strongest evidence we have comes from Britain and the Low Countries. By contrast, the new consumption patterns arrived in central Europe later, and to a lesser extent. To many poor regions in the east and south of the continent, they did not come at all until the nineteenth or even the twentieth century. We cannot speak of an 'industrious revolution' that affected all areas of eighteenth-century Europe equally.

The 'industrious revolution' relied on changes in the relative price of making something yourself compared to buying it. Partly, this depended on the value you placed on various uses for your own time: leisure, household production, and income-earning work. But it also depended on the prices you had to pay if you purchased goods. Prices were partly determined by the efficiency of merchants, traders, and peddlers, as we will see in the next section. But prices were also determined by the extent to which craftsmen and proto-industrial producers minimized production costs, introduced better techniques, and responded to consumer demand for quality and fashion. The efficiency and adaptability of industrial producers varied from one European region to the next, and were influenced by many of the same socio-political and institutional factors whose effects on agriculture we have already seen. All over eighteenth-century Europe, the costs of manufactures were often needlessly high, and the quality and selection needlessly uninviting, because of social and political rules directed at redistributing resources to powerful minorities rather than allocating them in ways that would benefit the economy at large.

One powerful minority was the privileged craftsmen based in the towns and organized into guilds. As the French economist Robert Turgot wrote in 1776, 'In nearly all the towns of our Kingdom, the practice of different arts and crafts is concentrated in the hands of a small number of masters, united in a corporation, who alone have the exclusive right to manufacture and sell particular articles.' France was no exception. In most European societies, towns claimed a legal monopoly over industry. Within towns, each branch of industry was the monopoly of a group of adult males, the masters of a particular guild or 'corporation'. Guilds almost always excluded women, bastards, foreigners, Catholics in Protestant territories, Protestants in Catholic ones, and Jews anywhere. Most of them discriminated against everyone except male relatives of their own male members. They tried to make monopoly profits by limiting the number of masters, punishing outside encroachment, preventing internal competition by prohibiting new tools and new products, imposing output quotas, fixing minimum prices to customers, and setting maximum rates to suppliers and employees. Guild masters justified all this by claiming they protected consumers from low-quality goods. But often they merely exploited their workers, overcharged their customers, and, as Turgot put it, 'retarded the progress of these crafts, through the innumerable difficulties encountered by inventors with whom different corporations dispute the right to exploit their discoveries'.

Urban guild monopolies had already largely broken down in the Low Countries and England before 1700. Competition among the numerous great Dutch and Flemish cities created unregulated interstices in the countryside, where rural craftsmen could play off one urban government against another and produce freely and cheaply in the resulting confusion. The English crown was unwilling to enforce the privileges of towns and guilds after the political crisis over 'monopolies' that peaked under the Stuarts. In any case, it was largely unable to enforce any domestic economic privilege, because, unlike most other eighteenth-century European states, it failed to establish a local-level bureaucracy on the absolutist pattern. Lacking the captive markets of the guild monopolist, eighteenth-century Flemish and British industrial producers could stay afloat only by minimizing costs, devising attractive products, pleasing customers, and responding fast to economic changes. Rural competition in turn energized urban guildsmen to change their ways, or go under. In eastern Europe, too, as 'refeudalization' reached its apogee in the eighteenth century, guilds were weakened by the great landlords, intolerant of any economic privileges save their own. A few strong princes also began to grant guild-free 'immunities and privileges' to favoured enterprises, such as the Saxon Elector issued to the Royal Meissen Porcelain Factory in 1710, 'to the end that the artists and artisans shall not be frightened off by the guilds or the jurisdiction of our local councils'.

But in most of central and southern Europe, guilds remained very strong. In some proto-industries, particularly in France, Switzerland, Saxony, and the Rhineland, guilds gradually lost their monopoly over rural stages of production after the early eighteenth century. But guilds continued to control urban stages of production, including the important finishing and marketing processes. The monopolistic practices of the urban guildsmen often cost their rural suppliers dear, and inevitably reduced competitiveness throughout the whole industry. Guilds remained even more powerful in southern and central Germany, Austria, Switzerland, Italy, Spain, Greece, and Bulgaria. Here, both crafts and proto-industries remained guilded until the very end of the eighteenth century, or even beyond. Rural industries simply formed new rural or 'regional' (rural-urban) guilds, with the explicit encouragement and enforcement of the state.

Even when guilds broke down, rulers often simply replaced the old monopolies of the guild masters with new monopolies for favoured groups of industrialists: the *Fabrik* (manufactory) privileges granted by German and Austrian princes, the *franquicias* of Spain. Industrialists sheltered behind their *Fabrik* monopolies, producing at high cost and making sales only because their royal patron kept out the competition and forced his subjects to buy their output. The Austrian Habsburgs granted *Fabrik* privileges to a worsted manufactory at Linz and a hosiery manufactory at Poneggen, which, despite their legal powers over thousands of rural outworkers and their protected domestic markets, failed ever to reduce costs to a profitable level, swallowed up huge state subsidies, and ultimately went bankrupt. The Prussian kings granted a long series of expensive monopolies, subsidies, and exclusive market rights to a silk *Fabrik* in Berlin, but it never flourished. By the 1790s, so notorious had its failure become that the Comte de Mirabeau wrote of the successful Krefeld silk manufactures that, although Prussian-ruled, had never been granted *Fabrik* privileges, 'Unhappy those manufactures, if ever a Prussian king should love them.' Although moving to the countryside could weaken guild and *Fabrik* privileges, they still kept costs higher than necessary in many industries.

Even when industry moved to the countryside and was not followed by the privileges of a guild or a *Fabrik*, it did not encounter the untrammelled market society Mendels described for Flanders. As we saw with agriculture, the rural economy was criss-crossed with institutional rules regulating the use of labour, land, and capital, and the exchange of food and other products. Inevitably, these affected how well industries could work. In societies where seigneurial and communal powers varied across short distances, such as Switzerland, England, Flanders, the Rhineland, and Saxony, proto-industrial workers settled where landlords and communities were weak. Above all, they clustered wherever seigneurial and communal rules failed to control migration, settlement, and occupational choice, since labour was by far the most important input into industry before the advent of the factory. In the Zürich highlands, for instance, weavers were excluded by villages with strong corporate rules, so they congregated in those whose regulations were weaker. In Leicestershire, framework-knitters proliferated in 'open' villages such as Shepshed, shunning 'closed' communities such as Bottesford where a single great landlord controlled settlement.

But in many parts of Europe, strong landlords and strong communities could not be avoided. Their rules might inflate costs, but industries could still arise and survive on the basis of proximity to lucrative markets or natural resource endowments (such as good sheep pasture for wool supplies, good water for linen-bleaching, or rich ore deposits). The Württemberg Black Forest, for instance, had very strong community institutions, which helped make its worsted proto-industry high cost, low quality, and technically backward. It nevertheless survived into the late 1790s because geography, trade barriers, and warfare protected its access to south German and Italian markets from more efficient competitors. Sometimes, strong communal institutions actually created an artificially cheap industrial labour supply, as in the Netherlands region of Twente, where village regulations excluded inhabitants who were not legally 'full peasants' from access to land, leaving linen production as their only option.

Strong landlords also affected the costs of industry. Sometimes, as in Mecklenburg, Prussia, or Sweden, they prevented their serfs from weaving or smelting iron, in order to protect their sources of agricultural corvée labour. But landlords sometimes encouraged industry where they saw profit for themselves. In Russia, as the German observer von Storch reported in 1797, 'Foreign capitalists establishing factories, manufactories or workshops may buy as many peasants or serfs as they require for their enterprises . . . it has become virtually impossible for anyone who does not possess his own serfs to enter the mining industry to advantage.' In Bohemia and Silesia, landlords sold monopolies over their serfs' yarn and cloth output to Nuremberg merchant houses, levied loom fees on serf weavers, and forced serfs to cart wood and ore for mines, ironworks, and glassworks. The 'Linen Triangle' of Silesia, Bohemia, and Lusatia became one of the largest linen proto-industries in Europe, despite primitive technology, because serf labour enabled it to undercut the free wage weavers of Westphalia, Flanders, England, and Ireland. But one must question whether the coerced serf weavers and serf miners of central and eastern Europe developed the new habits of diligent time allocation and market-oriented consumption that de Vries has termed the 'industrious revolution'.

Some systematic changes can be descried in European industry before the factory. Overall, between 1700 and 1800, proto-industries expanded while crafts stagnated or declined. Overall, household manufacturing gave way to both. Whether these changes presaged the rise of the factory is still an open question. It seems more likely that they, like the factories, were merely symptoms of deeper changes in the social framework surrounding all economic activity, whether industrial or agricultural. This is borne out by the fact that these changes occurred to widely varying extents, and with widely various consequences, in different parts of Europe. In many areas of the continent, as late as 1770 the industrial scene still looked very much as it had in 1670 or even 1570. Guilds and privileged towns were still powerful, except in the richest economies (England and the Low Countries) and the poorest ones (east of the River Elbe). Powerful landlords were successful either in forbidding rural industry where it would interfere with their agricultural interests (as in Leicestershire, Sweden, or Prussia), or in co-opting it as another source of seigneurial revenues (as in Languedoc, Silesia, or Russia). Corporate villages excluded proto-industry where it threatened communal resources (as in the Zürich uplands) or subordinated it successfully to their corporate rules (as in Twente or Württemberg). The privileged groups that had long regulated industry in the towns continued to do so. Those that had for centuries regulated the agrarian economy in their own interests extended control to the new rural crafts and proto-industries. High-cost industries were protected from competition by institutional privileges and geographical barriers to trade. Why should anything change?

Industrial change required two things to coincide: governments that were strong and stable enough to stop enforcing (or even to abolish) traditional institutional privileges; and markets that made it possible to use inputs in new ways, and sell output at a profit sufficient to make the risk of innovation worthwhile. Such a coincidence occurred in more and more regions of Europe during the eighteenth century. Slowly, some princes developed standing armies, tax systems, professional bureaucracies, and public finances that enabled them gradually to dispense with that old mainstay of early modern princes, granting economic privileges to favoured groups and institutions in return for military, fiscal, and regulatory cooperation. Gradually, in the interstices of poorly enforced institutional privileges, markets developed that allocated land, labour, and capital more efficiently, and let producers trade with consumers, without having to buy off innumerable corporate and feudal parasites along the way. The combination of strong governments with strong markets created an environment in which economic experimentation was both possible and profitable.

This did not make an industrial revolution inevitable, but it made it possible. By 1750 the combination of strong government and strong markets had been emerging slowly in a number of European societies for some time. With the spread of Newtonian science, new scientific ideas with potential industrial applications—what historians of technology have called 'macro-innovations'—had been proliferating in many parts of western Europe. But in the words of one of the great engineers of the Industrial Revolution, John Farey, 'The inventions which ultimately come to be of great public value were scarcely worth anything in the crude state, but by the subsequent application of skill, capital and the well-directed exertions of the labour of a number of inferior artizans . . . brought to bear to the benefit of the community.' Such fine-tuning proved to be easier in certain European countries. As one Swiss calico-printer remarked in 1766, for a new technique to be perfect it had to be invented in France and worked out in England.

Lively debate still rages about why this should have been the case. All the thousands of pages of controversy about the causes of the Industrial Revolution have still not come up with one clear, identifiable factor that Britain had and every other European (or Asian, or African) economy lacked. True, the agricultural revolution and an advanced financial system provided cheap sources of capital—but the Netherlands had these as well. True, agricultural productivity growth released labour, and guilds did not prevent it from taking work in industry—but by 1760 this was the case in parts of Flanders, Switzerland, and France. True, well-off farmers profiting from the agricultural revolution provided ready consumer markets for industry—but there were plenty of these throughout the Low Countries and other rich farming regions. True, a 'commercial revolution' (discussed in the next section) created an integrated grain market and lowered the costs for producers to reach consumers, without opposition from institutional privileges—but, again, England was not the only European economy whose trade, both domestic and foreign, was thriving.

Perhaps the best speculation, in the current state of our knowledge, is that, although each of these features could be found to some extent in other parts of Europe, England brought them all together. People who thought up better ways of producing things could obtain the necessary inputs in the required quantities at the lowest possible cost, without opposition from entrenched interest groups. And they could rely on being able to sell the output at a price and in a quantity that would gain them enough for it to be worth their while incurring the costs and risks of experimenting.

And experiment they did. The number of industrial patents in England expanded every decade after 1700, and a surprisingly large number were put into practice: Darby's coke iron furnace after 1710, Kay's flying shuttle after 1733, Paul's carding machine after 1748. As early as 1745, the French commentator Abbé Le Blanc remarked that 'England is the country where one finds the largest number of these machines . . . which truly multiply men by saving their labour.' Then, in the 1760s, the average number of patents issued in a single decade surpassed 200 for the first time. In an astonishing thirty-year period between 1760 and 1790, more than 1,000 inventions were patented in England, among them half a dozen that, along with the requisite 'micro-innovations', were to transform industry irreversibly: Arkwright's water frame, Hargreaves's spinning jenny, Crompton's mule, Watt's steam engine, Cartwright's power loom, Cort's iron puddling process. From 1770 on, English cotton production took off, and after 1780 iron followed suit. Productivity increased enormously, costs and prices plummeted, sales and output expanded fast. By 1784 the Marquis de Biencourt was describing in plaintive terms how the English were constantly making new discoveries: 'The whole of nature is unceasingly studied, requested, worked upon, fecundated, husbanded.'

This threw a spanner into the delicate equilibrium of eighteenth-century European industry. Hitherto, a slightly better technology in Flemish linen-making was counterbalanced by a slightly cheaper source of flax in Westphalia, slightly lower wage costs among Silesian serf weavers, or slightly greater proximity to key markets on the Swabian Jura. But, suddenly, competition among industries was no longer merely a matter of tiny cost differences, easily compensated for by local resource endowments, an artificially cheap labour force, high transportation costs, or protective legislation. The new machines and factories produced cotton textiles, small iron wares, and soon other manufactures, which could be profitably sold at prices a quantum leap below those of most existing proto-industries, whether in England or elsewhere in Europe. Machines often hugely improved quality as well. At a blow, machines and factories wiped out the tiny cost advantages on which so many eighteenth-century industrial regions had survived. Proto-industries throughout Europe began to feel the chill winds of competition. The stable and privileged industrial regime of eighteenth-century Europe began to break down.

The obvious move was for existing industries to introduce machines and factories. But for this the privileged groups already monopolizing industry had to recognize necessity, and bend to it. By the early 1780s, entrepreneurs in Belgium, northern France, Switzerland, and the German Rhineland were trying to set up factories and install the new 'English machines'. Quite apart from the technical challenges, the social barriers could prove insuperable, as was discovered by Brügelmann, a proto-industrial linen merchant in the Wupper valley, when he tried to set up the first English-style spinning mill in Germany in 1782. The state corporatism typical of eighteenth-century German industry meant that he could not just set up his factory, as in England: he had to get a *Konzession* (permit) from the state. But the Wuppertaler Garnnahrung, a privileged proto-industrial linen-trading corporation of which Brügelmann himself was a member, allied with the rural weavers' guilds to lobby against him. His application was turned down. Years later, Brügelmann got a permit, but from the ruler of a neighbouring territory with no existing industrial interest groups. In Silesia, the response of the institutionalized proto-industrial interests was even more fatal. The great feudal lords got the Hohenzollern rulers to prohibit machines and factories altogether, in order to protect their profits from their serf weavers. The result was a foregone conclusion: in 1820, the English traveller Russell was told how 'Thirty years ago, when the decay of the Silesian manufactures was only in its commencement, you might see weavers returning from the town to their distant villages, with tears in their eyes, and not a sixpence for the expectant family at home. The evil is now much more general.'

Institutional obstacles made it hard for many European industries to react to the coming of factories and machines with any flexibility. Some survived for a generation or two longer by devising other ways to lower their costs, mainly (as in Silesia) by lowering workers' pay. But undercutting the new machines was already difficult and became more so as factories spread outside England, and people learned to run them more efficiently. Other industries moved out of the direct line of fire: by 1850 many German and French industries had carved out modest niches in high-quality goods or raw materials that were difficult to mechanize, while their British, Belgian, and Swiss counterparts addressed the mass market with factory production. But technology did not stop moving into new sectors, and this was only staving off the evil day. Other industries tried to survive by persuading their governments to introduce protectionist barriers or new institutional privileges. Some Saxon cities even created new guilds of cotton-manufacturers, who tried to perpetuate old corporate monopolies into the factory era. These, combined with Napoleon's Continental System, protected some European proto-industries from English factory competition for another generation. But, after peace broke out in 1815, time ran out quickly for the old eighteenth-century industrial regime.

Responses to factory competition after 1770 thus varied widely across Europe. Many did not involve radical institutional reform, and thus it is not surprising that so many European economies did not even begin industrializing until well into the nineteenth century. A wide array of responses had to be tried, and fail, before privileged industrial interests could grit their teeth on change. Protectionism and deindustrialization could sustain existing institutional privileges, and these were chosen by some European proto-industries, or forced upon them, from the 1790s on. Devising new ways to reduce costs in order to compete with factories, or moving into as yet unmechanized lines of business, by contrast, required a degree of flexibility that put further pressure on rigid industrial institutions. Mechanization itself, which was the only long-term solution, required even more adaptation. Under intolerable pressure from rulers increasingly unsympathetic to old interest groups, and from markets that were more and more competitive, the industries that survived in Europe after 1800 were those that managed to free themselves from traditional institutional privileges. The eighteenth century itself saw only the beginning of these changes, and in many European countries they required the entire nineteenth century to diffuse or even get properly started. Moreover, in some European economies, new industrial and commercial interest groups soon obtained new legal privileges over the factory industries. But factories, even inefficient ones, required a new institutional framework. The stable industrial regime of the eighteenth century had contained the seeds of its own destruction. The destruction itself was often painfully delayed long into the nineteenth century.

Trade

'Trade makes the wealth of England,' wrote one French Foreign Office bureaucrat in 1736. The view that trade was the engine of economic growth was a central tenet of mercantilism, the European economic orthodoxy in the first half of the eighteenth century. After 1750 it was challenged by the physiocrats' insistence on the primacy of agriculture, but most French government officials still believed, as the French consul in London wrote in June 1789, that 'The wealth of England is nothing but the fruit of her large trade.'

This idea attracted later historians. Foreign trade did grow in many parts of Europe before the Industrial Revolution, and it grew earlier and faster in certain economies, such as England and the Low Countries, in which agricultural and industrial development was also advanced. Moreover, the eighteenth century also saw the growth of the British seaborne empire from its modest seventeenth-century beginnings into a fully-fledged colonial and imperial system. By the mid-eighteenth century, Europe, Africa, and the New World had been knitted together by the 'triangular trade', whereby European merchants exchanged manufactures (especially textiles and arms) for African slaves, which they shipped across to the West Indies and America to grow cotton, sugar, and other raw materials, which were then traded back to Europe to be incorporated into the manufactures that were exported to Africa (for slaves) and America (for slave-grown raw materials). A multitude of bilateral and multilateral trading links brought exotic goods into European households, spread European manufactures throughout the world, and made some handsome merchant fortunes. This trade was highly visible, it left very good records, and it seemed a new departure compared to the way the European economy had ever worked before. Surely this combination of long-distance commerce, imperialism, and slave-trading was what accumulated the capital, created the export markets, and captured the raw materials subsequently used in the Industrial Revolution?

This view is appealing, but the evidence is mixed at best. In Britain, long-distance trade and industry both grew remarkably during the eighteenth century, but which caused which? Did long-distance

commerce promise such huge profits—through exports of manufactures and imports of raw materials—that it stimulated British
industries to invent, invest, and expand? Or did the efficient and
flexible British industries produce goods that competed well on foreign markets, expanding sales there, and creating demand for colonial
imports? The role of foreign trade in economic growth is a fundamental question that economists have yet to settle even for the modern developing world, let alone for eighteenth-century Europe. It
seems likely, however, that the long-distance trade was at best a
'handmaiden' rather than an 'engine' of growth. All the figures suggest that British domestic supplies grew faster than foreign demand.
That is, it was the success of British industries that caused exports to
grow, not the success of British overseas trade that made industries
grow. Even for cotton textiles at the end of the century, the domestic
market could (and did) take up the slack when foreign markets failed.
The only argument that remains partly persuasive is that, without
cheap raw cotton from the American slave plantations, the Industrial
Revolution might have been delayed until linen or wool could be
mechanized. Those countries whose domestic economies were
flexible and efficient, such as Britain, probably benefited from
long-distance commerce, but would have industrialized anyway.

Nor is it clear whether the possession of colonies always brought
net economic benefits. True, most European imperial powers tried to
limit access to their colonies, subsidizing their own manufacturers'
exports to them, prohibiting colonies from buying foreign manufactures, preventing foreign ships from sailing there, and cornering
the best colonial exports for the mother country. Surely such legal
discrimination must have given those European economies that had
colonies a head start over others? Not necessarily. Even for Britain,
economists have calculated that the costs of defending and administering the colonies, enforcing the trade regulations, and giving prefer-
ence to colonial goods, outweighed the benefits. Colonialism, they
conclude, benefited naval interests, owners of plantations, and a few
subsidized manufacturers, at the expense of the economy at large; it
was essentially a device for redistributing resources from taxpayers to
special interest groups. Of course, if the resources extracted from
taxpayers to fund colonial defence and administration would otherwise have been lying idle, in a rigid and underemployed economy,
then it might be argued that there was no net cost to the economy.

But this assumption is implausible: certainly in eighteenth-century Britain, people had productive projects to which to allocate resources. Hence, it seems more likely that colonialism benefited certain social groups, but not the economy as a whole—not to mention the harm done to indigenous populations overseas. European comparisons cast even more doubt on the industrial benefits of colonialism: of the early industrializers, only Britain was an imperial power; Belgium and Switzerland industrialized next, without colonies; Holland, Portugal, and Spain, with rich colonial empires, are counted among the late industrializers of western Europe. The colonial trade generated prosperity for some individuals and regions, in a few economies in the west of the continent, but not on a scale fundamentally to alter patterns of growth in eighteenth-century Europe.

Yet a commercial revolution did take place in eighteenth-century Europe: not in the glamorous long-distance expeditions to exotic lands, but in the seemingly mundane business of regional exchange and local shopkeeping. For farmers to find the risks of agricultural innovation worthwhile, they needed to know they could sell their surplus at a profit, and that meant being able to reach consumers efficiently. For craftsmen or proto-industrial workers to risk specializing in goods they could not eat, they needed to know they could sell them and be sure of buying food. Trade made it possible for individuals and regions to begin specializing in the crops and goods their natural and social endowments made them best at producing. Trade also brought competitive pressures to bear on monopolists, forcing them to lower their prices and control their costs. But trade was costly, and where it was too costly it did not take place. The essence of the eighteenth-century commercial revolution was that it reduced the costs of trade so much that many exchanges began to occur that had never been possible before.

The most obvious costs of trade are the costs of transport. In 1700 both land and water transport were still extremely expensive in most parts of Europe. Water transport was much cheaper than land, with less draught power needed to move a given weight of goods. English coal, for example, doubled in price after 5 miles by road, but after 20–30 miles by water. Eighteenth-century roads were narrow, they were winding because they followed the contours of the landscape, and their surfaces were very poor. The best roads in central Europe at the end of the eighteenth century have been likened to present-day forest tracks. Water routes were not much better: many rivers were not navigable, building canals was costly and was as yet widespread only in the Netherlands, and only countries with long coastlines (such as Britain and the Low Countries, but also Denmark, Italy, Portugal, Dalmatia, and Greece) had access to almost all their regions by coastal shipping.

Road improvements that reduced transport times and breakages were a major component of the commercial revolution. The biggest problem was that no one owned roads, it was hard to charge for using them, so no one had an incentive to maintain them. During the eighteenth century, this problem was solved in France by the state, in England by the market, and in much of southern, central and eastern Europe not at all. The French Royal Road Administration expanded its budget from 870,000 livres annually in 1700 to 4 million livres by 1770, building a planned network of 40,000 kilometres of royal roads, and reducing the journey time between Paris and Lyons from ten days to five. England, by contrast, solved the problem through the 1662 Turnpike Act, which permitted the formation of tiny 'turnpike trusts', groups that invested in improving roads in return for the right to charge users a toll. By 1750, a network of turnpikes radiating out from London linked centres of population and economic activity across England, and between the 1740s and the 1780s the journey time from London to Birmingham fell from 2 days to 9 hours. By 1781, the French bureaucrat d'Aubarède was writing, in connection with plans for invading England, that 'the roads are superb'. Elsewhere on the continent, neither markets nor states made much of a start on improving land transport until the late eighteenth century. The Spanish crown did not begin a road-building programme until 1767, and even then the new royal roads addressed strategic rather than economic needs. Frederick II of Prussia regarded trade as politically destabilizing, so half of central Europe lacked proper highways till after 1780. As late as 1820, the English traveller Hodgskin described how in northern Germany the revenue from road tolls 'goes into the pocket of the sovereign, and he repairs the road or not as he pleases'.

River improvements and canals followed a similar pattern: they were carried out by private individuals in England, the state in France, and in many other European regions not at all. Canal improvements started in the Low Countries in the seventeenth century, where by the 1660s the canals were already carrying 38 million passenger-kilometres of transportation each year, and transport costs were so low that people sent their laundry from Amsterdam to be washed in the cleaner waters of Harlem and Gouda. England possessed only one river that was fully navigable, the Severn, but by 1760 river improvements (many inspired by Dutch engineers) had doubled England's endowment of navigable water to 1,400 miles. The real 'canal mania' started in 1760, with limited liability companies being set up by local landowners wanting to transport coal to salt-fields, ironworks, or big industrial cities such as Manchester, or by industrialists such as Josiah Wedgwood who needed a cheaper (and lower-breakage) method for transporting his heavy china. In France, by contrast, the canal network that grew up between the early seventeenth century and the 1730s was mainly inspired and financed by the crown, concerned to divert trade from the Habsburg possessions and incidentally help bring food into Paris. German princes' emulation of the French Bourbons was not limited to building mini-Versailles, but extended to the somewhat more useful activity of canal-building. But motives of princely display often, in both France and Germany, led to massive misinvestments. The Canal des Deux Mers, Colbert's pet project for connecting the Mediterranean with the Atlantic, was completed in 1691 but never used for any but local traffic; much of its length was out of use throughout the eighteenth century for lack of maintenance. In precisely the same way, the Dukes of Braunschweig-Wolfenbüttel spent huge sums making the Oker river navigable in 1741, but there was not enough ship traffic to justify the project and it was abandoned again by 1775.

But transport costs were not the only costs of trade. Even where roads, navigable rivers, or canals existed, the same privileged groups we have already seen at work in agriculture and industry also often secured institutional rights over them. At the same time as the French absolutist government was building roads and canals, it was also carving up the largest economy in Europe into a multitude of separate economies, by a complex system of internal tariffs. It then sold off the right to collect these tariffs to a set of officials (the 'Farmers of the Royal Customs'), creating an effective lobbying group for maintaining the internal trade barriers. During the eighteenth century, the great French seigneurs also revivified their ancient feudal rights to levy tolls on trade passing through their domains. In German-speaking central Europe, territorial fragmentation made the problem worse: not only princes and feudal landlords, but also privileged cities, charged innumerable tolls on road and river traffic. As late as 1820, an English traveller described in astonishment how 'There are no less than 22 tolls on the Weser betwixt Münden and Bremen . . . At every toll every vessel is stopped and her whole cargo examined . . . It is said the expence of collecting the tolls equals the receipts . . . Similar tolls and impediments are known to exist on every river of Germany.' The great German cities also possessed staple rights, entitling them to force farmers and industrial producers in the surrounding countryside to sell all their goods to town merchants, and to compel all goods passing through the city to be unloaded and sold to local merchants who had a monopoly over re-exporting them. In the Low Countries and England, the institutional weakness of cities and towns, which had lost their staple rights in the sixteenth or seventeenth centuries, was an important factor in their commercial strength.

A final component of the eighteenth-century commercial revolution was a transformation in the activities of merchants and traders. Since medieval times, the merchants in most towns in Europe had organized themselves into guilds, just like craftsmen. During the sixteenth and seventeenth centuries, the rise of new forms of commerce, such as the handling of proto-industrial products and the long-distance colonial trade, had seen the creation of new organizations called 'merchant companies'. A few of these presaged modern joint-stock companies, but most were simply guilds in a new guise. The merchants in a particular city, proto-industrial region, or overseas trade route would form a lobbying group, secure a state monopoly, and then act much like any other guild, excluding outside competitors, stifling internal competition, opposing new practices, and charging monopoly prices to customers. Some of the most important long-distance trading routes were dominated by such companies: the Merchant Adventurers, the Levant Company, the Dutch East India Company, the French East India Company, the Dutch West India Company, the English East India Company. Yet many of these companies failed financially in the short or long term, and those routes flourished most that were open not only to the monopolistic operations of the great companies but to small-scale trading by individual merchants.

The major contrast between the most advanced and the more backward trading economies in eighteenth-century Europe resided in whether privileged merchant companies also monopolized the proto-industrial trade, the inter-regional grain trade, and local retailing. In England and the Low Countries, urban merchant guilds had already lost control over these sectors before 1600. Throughout the rest of Europe, by contrast, there was hardly a proto-industrial region which was not the monopoly of a privileged trading company, which had the right to force local weavers, metalworkers or glass-makers to sell everything they produced to members of the company, often at disadvantageous prices. Sheltered behind their monopoly privileges, these companies failed to introduce commercial innovations that would have reduced trading costs. Whenever they could, they exploited their monopoly powers on regional markets to charge higher than competitive prices to customers. Guilded urban merchants also sought to keep the trade in grain, wine, industrial raw materials, indeed all 'merchant wares' in their own hands, using their lobbying power with rulers to limit the intrusions of unlicensed hawkers, peddlers, and informal shopkeepers, whose ability to lower the costs of trade benefited customers but threatened to eat into the monopoly profits of the established merchants. So ubiquitous were such merchant privileges as late as 1793 that, on a journey to Württemberg, the Göttingen professor Christoph Meiners described how commerce 'is constantly made more difficult by the form which it has taken for a long time. The greatest share of trade and manufactures are in the hands of close and for the most part privileged companies.' It was not until eighteenth-century rulers ceased to enforce these merchant monopolies that the costs of trade really began to fall outside the north-west corner of Europe.

The final element of the eighteenth-century commercial revolution is one we have already encountered: de Vries's concept of the 'industrious revolution'. De Vries argues that productivity growth in agriculture and industry, combined with the falling costs of trade, brought a richer array of cheap and attractive consumer goods within the budgets of poorer people. This meant that a much larger share of the population could now think of buying consumer items. This, he speculates, motivated people to change how they allocated their time. Traditionally, people had put a lot of time into leisure and 'household production' (producing things for their own use within the family), and relatively little into working for income in the market. In the eighteenth century, de Vries argues, they shifted time out of leisure and household production and allocated it to income-earning activities, so they could afford to buy the new consumer goods. This growth of consumption then became self-sustaining: increasingly, people began to define social esteem and class affiliation in terms of patterns of consumption and industrious behaviour, rather than in the traditional terms of birth, honour, corporate affiliation, legal status, or participation in sociability and leisure activities. This new interest in consumption and income-earning, de Vries argues, was itself responsible for drawing hitherto unused supplies of human time and ingenuity into productive activities, contributing to economic growth.

Empirical evidence that such an 'industrious revolution' actually occurred in eighteenth-century Europe is still not fully established, as we saw in the section on industry, and in some parts of the continent it probably did not take place in this period. However, for some regions of western Europe, there is evidence that during the eighteenth century people from ever wider social groups were consuming more traded goods. Even in Germany, as the political thinker Justus Möser demanded plaintively at the end of the eighteenth century, 'Can one conceive of anything which the shopkeeper does not now trade in, either secretly or publicly? Does he not watch out for all opportunities and crazes, in order to introduce something new, wonderful and foreign?' In societies where shopkeepers acted like this, there is even some indication that people were beginning to work more intensively. Partly, this was simply because, as discussed throughout this chapter, the institutional obstacles to productive work and low-cost exchange were being broken down. But it may also have been, as de Vries argues, because of social and cultural changes that oriented people more towards consumption and work, and less towards leisure and other ways of obtaining social esteem and political influence. As the Englishman John Bright wrote in 1756, 'See, as the Owners of old Family Estates in Our Neighbourhood are selling off their Patrimonies, how your Townsmen are constantly purchasing; and thereby laying the Foundation of a new Roll of Gentry! Not adorned, it's true, with Coats of Arms and a long Parchment Pedigree of useless Members of Society, but decked with Virtue and Frugality.'

The 'industrious revolution', no less than other aspects of eighteenth-century economic change, was evolutionary rather than revolutionary, and far from universal throughout Europe. The extent to which it could take hold in any society was profoundly influenced by socio-political and institutional factors. 'Sumptuary legislation' was issued by many European princes in the eighteenth century, precisely in order to stop the industrious revolution in its tracks. Rulers tried to prevent their subjects from spending money on 'needless luxuries' so they would be able to pay the taxes needed to finance the swelling tide of European warfare. The nobility and urban patriciate tried to stop their social inferiors from encroaching on traditional symbols of social demarcation. In many European societies, the nobility sought to defend its privileged status against incomers by genealogical codification, strict endogamy, or legal barriers. Where these attempts were successful, they hindered the emergence of a definition of social esteem and social status in terms of consumption or income, and blocked one of the main conduits of the 'industrious revolution'.

Nor must it be forgotten that there were many European societies, even at the end of the eighteenth century, in which privileged groups thoroughly cornered all consumption above the subsistence minimum. Contemporaries recognized that in such societies there could be no industrious revolution. As one western visitor to Poland observed in 1781, for 'the largest part of the nation . . . the drive to activity which is a consequence of the desire to happiness is lacking'. In this respect, as in so many others, the economic 'revolutions' so often associated with the eighteenth century in Europe were neither inevitable nor universal. Society and politics stifled economic revolution more often than economies revolutionized society.

4

Religion and culture

Derek Beales

Individual historians have saddled eighteenth-century Europe with a rich variety of contradictory titles: for example, in intellectual history 'the Age of Reason' and 'the Age of Enlightenment'; in political history 'the Age of Absolutism', 'the *Ancien Régime*', 'the Old European Order', 'the Reforming Century', 'the Age of Revolution', even 'the Age of the Democratic Revolution'; in social history 'the Aristocratic Century' and 'the Age of Politeness'; in economic history 'the Age of Commercialization' and 'the Age of Industrialization'; in religious history 'the Age of Scepticism' and 'the Age of Secularization'; and in the history of the arts 'the Age of the Baroque', 'the Classical Age', 'the Age of Sentimentalism', and even 'the Age of Romanticism'. Most of these titles are plausible for some parts of Europe in some parts of the period. A great deal depends on whether one is thinking of 'the short eighteenth century', 1715–89, the strict hundred years 1700–1800, or 'the long eighteenth century', 1688–1815. Once 1789 is passed, the French Revolution, its impact, and the reaction against it must dominate the story, at least in politics and related spheres, such as religion. Indeed, the French Revolution was such a colossal event that many historians have allowed the search for its origins and causes to constrain their view of the whole century: they see revolution as immanent in the France of Louis XIV and espy similar tensions in every other country. But in fact the beginning of historical wisdom about the eighteenth century before 1789, even with regard to France, is to forget the French Revolution. Many recent historians deny that a political, social, and religious upheaval such as actually occurred was inherent in the situation of France before 1789, and none of the other so-called revolutions that punctuated the 1780s elsewhere in Europe, in Geneva, Holland, and Belgium, much resembled the French cataclysm; even the 'American Revolution', earth-shaking though it seems with hindsight, was far less of a social upheaval than the French and had limited influence in Europe. Of course French society had been developing in ways that helped to make the Revolution possible and to give it its character. But many of its manifestations—mass democracy in a large state, mass nationalism, a citizen army bent on world conquest, total rejection of traditional religion, the attempt to democratize culture—had scarcely been imaginable before they actually appeared. Much the same can be said, as Sheilagh Ogilvie's chapter shows, about industrialization: sensational in retrospect, it was hardly dreamed of, even in Britain where it began, until the 1780s. Similarly, in the history of the arts Romanticism takes some finding before the last decades of the century. Historians who, having begun research on nineteenth-century Europe, move back into studying the pre-revolutionary period, feel that they might as well be working on the Middle Ages.

For the history of religion and culture, the period before the Revolution needs to be divided into two, roughly in the middle of the century. Until at least the 1740s the influence of Christianity and Christian churches still pervaded the lives of Europeans, in some respects even more than in previous centuries. Despite the fundamental differences between Catholic and Protestant countries, it can be said that in every state there was an established, legally privileged church and that the civil and religious rights of followers of other churches were either limited or non-existent. In every country education at all levels was almost entirely in the hands of clergy, usually of the clergy of one church only. Royal and princely courts, each in declared alliance with one of the Christian churches and usually in concert with the aristocracy, played at least as large a part as they ever had in government and in the shaping of culture. But from about the middle of the century, while some absolute rulers became still more powerful, the Roman Catholic Church and other established churches were thrown onto the defensive intellectually, politically, and culturally, as the ideas of the Enlightenment infiltrated the élites across Europe. The aristocracy too, as Christof Dipper's chapter shows, saw its unquestioned status challenged by the growing acceptance of wealth and merit as better personal recommendations than noble birth. Then, within four years from the outbreak of the French Revolution, the French Church was despoiled and outlawed, and the monarchy, the court, and the aristocracy abolished. Soon, under the direct or indirect influence of French armies, changes of similar tendency occurred in the Low Countries, Germany, Switzerland, Italy, and northern Spain. However, Britain, Austria and Russia escaped them, the most notable example of the diversity of European experience that is conspicuous throughout the century, even though in many respects it deserves to be called cosmopolitan. I aim in this chapter to illustrate both the common elements and the main divergences to be found in the religion and culture of Europe; to show how different were the tendencies of the first half of the century from those of the second half; and, so far as possible, to explain this shift and the revolutionary changes that followed 1789.

Religion, to mid-century

Among all the titles generally bestowed on the eighteenth century, 'the Age of Religion' and 'the Christian Century' are missing. They should not be, because at any rate in the first of my periods the churches were in many respects still gaining ground. But this achievement has been concealed, because historians have greatly exaggerated the immediate impact on religion of two developments of the late seventeenth century, first, the supposed 'end of religious wars' and, secondly, the 'scientific revolution' leading to what Paul Hazard entitled 'the crisis of the European consciousness' and dated to the years 1680 to 1715. Both developments need to be examined critically.

The Peace of Westphalia in 1648 certainly marked the end of religious wars within the vast lands of the Holy Roman Empire (which included modern Germany, Belgium and Luxembourg, Austria, the Czech Republic, Slovenia, and parts of Poland and of northern Italy). It ratified the existing territorial divisions and required many rulers, Catholic, Lutheran, and Calvinist, to tolerate worship by other denominations than the established one, on the basis of the conditions prevailing in each state in 1624. The resulting arrangements were often bizarre: Catholic abbots and abbesses became the patrons of Protestant parishes, two denominations might be entitled to worship 'simultaneously' in the same church and so might either fuse their services or agree a rota. Since the people of these lands no longer fought wars over religion and since, partly as a result, advocates of wider toleration became more numerous in Germany, religious feeling has appeared less important than before.

By 'the crisis of the European mind' Hazard meant the revolutionary impact of the works of geniuses such as Newton, Locke, Bayle, and Leibniz on our understanding of the universe and of ourselves, which opened the way to the Enlightenment, a movement that Peter Gay has identified with 'The Rise of Modern Paganism'. In 1687 Isaac Newton (1642–1727) expounded in his *Principia mathematica* his theory of gravitation, explaining in a manner not seriously challenged until the twentieth century the movements of stars, planets, sun, and earth and also of earthly bodies. It was the most striking achievement so far of human reasoning and observation, unaided by divine revelation and producing results contrary to most people's understanding of biblical and Christian teaching. John Locke (1632–1704) put forward in his *Essay Concerning Human Understanding* of 1690 his 'sensationalist' philosophy, the theory that everything in the human mind derives from sense impressions received after birth: there are no 'innate ideas', instincts, or inborn moral imperatives—hence 'original sin', one of the foundations of Christian doctrine, is untenable. Locke also published in the same year his *Two Treatises on Government*, which mounted so persuasive an argument for resting government on the basis of popular support that it not only inspired the American Constitution of 1787 but is still being translated into the languages of countries that suddenly find themselves with the hope of establishing such a government: Hungary, Turkey, and China are recent examples. Pierre Bayle (1647–1706) was an ardent advocate of complete religious toleration who, in his *Historical and Critical Dictionary* of 1697, assembled a vast pot-pourri of the inconsistencies, implausibilities, and downright impossibilities to be found in the Bible and other Christian writings, making it very difficult to accept much of the traditional baggage of the Church's teaching on history and chronology, miracles and holy relics. Gottfried Leibniz (1646–1716), a German polymath who rivalled Newton as a mathematician, exemplified by his wide-ranging contacts among Catholic as well as Protestant scholars the development of tolerant and ecumenical attitudes in 'the republic of letters'. The influence of these writers, all of whom were Protestants, helped to foster the growth among the educated of a more 'rational', 'reasonable', less dogmatic and 'mysterious' religion—and even, for a minority, of 'freethinking' and unbelief.

To take first 'the end of religious wars': though they had virtually ceased within the Empire, they continued to flourish elsewhere. From the siege of Vienna by the Turks in 1683 until the Treaty of Passarowitz in 1718 war was being waged against them almost uninterruptedly by the Habsburg emperors, who were generally supported by Britain and the Dutch Republic, and sometimes by Poland and the Pope. Although for long periods France was an ally of the Turks, this war was seen as a war of Christian (mainly Catholic) against infidel, and it made possible the recovery for Christian rule of huge areas long lost to it: virtually the whole of Greater Hungary (which then included Slovakia and parts of modern Croatia, Romania and the Ukraine and also, until 1739, Serbia. As between Protestants and Catholics, whereas in the international 'religious' wars of the sixteenth and seventeenth centuries alliances always cut across the denominational divide, after the Diplomatic Revolution of 1756 the alignment was more strictly confessional than ever before: Britain, the Dutch Republic, and Prussia versus France, Austria, and Spain. Within France the so-called religious wars had ceased, but in 1685 Louis XIV revoked the Edict of Nantes of 1598 under which Huguenots (i.e. Calvinists) had been granted certain civil and religious rights. The law now declared that to be French and Catholic were the same thing. Tens of thousands of Huguenots were forcibly converted to Catholicism, while large numbers fled the country, swelling the industrious elements in the populations (for example) of Britain, the Dutch Republic, and Prussia. Some stayed on in France yet remained Protestants, practising their religion more or less secretly. They suffered bouts of persecution as late as the 1780s, especially when France was at war with Protestant England.

Within the Empire the more peaceful and prosperous period that followed the Westphalia settlement gave the opportunity to all three denominations to advance their own position as against the others by aggressive proselytization. The least successful were the Calvinists, although they had the personal allegiance of the Hohenzollern kings of Prussia. But the Lutheran Church, until around 1670 apparently the sleepy servant of princes, then spawned an evangelical movement known as Pietism that promoted with marked success intense religious devotion in individuals, innovative educational work, and missionary activity. Its most powerful patrons were the rulers of Prussia. Frederick William I in particular, fierce Calvinist though he was, admired the spirit of the Pietists and employed them to help galvanize and purify not only the established Lutheran Church but also education and government in his dominions. Their chief institutions were the university of Halle, established in 1694, and the clutch of foundations made by August Hermann Francke (1663–1727) in the outskirts of the same town—schools of different levels and for different classes, a teachers' training college, an orphanage, a pharmacy, a library, a printing press, and a bookstore. From this Protestant powerhouse, which employed 3,000 people, ministers spread the influence of Pietism in person, by correspondence and by selling books and medical remedies, throughout Germany, Scandinavia, and eastern Europe and across the Atlantic. Missions were a novelty in Lutheranism, but the Pietists' greatest contribution was to education. As well as pioneering the training of teachers, they adopted more humane, though highly dirigiste, teaching methods. They promoted reading among all social classes, using the vernacular rather than the Latin still usually employed in secondary schools and universities; and they were among the first to teach subjects other than classics— geometry and mechanics to intending soldiers, history, geography, and modern languages to future officials. All this was still done, though, under the aegis of clergy in the name of religion, and the central element in Pietist education remained the teaching of the Bible and of the catechism (a question-and-answer statement of Christian faith).

As for the Catholics, there is a good case that it was not until the middle of the *eighteenth* century that the Counter-Reformation reached its apogee, in Germany and elsewhere. This statement may well astonish, since most historians have situated that movement squarely in the sixteenth century, with perhaps an extension into the early seventeenth when the Austrian Habsburg emperors, inspired by the Jesuits, sought to recover Germany for Catholicism in the Thirty Years War. But it was calculated, for example, that a total of fifty-one German princes converted from Protestantism to Catholicism during the seventeenth and eighteenth centuries, as Catholicism came to be seen as the natural support for absolute monarchy. It tilted the balance of religious power in the Empire when the Elector of Saxony,

Augustus the Strong, whose predecessors had protected Luther and who counted as the first among the German Protestant princes, converted to Rome in order to be able to accept the throne of Poland in 1697. He did not carry his subjects with him, but he and his successors fostered Catholicism in Saxony, leaving the leadership of German Protestantism to the Hohenzollern rulers of Prussia. Toleration was far from universal even in the Empire: the prince-archbishopric of Salzburg—one of the more than twenty states still ruled by a Catholic bishop—notoriously expelled all Protestants in 1731. This was a period of massive Catholic missionary endeavour. Most of one large country, Hungary, was won back to Rome from Protestantism in the eighteenth century by a combination of force and proselytization, and much of another, Poland, chiefly by missions. Until after the middle of the eighteenth century Protestants had reason to fear that intolerant Catholicism was still militant and still gaining ground.

In all Catholic countries, down to the 1770s, lay men and women of all classes, in their millions, continued to join in religious brotherhoods or confraternities under priestly supervision, of which the most famous were those associated with the Jesuits. These organizations had varying emphases but generally included more than one of the following objects: prayer, religious observances, processions and pilgrimages, maintenance of churches, religious education, poor relief, care of the sick and aged, and providing for funerals. The seventeenth-century devotion to the Sacred Heart of Jesus inspired the foundation of 1,088 confraternities in France and Italy between 1694 and 1769. A new devotion to the Eucharist, associated especially with St Alfonso de' Liguori (1696–1787), attracted a huge following. Pilgrimages to the sites of miracles and holy relics grew ever more popular, and the number of such places increased as 'tree, rock, spring, hill and cave were brought into relation with the Catholic faith'. Nearly all were connected with some aspect of the cult of the Virgin Mary. At Mariazell, the principal shrine in Austria, 120,000 to 150,000 people arrived annually in the seventeenth century, 188,000 in 1725, and 373,000 in the jubilee year 1753.

Perhaps the most telling indication that Catholic Reform reached its peak as late as the mid-eighteenth century is the evidence that the proportion of 'secular' (i.e. non-monastic) priests to population reached its highest known level around that time not only in France, but also in Spain and Italy. But it is often forgotten that Catholic countries still also contained thousands of monasteries and tens of thousands of 'regular' (i.e. monastic) clergy; and in fact they too— monks, nuns, and their houses—were still, overall, increasing in numbers until around 1750. The most striking gain was made by the various Franciscan Orders, among which the Capuchins grew from about 22,000 brothers in 1650 to nearly 33,000 in 1754. In the admittedly special case of Hungary the number of monasteries almost doubled between 1700 and 1773, and in Poland they increased by two-thirds. By the 1760s the lands of the Austrian Monarchy (which included, as well as modern Austria and the Czech republic, most of Belgium, Luxembourg, parts of southern Germany, some of northern Italy, Slovenia, and Croatia, and all of greater Hungary) contained a total of about 2,500 monastic houses. France possessed more than 8,000. In many countries there were more regular than secular clergy. Of all the Orders the most powerful were the Jesuits, who supplied nearly all the book censors, university professors, and royal confessors in Catholic Europe, and by precept and example dominated missionary activity. But they were by no means as rich as the old Orders, Benedictine, Cistercian, Augustinian, and Premonstratensian.

Although exact figures are rarely available, it is certain that in Catholic countries the Church owned very high proportions of the land—much more than had been left to Protestant Churches at the Reformation. In France the figure varied greatly from region to region, perhaps from as much as 40 per cent to as little as 1 per cent, but the average is thought to have been about 10 per cent. In Austria the average approached 40 per cent, in Bavaria over 50 per cent. Monasteries, taken together, commonly owned about half of all church land. There can be no doubt that the Church's wealth was still growing, because under the laws of 'mortmain' in most countries land once acquired by the Church could never be alienated, and rents from agricultural land were rising.

Despite 'the crisis of the European mind' described by Hazard, many indicators suggest that, long after his terminal date of 1715, Catholicism, far from being in discredited retreat, was in many countries still strengthening its intellectual hold on the élites as well as on the common people. Until at least the middle of the century a high proportion of Catholics' wills, in some areas the majority, stipulated that Masses should be said for the testators' souls. Though the *proportion* of theological and religious works among new publications was certainly declining overall throughout the century, there was a notable increase in the *total* number of such works that were published. As we shall see, France proved eventually to be the Catholic country most exposed and receptive to the 'crisis of the European consciousness'. Yet in the libraries accumulated by nobles in western France the proportion of religious books actually *grew* until around the middle of the eighteenth century. More surprisingly still, when in 1778–9 a relaxation of government controls in France led to a flood of reprints of works by dead authors, of over two million copies produced no less than 63.1 per cent were religious. Hence Dominique Julia can say of France that 'it was in the eighteenth century that the piety of the Catholic Reformation won the day, through the weight of books of hours, psalters, prayer books and lives of saints', and, going even further, that this was the time when France was at its most Catholic—indeed that the eighteenth century should be seen as 'the truly Christian century'.

While their numbers and wealth were growing, however, Catholics found themselves newly and bitterly divided by a doctrinal dispute. The Church's theology had never been monolithic, and one of the matters of debate had always been the relative importance of God's grace, the individual's faith, and his or her 'works' in procuring salvation. Among the Fathers of the Church, St Augustine had tended to emphasize grace and faith, and it is no accident that Luther, who contended for 'justification by faith alone', was originally a monk of one of the Orders that claimed to follow the rule of St Augustine. In opposing the Reformation, the Catholics, and especially the Jesuits, came to place stronger emphasis on the efficacy of 'works' such as prayer and worship, scholarship and teaching, serving the poor and sick, and raising lavish monuments to God. But the stress on faith, and therefore on individual conversion, was revived by Bishop Cornelius Jansen in his book *Augustinus*, published posthumously in 1640 and in part condemned by the Pope. This and other writings inspired a puritanical movement of religious devotion that came to be known as Jansenism. At first particularly associated with the nunnery of Port-Royal near Paris, the movement became fashionable in the middle years of Louis XIV's reign. But in his last years he came to see it as no less an affront to his absolute rule than the Huguenots had been. Having suppressed Port-Royal in 1709 and had its buildings razed to the ground two years later, he played a large part in procuring from Pope Clement XI the bull *Unigenitus* of 1713, which condemned many propositions found, or said to be found, in Jansenist writings. It was a victory for the Jesuits, the promoters *par excellence* of the Counter-Reformation and of papal supremacy, and therefore it appeared to strengthen Rome. But the bull was a botched and one-sided document, to which many Catholics found it impossible to subscribe. The controversy led to bitter and prolonged disputes in France and other Catholic countries. Some rulers dealt with the matter by forbidding all discussion of the issues involved. In France, however, the government under Cardinal Fleury unequivocally took the side of the Pope and in 1730 incorporated *Unigenitus* into the country's law, effectively encouraging the persecution of Jansenists by orthodox clergy. Julian Swann's chapter explains the political implications and dangers of the French situation, which became fully apparent only after 1750. For Catholicism as a whole the internal divisions over Jansenism were to prove as damaging as the threat of the radical Enlightenment.

From all this it will be evident that the doctrines of Bayle, Locke, and Leibniz had made remarkably little impression in France by mid-century; and they had made still less in other Catholic countries.

Culture before the middle of the century

The period between roughly 1685 and 1750 saw an efflorescence in the arts, especially in architecture and music, that few other ages have equalled. The overwhelming proportion of this cultural achievement was commissioned by rulers, nobles, and the churches, especially the Catholic Church, its bishops, and its abbots. These groups almost alone had the land that, together with the taxes and other exactions that they had the right to levy, provided sufficient revenue to fund the enormously expensive palaces and churches that were erected in their thousands during the period. The buildings, moreover, were designed to exploit and embrace many other arts—sculpture, painting, furniture-making, organ-building—and to create facilities for theatrical and musical performance; and so it was these same lay and ecclesiastical grandees who provided the main career opportunities for painters, sculptors, playwrights, and musicians. The overriding purpose of these great buildings and their vast parks was to impress: to signal—and usually to exaggerate—the standing, power, and wealth of the authorities that had commissioned the work. The buildings were further conceived as the theatres where these personages who claimed and were acknowledged to be raised above ordinary mortals, to be semi-divine—kings, princes, aristocrats, bishops, and abbots—acted out their public 'representative' roles with elaborate ceremony, and, in the case of churches, where God and his Church were similarly glorified. People seldom distinguished clearly between the exaltation of God and that of his earthly representatives. The Abbot of Ottobeuren in south Germany, one of the numerous abbots who was also the ruler of a principality, when criticized for pouring his abbey's resources into a complete and sumptuous rebuilding of the house and its church, declared: 'My intention is no other than to build such a house of God as is fitting for the Holy Order and the abbey in honour of the Holy Trinity, to whom alone I have dedicated it. I have imagined that I would acquire merit in the eyes of God and men . . .'. The confusion or overlapping between the religious and the secular was highlighted by the existence of such ecclesiastical states and by the leading role accorded to the higher clergy in nearly all of the many provincial 'Estates' (representative assemblies) of Europe.

There were few exceptions in this period to the dominance of rulers, aristocrats, and churchmen as patrons. Even in Italy, where city states controlled by merchant families had largely created the Renaissance, cities had now lost most of their independence, having fallen under princely rule or, in the case of the surviving republics, under aristocratic control; and many were actually declining in wealth and population. Nearly all the towns that flourished in this period did so because they were the seat of a ruler's court. Vienna was the most notable example. It more than doubled in population because, after the withdrawal of the Turks, the great nobles of the expanding Austrian Monarchy built palaces in the city in order to have access to the patronage of its powerful Habsburg rulers and to the prestige and pleasures of their court. New residences or capitals were founded, for example, by Louis XIV at Versailles, Peter the Great at St Petersburg, and the Palatinate electors at Mannheim. Louis was removing himself and his government from the turbulence of Paris, Peter was trying to shake off the Asiatic influences of Moscow, the Elector Palatine, newly converted to Catholicism, was escaping from the Protestant ambience of Heidelberg. Only one of them, Peter the Great, had economic and strategic considerations among his motives, the desire to increase trade with the West and develop a powerful navy. Dozens of other rulers rebuilt their town palaces and also created summer residences or pleasure palaces a few miles from their capitals, like Schönbrunn near Vienna or Nymphenburg near Munich, in some cases, as with Potsdam near Berlin, creating a significant town as well. But it was only in a few rare continental cities that grand public and private buildings were being commissioned by citizens as a by-product of economic success, as in Bordeaux, enriched by the Atlantic (including slave) trade, or that the city authorities were the employers of a major artist, as in Leipzig with its expanding international fair, where J. S. Bach presided over the city's music from 1723 to 1750.

Even in Britain, where the situation was to change so dramatically later in the century, down to about 1720 the major architectural enterprises were: the royal hospitals of Chelsea and Greenwich and the enlargement of Kensington and Hampton Court palaces; grandiose country houses for the high aristocracy such as Chatsworth for the Duke of Devonshire, Petworth for the Duke of Somerset, Castle Howard for the Earl of Carlisle, and Blenheim for the Duke of Marlborough; and the continuing work on Sir Christopher Wren's new St Paul's, consecrated in 1697, and on the fifty-odd City churches he was rebuilding after their destruction in the Great Fire of 1666. Although, as we shall see, London was growing rapidly and supported a unique culture, the most striking counter-example to royal and aristocratic building before 1750 was the re-creation of Bath, by far the grandest of the numerous spas that became fashionable in England in the early eighteenth century. Serious rebuilding began in Bath under Queen Anne, but John Wood's grand-scale scheme dates from 1725. Royalty and aristocracy had little to do with its conception, the profits of commerce and industrialization nothing whatever. On the other hand, it was a commercial enterprise, built to attract royalty, aristocracy, and other wealthy persons to its spa, to its classical squares, circus, and crescents, and to the associated entertainments—providing from below what in other countries grandees supplied from above.

Almost all major buildings of the age were in some sense classical, but the early eighteenth century is associated with a particular form of classicism, 'the baroque', a name applied to all arts and to the age as a whole but easiest to define in relation to architecture (with which in any case the other arts were commonly integrated). It is based on the classical forms that had been revived and glorified, as against the Gothic style, in the Renaissance: columns, round arches, pediments, and domes. But the aim is no longer to convey a pure, stately, geometrical, historically correct, 'classical' repose. The most characteristic baroque buildings assert themselves, and aim to overawe, by their vast or simulated scale and grandeur and by the elaboration of their applied ornament and decoration. Their classical forms are often so teased and contorted that buildings come to resemble huge stage sets, manipulating space and light, deceiving observers and drawing them into their fantastic constructions. The accompanying statues, furniture, and frescoes are designed to awe and amaze the observer by their virtuosity and emotionalism. All is movement. Goddesses and angels appear to be in flight, heroes and horses burst from the frames of windows and ceilings, miracles and martyrdoms take place before our eyes. This is 'virtual reality' *avant la lettre.* Artists consciously aimed to depict an ideal nature, as landscape gardeners worked to create it.

Though the secular examples of the baroque style are very numerous, reaching beyond Catholic Europe to Castle Howard and Blenheim in England and to several of the palaces in and around St Petersburg, it was especially associated with the general rebuilding and refurbishment of the churches of Catholic Europe during the last century of the Counter-Reformation. Its Roman creators consciously countered Protestantism's reserve, austerity, and iconoclasm by their demonstrative emotionalism and theatricality, their insistence on colour and statuary, their appeal to all the senses. More specifically, baroque church architecture was designed to suit the liturgical changes required by the theological emphases of the Counter-Reformation, such as the exaltation of the Mass and therefore of the high altar, reverence for the saints and their physical relics, and better facilities for the confessional—all anathema to Protestants. However, both Reformers and Counter-Reformers laid a new emphasis on preaching. A good many Protestant churches were adorned with baroque pulpits, organ case, and domes—the dome of St Paul's Cathedral was the first dome to be designed in Britain—but they could never include the whole gamut of baroque paraphernalia.

Among the most notable examples of ecclesiastical baroque are the great abbeys of Austria and southern Germany, such as Melk and Ottobeuren, or Einsiedeln in Switzerland and Strahov in Prague, with monumental staircases to assert their secular grandeur and gorgeous libraries to house the vast collections of books and natural specimens they were systematically acquiring; the numerous pilgrimage churches of the same areas, mostly built under monastic auspices, like Vierzehnheiligen and Die Wies, both from the 1740s; and the rather earlier church of St Charles Borromeo in Vienna, designed by J. B. Fischer von Erlach, which contrives to bring reminiscences of Trajan's column and of Turkish minarets into harmony with classical dome, portico, and pediment.

The most famous secular building of the age, then as now, was the palace of Versailles. It was in 1682 that construction was far enough advanced for Louis XIV to set up his court there. Perhaps the most celebrated of its features, the Sun King's *levée* in the centrally placed royal bedroom where great nobles took part in the formal dressing of the monarch, began in 1701. The building is baroque in its huge scale, in being integrally related to a vast formal park, in having an immensely long façade that is partly recessed, in its lavish internal decoration, and in certain of its elements—for example, the royal chapel of the early 1700s. But the details of its architecture, as of most French building, are much more restrained and traditionally classical than is commonly found in the contemporary buildings of Spain, Portugal, Italy, Germany, and the Austrian lands, the true homes of baroque. Culturally, Versailles made a sensational impression, enhanced by the successes of Louis's rule and the splendour of the literature he patronized, especially the plays of Molière and Racine, and by his deliberate cultivation of civilized and civilian behaviour and dress. All this helped to establish French as the polite language of aristocratic society across most of Europe. Frederick the Great notoriously declared —in French—that all German rulers were ruining themselves trying to emulate Versailles and its ways.

In fact, though, the all-pervading influence of Versailles is a myth. Many of its characteristics were copied only rarely. Whereas Louis's purpose was never to live in Paris again, the great majority of the rulers who built new country palaces continued to reside for substantial parts of the year in their capital cities. Whereas he took the principal ministries with him to Versailles, virtually no other ruler transplanted the government machine: the only major example is

Caserta, near Naples, begun in the 1740s. Few copied Versailles's architectural style, though there were direct influences, for example, on the Charlottenburg palace built by the first king in Prussia, Frederick I, for his wife, starting in 1700, and on Boughton, Petworth, and Hampton Court in England; and a number of the architects concerned went on to help in the building of palaces in the duchy of Lorraine and in Germany. Most German palaces, like Prince Eugene's Belvedere in Vienna or that of the prince-bishop of Würzburg, were much more flamboyant. The fantastic etiquette of the *levée* was adopted almost nowhere. Peter the Great, impressed by what he saw when he visited Versailles, built a palace called Peterhof, which, though more baroque in style, was intended to vie with it in its scale and opulence and the number of its fountains. But he did not relish the formality of court life, was both coarse and brutal, and showed more interest in economic, scientific, military, and naval matters than in literature. Whereas Louis deliberately attracted the French nobility to Versailles as an alternative to employing them in affairs of state, Peter created a nobility of service. Charles XII of Sweden, determined to be absolute, had been no less determined to endure the hardships of a soldier's life, constantly campaigning outside Sweden until his death in 1718. Frederick William I, contemptuous of his father Frederick I's cultural aspirations, cut down the ceremony at his coronation to the point that it cost 0.05 per cent of his predecessor's, avoided using French, and reduced the expenditure on the members of the academy his father had founded, describing them in his accounts as the 'royal buffoons'. He devoted himself instead, with remarkable success, to the creation of the best army in Europe, requiring his nobles to serve in it as officers, always wearing uniform himself, and turning Prussia into 'an army with a state attached'. Neither Russian nor Prussian nobles found it easy to get their sovereign's permission to travel and sample the civilization of western and southern Europe. In complete contrast both to these militarists and to Louis, two major rulers of the early eighteenth century, Charles VI of Austria (1711–40) and John V of Portugal (1706–50), decided that their ideal residence was a palace-monastery, like the Escorial of Philip II in Spain: Charles started a grandiose rebuilding of the Augustinian house at Klosterneuburg, John completed a vast new palace-monastery at Mafra. These projects are further evidence of the continuing allure of traditional Catholicism down to the 1740s.

The age is pre-eminent too for its music, embracing as it does virtually the whole lifetimes of J. S. Bach (1685–1750), G. F. Handel (1685–1759), Antonio Vivaldi (1678–1741), and the Scarlattis, Alessandro (1660–1725) and Domenico (1685–1757). Its most extravagant and characteristic form was *opera seria*—that is, performances, usually in court theatres, of operas that consisted chiefly of a string of recitatives and arias in Italian, which portrayed the feelings of classical gods and heroes in complicated mythical situations against a rapidly changing backdrop of extremely elaborate and expensive sets. At certain points the singers would be replaced by dancers performing a 'ballet'. These grand operas were often—in Vienna, Dresden, and Berlin, for example—directly commanded and funded by the ruler for special court occasions such as name days and weddings; all members of the audience were his invited guests; the plots were selected so that the hero could be plausibly identified with the ruler or the principal characters with the bridal pair; the feelings expressed in the words and music were elevated and restrained; and there was very little in the operas of what we would call dramatic action. They were essentially ideal expressions of the ruler's grandeur, like baroque palaces, and courts were felt to be inadequate if they lacked either. Among the most successful composers of such operas were J. A. Hasse (1699–1783), who dominated the sumptuous productions of the Saxon court for decades and was admired by both Maria Theresa and Frederick the Great; and Handel, who worked mainly in the very different circumstances of England.

Opera had originated in Italy, and Italy remained its home, where, though organized by courts and grandees, it was a genuinely popular art. North of the Alps a great city might possess only one opera house, usually attached to the court, but in Venice there were at least seven. Here, as in other places where the court was not in full control, like Prague, Hamburg, and London, many of the seats were for sale and the theatres often performed less serious works, perhaps in the vernacular, like the 'masquerades' and 'ballad operas' of London or the comic operas (*opere buffe*) and *intermezzi* of Italy, of which the most famous was *La serva padrona* of 1733, composed by the young Neapolitan G. B. Pergolesi (1710–36). In London the court and the aristocracy combined to subsidize *opera seria*, largely provided by Handel, for most of the period from 1710 to 1741. But thereafter, since the public would no longer support it, even these wealthy promoters could not afford to maintain it.

Since all significant churches, except those of the Calvinists and the Orthodox, had sizable musical establishments of voices and instruments to perform the liturgy, the Church was the major patron of composers and performers. In Vienna, for example, before the economical reforms of Joseph II, nearly 300 musicians received regular, if usually meagre, incomes from one or more of almost 100 ecclesiastical establishments. The Church provided nearly all the musical training there was, and the 'conservatories' of Italy amounted to musically oriented orphanages run by clergy (like Vivaldi). To provide a semi-religious alternative to opera during the solemn periods of the Church's year when it was banned, oratorios on sacred themes had been developed in Italy and quickly spread to other countries. In 1720 Handel began composing English-language oratorios and by the 1740s their popularity had become so great that they superseded opera on the London stage. J. S. Bach never obtained a major court appointment and hence never wrote an opera. His chief output was of German-language church cantatas and settings of the story of Christ's Passion from the New Testament. The music of oratorios and passions, concerned with religious themes and unsupported by the panoply of court theatre and scenery, appealed much more directly to the emotions than *opera seria*. Working in the part of Europe where organs, mostly to be found in churches, had reached their highest development, Bach wrote the greatest music ever composed for that instrument.

At the beginning of this century of strutting absolute rulers and Catholic *revanche* the two major Protestant states, the Dutch Republic and constitutional Britain, stood apart as havens of religious toleration and of relatively free speech and publication. By 1750 the Dutch Republic's decline was manifest and Britain had established its preponderance. As compared with the other Great Powers, it was politically, socially, religiously, and culturally a special case. Not only had serfdom disappeared centuries previously, whereas it was present almost everywhere else in Europe and growing ever more restrictive in eastern countries; but also the legally privileged aristocracy was uniquely small, a mere 200 people, probably less than one-hundredth of the number of privileged nobles in Prussia and less than one-thousandth of the number in France. Since 1688 the monarch had been required by the constitution to observe 'the statutes in parliament agreed on'. In 1689 some dissenters from the Church of England were given legal rights to worship in their own way and to conduct schools. In 1695 the legal provision for the censorship of books by ecclesiastical authority before publication lapsed—though this still left authors at risk from prosecutions at a later stage. Even the maverick Quakers obtained a right of access to the king. It is true that the established churches none the less retained much social and political power and the allegiance of the majority of the population; that in England the right of Dissenters to hold office was not fully conceded, the universities were Anglican monopolies and Catholics remained severely disadvantaged; that Catholics were even worse off in Ireland despite the fact that there they constituted the large majority of its population; that most Anglican clergy remained traditionalists in doctrine and rejected the 'reasonable' undogmatic religion advocated by Locke and his followers; and that a 'moral reformation' movement and stirrings of the evangelical revival are to be found in this period. But, at a time when most of Europe was dominated by absolute rulers with the power to legislate on their own, and much of it by a monopolistic church that strictly controlled what people could read, Britain was startlingly free.

It was essentially in Britain during this period that a public, public opinion, and what Jürgen Habermas christened 'the public sphere' first arose. Perhaps the essence of 'the public' is that those who make it up are anonymous and always changing. A court might involve thousands of people, but they were in principle known to those in charge. Church congregations, though much wider than the public in this period, were also in principle known to the authorities by baptism and other rites of passage. Moreover, courtiers and worshippers were not advertised for: they were under pressure to attend. In return they did not pay for admission, except in indirect ways such as buying offices and paying tithes. They were in principle passive, commenting only privately, whereas the public is in principle active and expects to be able to read critical reviews. Among the innovatory aspects of the public sphere in Britain in this period, all admired and sooner or later copied elsewhere so far as local circumstances permitted, were: the first true national daily newspaper, the *Daily Courant*, founded in 1702; the proliferation of provincial newspapers, usually weekly, which numbered about forty by 1750; and the first 'polite' journals, the *Tatler* (1709) and the *Spectator* (1711), the latter a daily run jointly by Joseph Addison and Richard Steele, which catered for a 'general public' of non-aristocrats with short, unpretentious, amusing, sometimes gently satirical essays about contemporary society, with a bias towards 'moral improvement' and special attention to female readers. The first novel to have a runaway success was Defoe's *Robinson Crusoe* of 1719, which, like his *Moll Flanders* of 1721, appealed to both a popular and an educated readership; Alexander Pope was the first poet who had the talent and the audience to make a good living out of his art; the first composer and musical impresario who made a fortune from a paying public was Handel; and the first scientist to receive a state funeral was Newton. By modern standards, newspapers and periodicals had very small circulations: Addison reckoned on 3,000 for the *Spectator* in 1711, which he thought meant he had 60,000 readers; the *Gentleman's Magazine* may have achieved a circulation of 10,000 in the 1740s. But these sales were prodigious by previous and continental standards. Addison wrote: 'It was said of Socrates that he brought Philosophy down from Heaven to inhabit among Men; and I shall be ambitious to have it said of me, that I have brought Philosophy out of Closets and Libraries, Schools and Colleges, to dwell in Clubs and Assemblies, at Tea-Tables and in Coffee Houses.' It was the first age of 'voluntary associations'. Clubs, nearly always for men only, multiplied, virtually untroubled by the law, whereas abroad they were restricted as dangerous. Freemasonry, which was reorganized in Britain from 1717 as a network of gentlemen's clubs with secret ritual and charitable, tolerant, and fraternal principles, was there considered respectable and harmless. When it spread to the continent it was condemned by the Pope, first in 1738, and regarded as anti-religious and politically subversive. During this period, too, commercially organized concerts became a regular feature of life in London and major towns, at a time when they were virtually unknown elsewhere. In 1732 the pleasure garden at Vauxhall was opened, soon to be joined by Ranelagh and others, places where on payment of an entrance fee anyone could go to enjoy food, drink, theatre, music, and less respectable diversions. This was an example of freedom and of social mixing astonishing to travellers from the continent. As late as 1782 Carl Philipp Moritz wrote of Ranelagh:

I looked down on the concourse of people . . . and then I could easily distinguish several stars, and other orders of knighthood; French queues and

bags contrasting with plain English heads of hair . . . old age and youth,
nobility and commonalty, all passing each other in the motley swarm . . .
Even the poorest families are at the expence of a coach, to go to Ranelagh, as
my landlady assured me.

Religion, enlightenment, and culture from mid-century to 1789

On almost every front the churches, especially the Catholic Church,
were in retreat from around 1750, and still more obviously after 1770.
Charles VI's palace-monastery was left unfinished when he died in
1740; his successor, Maria Theresa, pious though she was, had little
sympathy with the project but a good deal with Jansenism. It was in
1740, too, that Frederick the Great, an unbeliever, succeeded to the
throne of Prussia and immediately widened religious toleration,
restored the Berlin Academy, and relaxed the censorship, especially in
favour of works sceptical of traditional theology. Cardinal Fleury died
in 1743, and Louis XV's government, short of money because of the
costs of the War of the Austrian Succession, soon began challenging
the Church's tax privileges—though the king lacked the tenacity to
carry his point. John V's palace-monastery at Mafra was never occupied, and his successor, José I, coming to the throne in 1750, entrusted
power to the ruthless minister universally known as Pombal, who
began an assault on the Jesuits that led to their expulsion from
Portugal in 1759, France in 1765, Spain and Naples in 1767, and ultimately to the suppression of the whole Order by the Pope in 1773. All
Catholic governments tightened up legislation against mortmain. In
1766 a commission was set up in France under Bishop Loménie de
Brienne to reform the monasteries, and its report eventually led to
the suppression of a few small Orders and over 400 houses. During
the late 1760s and in the 1770s Maria Theresa imposed more and more
controls on the Church in the Austrian Monarchy. Then her son
Joseph II, who ruled from 1780 to 1790, set about subordinating the
Church to the State, dissolved all brotherhoods and nearly half the
monasteries, granted a measure of toleration to the main Protestant sects and to the Jews, greatly relaxed the censorship, made
marriage a civil matter, rewrote the Church's liturgy, began a

sweeping reform of parochial provision, and removed the training of clergy from the control of bishops and monasteries, concentrating it instead in state-directed general seminaries. France at last restored a measure of toleration for Protestants in 1787. In many parts of Catholic Europe monastic and priestly vocations fell off, and the number of bequests for Masses in Catholics' wills dwindled, as did other manifestations of baroque piety. As for the papacy, the defects of the bull *Unigenitus* made its claim to infallibility in matters of dogma contemptible even to many Catholics. When in 1768 Clement XIII reacted to lay rulers' curbing of Church power by reviving the rusty weapons of excommunication and deposition, he succeeded only in provoking ridicule and retaliation. By the 1780s, at least among the upper classes, dogmatic religion seemed to be giving way among both Catholics and Protestants— as even among practising Jews—to a generalized and tolerant benevolence uninterested either in the ancient ideal of asceticism or in doctrinal precision. This bare recital of course needs elaboration and modification, but there can be no question that, overall, baroque piety, monasticism, clergy numbers, dogmatism, religious intolerance, and the respect of rulers and laymen for ecclesiastical authority, especially of Catholics for the papacy, were all declining—a reversal of most of the trends of the first half of the century.

Why did this remarkable shift occur? Was it, as is often suggested, straightforwardly attributable to the Enlightenment? In order to answer this question, it is necessary first to try to define and describe the Enlightenment. Let us start with the word. Down to the eighteenth century one of the commonest meanings of the adjectives 'enlightened' in English and *éclairé* in French was 'illuminated by faith'. Christ had brought 'a light to lighten the Gentiles'. A convert was said to have 'seen the light'. But during the century it became normal to think of light as coming rather from the advance of secular knowledge and philosophy; and 'enlightened' and *éclairé* acquired the meaning 'sympathetic to the new tendencies of thought'—namely, those that had emerged during 'the crisis of the European consciousness'. At the time the concept of 'the Enlightenment' as a movement did not exist, and only in German was an abstract noun regularly used that is directly translatable nowadays as 'enlightenment', *Aufklärung*. In French the nearest equivalent nouns were and are *les*

lumières and *philosophie*, and the leaders of the French Enlightenment liked to be known as *philosophes*.

In the 1780s the meaning of *Aufklärung* became a matter of lively
discussion in Germany, and in 1784 the great philosopher Immanuel
Kant, in his tract *What is Enlightenment?*, wrote:

> If it is now asked whether we at present live in an *enlightened* age, the answer
> is: No, but we do live in an age of *enlightenment*. As things are at present, we
> still have a long way to go before men can be in a position (or can even be put
> into a position) of using their own understanding confidently and well in
> religious matters, without outside guidance. But we do have distinct indica-
> tions that the way is now being cleared for them to work freely in this
> direction, and that the obstacles to universal enlightenment, to man's emer-
> gence from his self-incurred immaturity, are gradually becoming fewer. In
> this respect our age is the age of enlightenment, the century of *Frederick*.

Kant thus, as he acknowledged, 'portrayed *matters of religion* as the
focal point of enlightenment'. Voltaire, the French writer generally
accepted as the leader of the European Enlightenment, took as his
war cry Frederick the Great's motto, 'Écrasez l'infâme', by which they
meant 'Smash bigotry and superstition'. So from their standpoint too
matters of religion were the focal point of enlightenment.

There is a sense in which any intellectual movement of the period
had to focus on religion, since virtually all education (other than legal
and medical) was in the hands of clergy. Many Catholic teachers,
whose leaders until the second half of the eighteenth century were the
Jesuits, had striven either to suppress or to annex ways of thought
apparently hostile to orthodoxy. Hence Jansenist attitudes were
banned, while the Jesuits' reworking of Descartes's deductive rational
philosophy dominated French university education—they had
underpinned (or undermined) the foundation of Descartes's system,
Man's awareness of himself, by subordinating it to the will of God.
Anyone who questioned this adaptation or other officially approved
views came up against ecclesiastical authority—bishops and mostly
Jesuit-dominated universities with the power to censor writings and
have their authors punished by the state. But lively minds naturally
rebelled against these restrictions; and, paradoxically, the rigorous
rationalism of Cartesian theology evidently helped to prepare pupils'
minds for rationalist approaches of a more sceptical character.

One of the chief emphases of French Enlightened writers such as
Voltaire was on the merits of the inductive method, which seeks to

establish truth by experiment and observation, as against the deductive method of theology and of metaphysics, which erects a system of explanation from first principles. With this went both the acceptance that much was still unknown about the world and the desire to find out more, which reinforced the demand for freedom of enquiry, speech, writing, and publication. In describing these sceptical and critical attitudes as *philosophie* they were deliberately giving the word a new meaning, overlaying its earlier connotations of metaphysics and Stoicism. Questioning of some Christian beliefs, especially Catholics' belief in frequent miracles and in the authenticity and efficacy of the relics of saints, followed naturally, and many of the great writers of the French Enlightenment enjoyed deploying their talent for ridicule to scoff at the Church and its doctrines.

Protestantism demanded fewer beliefs from its adherents than Catholicism did, and neither in Britain nor in northern Germany was Enlightenment nearly so hostile to the established churches and their claims as in France. But Kant and Voltaire were united in rejecting the intellectual authority of the Church and asserting the right of laymen to pronounce on matters that the clergy considered to be within their monopoly. The Enlightenment has to be seen as a laicizing movement. It was also a secularizing movement in a certain sense, in that many of its leaders sought to emancipate from divine and ecclesiastical interference almost all branches of knowledge, including history, law, anthropology, and natural science—not to mention politics. Newton's God set the solar system to work but intervened no more; perhaps, suggested Voltaire, there have been no genuine miracles since the time of Christ; polygamy, insinuated Montesquieu in his *Persian Letters* of 1721, is just a social custom like any other; Christian morality, declared the Italian Cesare Beccaria in his *Crimes and Punishments* of 1764, properly has nothing to do with law. The criterion by which to judge laws and policies, as Beccaria, Jeremy Bentham, and many less radical writers argued, is their 'utility', their calculable benefit to those now on earth. Even so, in only a tiny handful of thinkers, such as Frederick the Great, Baron d'Holbach, or David Hume, is there a fundamental challenge to Christianity. 'The Rise of Modern Paganism', in the natural sense of those words, is not an appropriate title for the Enlightenment in general, even in France. It is likely that Voltaire himself meant what he said in his eloquent defence of the existence of God. Many clergy were promoters of the new views, if less prominently in France than in Germany and Britain. In time the objective study of Nature was easily sanctified by such as the Anglican clergyman, William Paley, into 'natural theology', and German Protestant theologians found no great difficulty in harnessing Kant's philosophy to their cause. The Enlightenment is much more like a heresy than a denial of faith. It sought to restrict, rather than eliminate, the influence of Christianity in intellectual life and the activity of the Church in politics, education, and society. But it was anathema to the papacy—as it still is—and to a large body of conservatively minded clergy and laity.

Though many of the major works of the French Enlightenment had been published earlier, it was only around the mid-century that it began to capture the élites. Even thereafter the story of its diffusion is fitful and contradictory, largely because of the chaotic structure of the *Ancien Régime*. Writers and publishers of critical or advanced books had always to guard themselves against the risk of prosecution. So such writings were usually published anonymously and often with a fictive imprint; if they could not safely be published even anonymously in France, they would appear under the imprint of a foreign city and be imported clandestinely into France; as court factions battled for influence, there were times when the authorities appeared sympathetic, and then suddenly they would become restrictive again. On the other hand, the identity of the authors of anonymous publications was often generally known. The *Persian Letters*, a brilliant early example of the device of criticizing the French government and western society through the imaginary correspondence of an astonished foreigner, appeared anonymously. But top people knew it had been written by Baron de Montesquieu, a judge of the Parlement of Bordeaux, and he was made a member of the French Academy on the strength of it. More provocatively, Voltaire brought out in 1734 his *Lettres philosophiques*, first published in English in the previous year, a work in which he enthusiastically, but of course anonymously, commended to his compatriots the thought of Bacon, Locke, and Newton, Britain's constitution, its religious toleration, its commercial institutions, and the hitherto despised plays of Shakespeare—all of which he had come to know while exiled in England from 1726 to 1728.

In 1736 the future Frederick the Great, as crown prince, sent a letter to Voltaire out of the blue, praising some of his more literary works in the most flattering terms, asking to be sent his other works and urging him to come to Prussia. This letter began a lifelong correspondence, the existence of which soon became generally known with the connivance of both parties. Frederick, having seized Silesia from Austria in 1740, showed during the resulting War of the Austrian Succession, in alliance with France, that he was a general of genius. If cultural historians are liable to underrate the influence of religion, they usually ignore military and diplomatic history altogether. Yet these actions of Frederick profoundly affected the development of the Enlightenment across Europe. His friendship gave the *philosophe* and his cause a new status. The Pope applauded Voltaire's play *Mahomet*, old Cardinal Fleury employed him as an unofficial envoy to Berlin, and Louis XV made him historiographer royal and a lord of the bedchamber. Before long he fell out of favour again at Versailles, but he was now a wealthy man with so high an international reputation that he became virtually an independent power, safe from the French government in his Swiss chateau. Hence he was able to wage a brilliant, arduous, and successful campaign to rehabilitate Jean Calas, a Protestant of Toulouse executed in 1762 for allegedly murdering his son in order to stop him converting to Rome.

In 1748 there appeared the period's most influential work of political theory, Montesquieu's *The Spirit of the Laws*, another book that praised the English constitution and criticized the French monarchy's absolutist aspirations. But the French Enlightenment's real breakthrough came with the publication of the *Encyclopédie*. It started as a project to translate into French the two-volume *Chambers' Encyclopedia* of 1728, one of the many initiatives of the Scottish Enlightenment, but developed, with government encouragement, into a much bigger scheme for a largely new encyclopaedia. In 1747 Jean d'Alembert, a brilliant mathematician, and Denis Diderot became joint editors—extraordinary choices because they both had radical religious views, but this was a moment when prominent ministers were progressive. In 1750 d'Alembert's prospectus appeared, glorying in the progress of science and promising to provide a universal account of useful knowledge. The first seven volumes were published, one a year, from 1751 to 1757, despite a papal condemnation and the violent hostility of the Jesuits. But then, in the changed situation of the Seven Years War, with Prussia now the enemy of France, the government forbade its continuation. By one of the more delicious ironies of the *Ancien Régime*, Malesherbes, the head of the censorship, was privately a supporter of freedom of the press: he warned Diderot beforehand that the materials for the *Encyclopédie* were about to be seized and then took them into his own house to safeguard them. Not until the war was over could the remaining ten volumes of text be published—at the end of 1765, the *annus mirabilis* in which the judgment on Calas was reversed and the Jesuits were expelled from France.

About 300 writers had contributed to the *Encyclopédie*, and so it was far from uniform in its attitudes. But many of the 72,000 articles mocked what the authors saw as superstitions, Christian and non-Christian, and sought to promote Enlightened opinions, in some cases even venturing to challenge the absolutist pretensions of Louis XV. Tendentious though it was, it was easily the most complete encyclopaedia available for many decades, and by far the most entertaining ever published, especially as the text was accompanied by eleven volumes of marvellous plates illustrating natural phenomena, industrial and artistic methods, and historic artefacts, from the Giant's Causeway to the Dresden opera orchestra, the manufacture of pins to Noah's ark. Four thousand people subscribed initially, and by 1789 about 25,000 copies of this huge and expensive work had been sold, just over half outside France. It contributed as powerfully as any product of the French Enlightenment to the spread of *philosophie* across Europe, and within France to the situation lamented paranoiacally by the General Assembly of Clergy in 1780: 'the *philosophes* are no longer a party, they are popular opinion.'

Despite all this, it was by no means the case that the writings of the *philosophes* were mainly responsible for the retreat of the Church, even in France. A much wider explanation is required. In the first place, baroque, like all dominant and aggressive cultural and intellectual movements, in due course provoked a general reaction. By the middle of the century, many kings, princes, bishops, and nobles had clearly become reluctant to 'represent', act out, their status and grandeur. They wanted instead to be able to enjoy as much of their wealth as possible in seclusion, out of the public gaze, even incognito: Louis XV escaped from Versailles for four-fifths of the year. More of them now saw themselves as professional commanders-in-chief and heads of the civil service rather than as sacred, ceremonial father (or mother) figures. Frederick the Great is again the supreme example, shunning ceremony, leading his armies, answering all major dispatches himself, maintaining his father's standards of probity in the administration, and publicizing himself as 'the first servant of the state'. His much admired 'palace', Sanssouci at Potsdam, begun in the mid-1740s, would be better called the quintessential bachelor pad, designed to house only himself and a few intimates and to provide the backdrop for his private reading, music-making, conversation, and connoisseurship, all of which were largely insulated from his activities as a ruler. Joseph II, trying to emulate him, always wore uniform, joined his troops annually in camp, travelled frenetically and without pomp around his dominions and to France, Italy, and Russia, abolished almost all the monarch's regular public appearances, and lived for long spells in a small private villa in the Augarten, a hunting reserve that he had opened to the public as a park. If successive Russian empresses, Elizabeth and Catherine, defied the trend by truly lavish expenditure on court and palaces, Catherine at least was a hard-working and highly effective head of the administration and liked to waive etiquette with *philosophes* and her numerous lovers.

It was symbolic that the taste for grand formal gardens in the French manner, attached, as at Versailles, to a bombastic palace, was giving way to emulation of the 'English' garden, in which the natural contours, instead of being flattened and geometrically regularized, were exploited or enhanced to make a 'picturesque' landscape setting for a less assertive house and for a range of temples, follies, and ruins artfully disposed. Palladianism, the style of these new country houses, derived from a pre-baroque classicism brought from Italy by Lord Burlington and displayed at his own Chiswick in the 1720s—as Pevsner says, 'so chaste outside and so sumptuous inside'. The most elaborate of these gardens was being created at Stowe from the 1730s. In France baroque was displaced by rococo, again architecturally less elaborate but bringing lighter and more elegant decoration to interiors, as exemplified in many Parisian *hôtels* (noble houses) and by the work of French artists at Nymphenburg.

With the decline of baroque in general went a decline of baroque piety in Catholic countries, at least among the literate classes: it was replaced by a simpler, more personal, less costly, and less ostentatious devotion. The attitudes of the later Counter-Reformation, and particularly of the Jesuits, seemed too strident and triumphalist now that the external threat to Catholicism had disappeared and its position seemed secure. A strong reaction developed within the Church itself, of which perhaps the most important representative was Lodovico Antonio Muratori (1672–1750). Parish priest, librarian to the Duke of Modena, pioneer of Italian medieval studies, indefatigable correspondent across denominational boundaries, Muratori, towards the end of his long life, became known also as an advocate of church reform, most notably in his book *Of the Well-Ordered devotion of Christians* (1747). His aims, as he knew, were not dissimilar from those of the early Counter-Reformation, even of the Reformation. The Church, he held, must be shorn of the unwarranted and unappealing accretions of doctrine and ritual added since the days of the Primitive Church. Monks and nuns were too numerous and comfortable, and their Orders too rich. The overweening power of the Jesuits needed to be broken, and those Orders should be dissolved that were corrupt or did not contribute to parochial or missionary work or to other 'useful' activities such as education and caring for the sick. The people should be encouraged, as they had not been, to read the Bible in the vernacular. It is wrong, said Muratori, to convert heretics forcibly; they should be granted a measure of toleration, creating a freer situation within which the true Church can seek to convince them of its credentials. Above all, the education and preaching of parish clergy must be improved, and their numbers and standing enhanced. These views, which, like all views critical of the Church establishment, were loosely described as Jansenist and are now seen as part of a 'Catholic Enlightenment', became especially influential in northern Italy, southern Germany, and Austria. They appealed to bishops, parish priests, and laymen who thought the Jesuits and monks in general had too much of the wealth and power of the Church, and even to monastic Orders such as the Benedictines and Augustinians, jealous of the Jesuits' monopoly in education and critical of their theology. Some representatives of all these groups cherished a genuine desire for church reform. It was hoped that Benedict XIV (1740–58), an exceptionally liberal Pope and a friend of Muratori, would act in this sense, but he did little: there were too many obstacles in the way of a Pope trying to change long-standing practices, especially in countries like France over which his predecessors had virtually surrendered jurisdiction. Good parochial provision was seen by governments and philosophers as an essential element of a good society. Since the Pope could not or would not act, it was argued that others must. Febronius' provocative book *On the Condition of the Church* (1763) demanded similar reforms to Muratori's while maintaining that they should be carried out by individual bishops, especially prince-bishops. Others declared that it was the duty and the mission of secular rulers to reform the Church themselves, a view of which Joseph II was the embodiment.

Such an approach was not readily accepted in France, where very few thinkers would entertain the notion that despotism or absolutism could be Enlightened and most denounced the spasmodic efforts of Louis XV to act as the absolute ruler he claimed to be. In Britain there was no question of the government attempting major reforms of any kind. But in Germany dozens of rulers were acknowledged to be absolute in the sense of having the legislative power, and the received version of contract theory was Hobbes's, as popularized by Samuel Pufendorf in the seventeenth century and taught in German universities, that the people, in making their pact with the ruler, had surrendered all their rights to him. Pufendorf included among the sovereign's rights control over the Church, which Protestant princes had already successfully asserted at the Reformation. It was one of the strands in the story that German Catholic rulers too came to accept Pufendorf's position. Joseph II, as usual, was the most extreme. Faced with the situation that important powers over the Church in his territories were exercised by the Pope, by bishops whose sees were beyond his frontiers and by the superiors of religious Orders, he ordered the bishops to take over many of the functions of the Pope, severed the links between the monks and nuns in his territories and their foreign superiors, and fought to make the diocesan map coincide with the political.

Catholic Enlightenment can be seen to have affected the attitudes of laymen and the ecclesiastical reforms of governments at least as much as the French Enlightenment did. But neither of them had much to do with the most important single incident in Church history between 1750 and 1789, the fall of the Jesuits. Portugal was generally held to be the most obscurantist and priest-ridden of the Catholic countries of Europe, and yet this was where the assault on the Jesuits began. It was manifestly not due to pressure from below; it was essentially the work of Pombal, who was given virtually complete power by the king after the catastrophic Lisbon earthquake of 1755. It was not on religious grounds that the Jesuits fell foul of Pombal's regime, but because they were effectively running a state within a state in Portuguese territories in South America, thus defying his absolutist principles. He forced them to give up protecting the Indians and their traditional society, intending instead to encourage intermarriage between races with a view to the maximum growth of population. Then he found it possible to implicate them in an attempt to assassinate the king in 1758, and in the following year they were expelled from all the dominions of Portugal without pensions, and all their property was seized.

France was the next country to expel them, and after the event d'Alembert wrote a pamphlet claiming that the *philosophes* were responsible. This was obviously untrue. It was French Jansenists, who constituted a substantial minority of members of the Parlement of Paris, who were the spearhead of the attack on the Order. They were able to take advantage of another disastrous colonial imbroglio of the Jesuits, the default of a grand enterprise organized by Father La Vallette in Martinique that had led to serious losses for many French investors. The Parlement forced the expulsion on a reluctant king. In Spain, on the other hand, the prime mover was King Charles III, using the pretext of a riot in Madrid, supposedly fomented by the Jesuits. He became determined to persuade other Catholic Powers to expel them, made it the price of his alliance, ensured that a compliant Pope, Clement XIV, was elected in 1769, and continued to exert pressure until he dissolved the Order. Austria had declined to act itself—this was a matter on which Joseph II was not extreme—but acquiesced in the papal decree.

The symbolic significance of the suppression was immense: that the papacy had been compelled to abandon the very Order whose members made a fourth vow of obedience to Rome, the Order most prominent in promoting baroque piety and in furthering the Counter-Reformation. But the tangible results were highly important too. Hundreds of brotherhoods associated with the Jesuits had to be dissolved. Still more significantly, all Catholic states now had to reorganize their university and secondary education. Although much of it remained in the hands of clergy, and in some countries ex-Jesuits continued to teach, the measures taken amounted to a purge of many of the most influential and able professors in every Catholic country. Some Jesuits had been intellectual reactionaries, but others had set high, international standards of teaching and scholarship and had been abreast of Enlightenment thought, even if they criticized much of it. Overall the role of regulars was diminished and that of secular clergy and even laymen enhanced. In the short run governments could not fully match the scale of Jesuit provision, but some institutions, like the Portuguese university of Coimbra, were expensively and radically remodelled; and the new system was naturally more subservient than the old to the state and its priorities, especially its need for well-trained civil servants.

Other aspects of Enlightenment too owed less to the *philosophes* than they and historians have maintained. It was the triumph of the British in both the war of the Austrian Succession and the Seven Years War, aided by Prussia in the latter, that made the rulers and ministers of Catholic countries, such as Prince Kaunitz in Austria, consider seriously whether, in order to be able to match the revenues and armed forces of these Protestant states, they might not have to follow their example and suppress monasteries, take away most Church land, bring in religious toleration, and, to increase the population, even allow priests to marry. Kant's claim that the Age of Enlightenment was the century of Frederick comes to seem less extravagant if one adds to his patronage of *philosophes* and their ideas the brilliant success of his foreign policy and generalship, without which the Protestant triumphs of these wars might never have occurred and Catholic states might not have felt compelled to re-examine their ecclesiastical policies.

It was one of the achievements of the age to end the witch crazes that had erupted fitfully in Europe since the late fifteenth century, causing many thousands of women to be tortured and killed, in most cases burned to death. Protestant authorities had been if anything more inclined than Catholic to believe in witches, demonic possession, fornication with the devil, and so forth, and to try to stamp out these enormities by ferocious persecution. The campaign to bring it to an end cut across confessional boundaries: Descartes was saluted by the Pietist philosopher Christian Thomasius as the man who dealt the final blow to the superstition. The Dutch Republic had its last case in 1610, England in 1710. Louis XIV clamped down on witch-hunting in 1682, Frederick William I in 1728. But serious controversies were raging about it still in Italy during the 1750s and in Bavaria during the 1770s; a bout of witch-burnings occurred around 1755 in Hungary; in

Germany the last execution was in Catholic Kempten in 1775, in Spain in 1781, in Protestant Switzerland in 1782, and in Poland in 1793. In most cases government action was necessary to put an end to such proceedings, and it was Maria Theresa and her ministers who abolished the practice in Hungary in 1766, overriding local opinion among both nobles and people. The arguments used in her decree are especially striking, since they come from a devout Catholic ruler who loathed the *philosophes*:

It is well known, what an intolerable level has lately been reached by the craze concerning sorcery and witchcraft. Its foundations were laid by the inclination of the idiotic and vulgar crowd towards superstition ... Any event which has seemed to them hard to explain (although merely caused by accident, science or dexterity) has been ascribed to the activity of sorcerers and witches. Even natural events like tempest, animal diseases or human illnesses have been considered to be caused by them.

There lay behind this decree, first, the influence of Catholic writers including Muratori, one of whose many works had been directed against belief in witches; secondly, the efforts of Gerard van Swieten, Maria Theresa's Dutch physician, librarian, and reformer of the censorship and of education; and, thirdly, the alarm felt by the government at the rise of a new superstition, belief in vampires.

The last quotation is a strident example of the normal contempt of the Enlightened upper class for popular attitudes. Many aspects of baroque culture had appealed to ordinary people as much as to the aristocracy: pilgrimages, brotherhoods, colourful depictions of religious themes, miracles, relics, and passion plays. The numerous feast days of the Church provided the poor with holidays and entertainment. In any case, all churches' services and ministrations were in principle available to all men and women. The appeal of Protestant hymns and psalms cut across all boundaries. But governments insisted on challenging these popular elements of religion. Catholic rulers and the Pope collaborated in cutting down the number of feast days, hoping to reduce both disorder and idleness but causing discontent. Joseph II's liturgical changes aroused strong popular opposition, as did Frederick the Great's attempt to impose on the Lutheran Church a more Enlightened hymnbook. In Britain measures relaxing the laws against Jews (1753) and Catholics (1778–9) provoked alarming riots in London, which seriously delayed the process of liberalization.

In the secular sphere, the *commedia dell'arte* in Italy and France and *Hanswurst* in Germany had been enjoyed by all classes. But the Enlightenment—even the Catholic Enlightenment of Austria—self-consciously disrupted this harmony. Popular amusements, it was declared, needed to be purged of coarseness, paganism, disorderliness, and cruelty. Most literary pundits of the 1760s and 1770s wanted to abolish traditional popular theatre, as Sonnenfels in Austria wished to suppress *Hanswurst* and establish instead more elevated forms of drama, intellectual and moralistic, such as the plays Lessing, Goethe, and Schiller wrote in the 1770s and 1780s. Humanitarians and Evangelicals sought to abolish pastimes such as cock-fighting and bear-baiting. Further, the grandees' pursuit of privacy and 'simplicity' actually withdrew them from contact with the poor; and the growth of middle-class self-consciousness and the cult of respectability, especially in Britain, created new and complicated social exclusions and snobberies.

During this period the history of culture becomes more complex and contradictory than in the first half of the century—or ever before. By the 1770s, for example, the visual arts had lost the stylistic unity of the baroque period. The most powerful impulse of the time can be summed up as neoclassicism, a reversion to the purist attempts of the Renaissance to reproduce classical models. But this tendency was far from homogeneous, partly because the models themselves were multiplying and diversifying. As well as by the work of Palladio, architects and artists were inspired by new discoveries of authentic Roman buildings, statues, and paintings during the excavations at Herculaneum and Pompeii from the 1730s, and then by Greek temples, first those of southern Italy and later, after the seminal journey of James Stuart and Nicholas Revett to Athens in 1751–5, those of Greece itself. The first modern reproduction of a Greek Doric temple front in Europe was built by Stuart at Hagley in 1758. In addition, and even more remarkably, Gothic was being revived, half playfully, by Horace Walpole from 1749 onwards at Strawberry Hill—to quote Pevsner again, 'a place . . . both amusing and awful, Rococo and romantic'. The diversity and inventiveness of the styles employed in Britain at this period reflect, negatively, the lack of a powerful monarchy capable of imposing artistic criteria and, positively, the wealth, taste, and intelligence of the British upper classes: Hagley was built for Lord Lyttelton, Walpole was the son of the Prime Minister.

Another conspicuous element of stylistic eclecticism was the *chinoiserie* decoration to be found in palaces all over Europe.

Somewhat similar trends can be discerned in music. The successful assault mounted in England against *opera seria* was paralleled a decade later by an attack on the similarly pompous French form, *tragédie lyrique*. Jean-Philippe Rameau was the dominant composer in this field, as he was the major contemporary writer on musical theory. After he declined to write the musical articles for the *Encyclopédie*, the task was assigned to Rousseau, whose contribution to the project consisted of one article on political economy and nearly 400 on musical topics. In this as in almost every other sphere, he was the enemy of the Establishment. He denounced the theories and music of Rameau, rejecting counterpoint itself as the bane of music; and in 1752, to show what ought to be done, he composed an opera of extreme naïvety, *Le Devin du village* (*The Village Soothsayer*). Paradoxically, this achieved a huge success at the court of Louis XV and elsewhere. The cult of simplicity was one of the influences behind Gluck's 'reform opera' *Orfeo ed Euridice*, first produced at the Vienna court theatre in 1762. Gluck's claims for it included the unprovable assertion that he was reviving Greek practice, but he was justified in maintaining that he gave the words a new importance and more effectively involved his hearers' emotions.

Italy still provided a high proportion of all successful musicians, but in this period the German lands are agreed to have produced the most notable composers, pre-eminently Haydn and Mozart. Helped by the keen interest displayed by many of the wealthiest nobles, such as Haydn's patron Prince Esterházy, by the musical establishments of the great monasteries, and by Joseph II, various musical genres reached unsurpassed levels in the Austrian Monarchy. The emperor had renamed the court theatre the *Nationaltheater* in 1776, and for some years it made a point of producing works in German, most famously Mozart's opera *Die Entführung aus dem Serail* (*The Abduction from the Seraglio*) (1782). But the audiences at the court theatre perversely preferred Italian opera and so the German troupe had to be sacked. Since Joseph drew the line at *opera seria*, Mozart turned to writing his transcendent comic operas in Italian, *The Marriage of Figaro* (1786), *Don Giovanni* (1787), and *Così fan tutte* (1790). But the less aristocratic public of the Vienna suburbs took delight in his *Magic Flute* of 1791, a glorious hotchpotch of fairy tale, farce, and

Masonic ideology with a German libretto. More novel still was the explosion of secular instrumental music such as piano concertos, developed chiefly by Mozart, and string quartets, especially associated with Haydn, genres fostered less by a concert-going public than by private and semi-private performances for rulers, noblemen, and wealthy commoners. The Viennese public sphere was much less well developed than London's, which supported Haydn's concerts enthusiastically on his two visits in 1791–2 and 1794–5, giving him a financial return far beyond anything attainable in Austria.

Contradictions and complexities are even more evident if one looks beyond the élites. Literacy was growing fast in many countries. In some places the proportion of persons able to sign their wills or the marriage register almost doubled during the century: in London and Paris it reached on one or other criterion 90 per cent for men and nearly 80 per cent for women. But of course the poor on the whole did not make wills, and by no means all marriages were registered. Although levels were far lower in such places as the kingdom of Naples, the differences were not simply a matter of prosperity or of Protestant versus Catholic. In some Catholic areas, like the Electorate of Trier, percentages were reached that matched those found in London. The public too was growing, and at a faster rate. In Germany sixty-four new periodicals were published each year in the first decade of the eighteenth century, 331 in the 1750s, and 1,225 in the 1780s. (Of course many were short-lived, and few had wide circulation.) New amenities were beginning to be offered to the public, usually by Enlightened rulers: parks like the Prater and the Augarten in Vienna, art exhibitions like the Paris *salons* and the Royal Academy's open days, museums like the Uffizi and the specially built Pio-Clementino in the Vatican. As urban population began to grow at a tremendous pace in Britain, the West End of London was built up, and cities old and new supplied themselves with facilities such as reading-rooms, theatres, assembly halls, circulating libraries, hospitals, infirmaries, dispensaries, and suburban churches.

All this can easily be represented as of a piece with Enlightenment. But the education that brought about these great increases in literacy had nearly always been given in a religious context, with a view to inculcating some brand of Christianity. If many pupils advanced beyond this grounding, probably more did not. The public, however large potentially, was in practice only a very small proportion of the literate. Even in England in 1760 the total number of copies of registered newspapers sold was under ten million a year, that is 30,000 a day for a population of six million. Against this background it is not so surprising that the largest new popular movement to develop in Britain during the period should have been religious, and stridently opposed to most of the tendencies of the Enlightenment: Methodism. Its founder, John Wesley, was a clergyman of the Church of England who had been influenced by German revivalist movements related to Pietism. In 1738 he experienced religious conversion, which led him to embark on strenuous preaching tours around England with the object of saving souls, journeys that continued on and off for more than fifty years. He revived Calvinist doctrines of grace and conversion, and deliberately worked to stem the very tendency that now seems to have characterized the age—namely, the weakening of dogmatic belief. The numerous adherents he won were strictly organized into 'classes' of twelve, grouped into circuits and finally into a 'connection' with an annual conference, over all of which he exercised autocratic authority from above. Much use was made of printed sermons, hymns, and pamphlets, and town populations responded better than rural. Methodism showed that dogmatic religion could prosper in the public sphere and in new industrial environments. It also showed that loyalism, royalism, and social conservatism, all ardently espoused by Wesley and inculcated in his followers, could command wide support. When he died in 1791, the number of committed members of his classes was over 70,000, and the movement clearly influenced immensely more people than that. These are far larger numbers than were attracted by Freemasonry or by Jacobin clubs. Methodism was not yet technically a separate denomination, but in effect it was by now distinct from the Church of England. None the less, its influence had much to do with the rise of the Evangelical movement within the Church, which had similar aims and methods.

Methodism was one form of revolt against Enlightenment. Of course Jesuits and, after 1773, ex-Jesuits and their sympathizers continued to attack it: among them the Belgian F. X. Feller was particularly effective. But, in addition, tendencies arising within the Enlightenment threatened to subvert it. In nearly all of them Rousseau, once the friend of Diderot and a large-scale contributor to the *Encyclopédie*, played a major part, and it will give unity to the discussion to focus on his role. Even before the *Encyclopédie* began publication, in 1750, he wrote a prize essay called *Discourse on the Arts and Sciences*. In it he attacked almost everything that the *philosophes* stood for. Science is evil, harmful, and vicious; luxury is wicked; Athens was a model of corruption, Sparta of virtue, civilization and the arts bring falsity and servility. 'Give us back', he urged, 'our innocence, ignorance and poverty.' In 1754, in his *Discourse on the Origins of Inequality*, he extended his critique to property, marriage, language, laws, and war. All are deplorable products of civilization—even though civilization may well be necessary. Voltaire wrote to him: 'I have received, Sir, your new book against the human race . . . One starts wanting to walk on all fours after reading your book. However, in more than sixty years I have lost the habit.' Rousseau was to push some of these arguments still further in *The Social Contract* of 1762, denouncing all existing societies except (perhaps) the republic of Geneva, and glorifying city-state or rustic democracy.

Having rubbished civilization, he moved on to belittle reason. In *The New Héloïse* (1761) and *Émile, or Education* (1762)—didactic epistolary novels that owed much to Richardson's *Pamela* (1740) and *Clarissa* (1747–8)—'sentiment' or emotion triumphs over reason not only in romantic love but also in education: human nature is inherently good; the individual's spontaneous responses must be respected. Between 1761 and 1800 *The New Héloïse* achieved seventy-two editions, an unrivalled publication record for any French work of this period. Seminal though these books were, they were only contributions to a Europe-wide movement of sentimentalism, disrupting the heroic and moral traditions of earlier literature and exalting the individual's feelings above the rules laid down by religion and society. It is no great step to Goethe's *Sorrows of Young Werther* (1773), another best-seller, in which a self-absorbed, idealistic young man commits suicide because he feels alienated from society and because his beloved proves unattainable—a book taken as justifying suicide, an action unequivocally condemned by the churches.

Intellectual and cultural development during the eighteenth century, at the élite level, was exceptionally cosmopolitan, or at least European, particularly after the middle of the century. A 'grand tour' was *de rigueur* for the sons of wealthy families. Books that made an impact in one country, especially if they were written in French or translated into it, were commonly being discussed at the other end of

Europe within three or four years. The distribution of the *Encyclop-édie* and the success of *The New Héloïse* have already been mentioned. Voltaire was recognized in educated circles everywhere as a brilliant writer and the leader of Enlightenment, even though most of his readers thought him too radical and too critical of religion. *The Spirit of the Laws*, published in 1748, was cited in the House of Commons, and was being read avidly in Bratislava and St Petersburg, by 1751. Beccaria's *On Crimes and Punishments* of 1764 was translated from Italian into French in 1766 and quoted liberally in Catherine the Great's *Instruction to the Legislative Assembly* of 1767. She even used notes taken at Adam Smith's lectures in Glasgow. She tried to persuade numerous writers, sculptors, architects, and musicians to go to St Petersburg. If she failed with d'Alembert and Voltaire (with whom she none the less continued to correspond), with Rousseau and Beccaria, she succeeded with Diderot; the sculptor Falconet came to create the famous statue of Peter the Great; among architects, if she could not tempt James Wyatt, she captured Cameron the Scot and the Venetian Quarenghi, fresh from building a cathedral for the Pope at Subiaco; and among composers she attracted Cimarosa and Paisiello. Even in the case of Russia, the traffic was not all one way. She commissioned from Wedgwood a vast 'Frog' service, requiring him to depict on it British 'Gothic' buildings. Wedgwood did not fully understand what she meant, and nor probably did she; but the commission was invaluable to him, and she must have contributed by it to the Gothic revival in Britain.

Many, though certainly not all, Enlightened writers and reformers thought that their principles were applicable everywhere: Voltaire, Beccaria, and Bentham all laid down what they considered universally valid principles of law reform; Joseph II was determined to make uniform the laws and administration of his far-flung provinces, whether Flanders or Galicia, Lombardy or the Bukovina. Geographical, historical, and linguistic differences were to be overcome; national feelings, so far as they existed, were ignored. A major exception to this tendency was Montesquieu, who argued that laws positively ought to vary from country to country, according to climate, custom, history, and the nature of the regime. But it was only during the second half of the century that the glorification of national feeling, identity, and separateness seriously began. Rousseau again was prominent. Asked to advise the Poles on constitutional reform, he wrote *Considerations on the Government of Poland*, published in 1782, in which he complained that 'today there are no longer Frenchmen, Germans, Spaniards, even Englishmen . . . there are only Europeans. All of them have the same tastes, the same passions, the same customs.' He recommended the Poles, by contrast, to glory in their nation, in their language, in their history and literature; their children should be educated only by Poles, should learn their nation's traditional songs and play its traditional games—if necessary, they should invent some—in order to create a national identity and a true patriotism.

This line of argument had special resonance in Germany, where the ramshackle Empire became a focus for national sentiment as a reaction developed against the dominance of French culture and in favour of literature in the vernacular—a movement so successful that from the 1770s Germans produced some of the greatest literature of all time. The most important German theorist of nationality was Johann Gottfried Herder, Lutheran minister of the court church in Weimar where Goethe and Schiller also worked, who identified the *Volk*, the people, as the most important unit of society and culture, with its distinctive language as its most important characteristic. At the same period Joseph II's attempts at homogenization of his lands, which included prescribing German as the language of administration in 1784, led to strong national reactions in all save the German lands of the Monarchy, including the revival of Flemish in Belgium, and in Hungary demands for the use of Magyar—though it was the restoration of Latin as the country's official language that was conceded in 1790! The Romanian nation of Transylvania—distinguished from the others by its affiliation to the Greek Orthodox Church as much as by its language—demanded parity of privileges in the *Supplex libellus Valachorum* presented to Leopold II in 1791.

Rousseau adopted yet one more position that runs counter to Enlightenment as ordinarily understood. In his *Émile*, the book in which he put forward his educational theories, he included the *Profession of Faith of a Vicar in Savoy*. It purports to be the mature credo of a Catholic priest, and it attacks both the perceived weaknesses of the Established churches and the anti-religious tendencies of the *philosophes*. The vicar was to be a dedicated, sympathetic, conforming shepherd of the flock. But he was also to teach a tolerant and undogmatic 'natural religion' based on sentiment, on the infallible dictates of conscience, and on the feelings of the heart, since it is these emotions that lead people to believe in and pray to God or 'the Supreme Being'. For anyone who accepted the gospel story or the decrees of the Church, this was absolute heresy, or a call for a quite new religion, and Rome of course condemned it. It was held to supply the philosophical basis for the revolutionary Cult of the Supreme Being during the Terror of 1793–4. But in another light it can be regarded as a version of the widespread demand among Catholics for better parochial clergy and, momentously, as 'leading to the reawakening of the religious spirit in France' and 'to the return of the Enlightened classes to the faith and the yoke of the Church' that were to follow the hiatus of the Revolution.

Epilogue: the French Revolution

Although European religion and culture changed so significantly between 1750 and 1789, there is no sign whatever that any of its rulers or more than a handful of their subjects yet dreamed of the drastic measures that were to be taken by the French Revolution against the Church. Bishop Loménie de Brienne was considered a *philosophe*, but his commission on French monasteries, when assessing the merits of individual Orders and houses, took as its criterion of their worth the strictness with which the old monastic rules were observed. Joseph II's test, on the other hand, was utility; but for him a monastery's utility usually meant its capacity to supply parish priests. Neither Brienne nor Joseph II diverted the property of the suppressed monasteries to secular purposes: it went into a religious fund. The French Church was in some ways in special need of reform: the king controlled all its major appointments, all its bishops were aristocrats, and it was normal to appoint as 'commendatory' abbots princes, nobles, bishops, ministers, often laymen, who received a handsome income from their monastery but performed no duties for it. When in 1788–9 the people of France, divided by region and into clergy, nobles, and third estate, stated their grievances for the forthcoming Estates-General in their *cahiers*, they professed both strong attachment to the Church and an expectation that the king would reform it. But only 4 per cent of *cahiers* of the third estate wanted the regular clergy abolished. There was even some sign of regret at the suppression of the Jesuits, and the educational and other 'useful' work of monks and nuns was applauded, though little sympathy was shown for purely contemplative Orders. There was much criticism of tithe. But what was most generally desired was a fairer distribution of property within the Church so that there would be more, better, and better-paid parish priests.

Harold Macmillan once declared that what determined the actions of governments was 'Events'. This was never so true as of the French Revolution. Its headlong rush towards extremism cannot be understood except in the context of a narrative, though here there is room only for a very selective account. At the beginning of the Revolution the clergy, like the nobility, abandoned their position as a distinct estate of the realm and united with the third estate to form the National Assembly. Threatened by plots, riots, *jacquerie*, and pressure from the newly emancipated crowds and journalists of Paris, the Assembly quickly moved far beyond the wishes of the people as expressed in the *cahiers*. It refused to declare Catholicism the religion of the state, granted complete religious toleration and freedom of speech on religious matters, and on the notorious night of 4 August 1789 abolished the privileges of the clergy and the nobility, including the Church's right to tithe. The momentum increased when in October the Assembly was told that the government was bankrupt. The property of the Church was now seen as a public resource; it was generally agreed that the economy would benefit if lands hitherto held in mortmain were rendered saleable; and politicians asserted that the purposes of the Church and the wishes of donors would be sufficiently respected if the state undertook to supply the necessary funds to provide church services, education, and charity. On 2 November all the Church's lands were declared to be at the disposal of the nation, though the clergy were promised a decent salary in return. In February 1790 those religious Orders that were not devoted to education, hospitals, or charity were declared dissolved, and the taking of religious vows was forbidden. A month later it was decided to sell off all the Church's property to raise money for the government. The whole structure of the Church was then reorganized in the Civil Constitution of the Clergy of 12 July, which removed what was left of the Pope's jurisdiction in France, abolished many acknowledged abuses, redrew the map of dioceses and parishes, redistributed clergy incomes, and provided for the election of priests and bishops. The Age of Secularization had certainly arrived in France, in five senses at least: first, the state was no longer formally bound to a particular church; secondly, the state had presumed to remodel the structure of the Catholic Church without previously consulting it; thirdly, *all* Church property had been seized by the state; fourthly, the secular powers and privileges of clergy had been abolished; and fifthly, laymen, even Protestants, had been given the right to take part in the election of clergy at all levels. The Protestant Reformation itself had been less drastic.

Impatient when Pope Pius VI did not quickly give the scheme the expected blessing, the Assembly, in a decree that the king ratified on 26 December 1790, required the clergy to swear an oath accepting the Constitution. At this point the Catholic, clerical backlash first became conspicuous. Only seven bishops out of 160 took the oath, and nearly half of the lower clergy refused it too. The Pope's public condemnation of the principles both of the Revolution and of the Civil Constitution, issued in the middle of the oath-taking process in March and April 1791, influenced and in some cases changed the decisions of the priests, as did the attitudes of their congregations, which were divided partly on geographical lines: the north-west, the north-east, Alsace, and the southern central region produced 'refractory' majorities; Paris and a huge area around it, together with the south-east, yielded high proportions of 'constitutional' clergy. Most of the old bishops emigrated, and so the leaders of both groups within France were new men. The schism within the Church was an essential element in the civil war that ravaged France for the next ten years.

Meanwhile, in almost every other country counter-revolutionary tendencies were gaining ground. Although liberals and radicals welcomed the outbreak of the French Revolution, opinion soon swung the other way, inspired by the extraordinarily prescient denunciations of Burke's *Reflections on the Revolution in France* of 1790. In Belgium, indeed, a revolution of a totally different stamp took place in late 1789. It was dominated by a conservative party, inspired by Feller, hostile to the emperor's reforms, and financed and organized by some of the great monasteries he had not dissolved. At a time when Louis XVI was still apparently collaborating with the Assembly, the rebels in Brussels declared their ruler deposed. It was only by conceding many of their demands in 1790 that the new emperor, Leopold II, made the short-lived reconquest of these provinces possible. The situation that faced him in Hungary was nearly as dangerous, and in order to secure his position as ruler of the Monarchy he was forced to abolish throughout his territories the general seminaries and other ecclesiastical innovations of his predecessor, to agree that he would dissolve no more monasteries, and to give the impression that he would allow some suppressed houses to be restored.

France went to war with Austria and Prussia in the spring of 1792, and with Britain in the following year. In the meantime the execution of King Louis XVI had made the revolutionary regime a pariah to foreign powers. Early military defeats put it in such danger that the extremist Committee of Public Safety set up by the Convention, the current elected assembly, imposed in the summer of 1793 a highly repressive and bloodthirsty regime—'the Terror'—with the object of mobilizing society against both external and internal enemies. Refractory priests, monks, and nuns were seen as traitors to the Revolution: thousands went into exile or were imprisoned, massacred, guillotined, or deported. Not content with having divided Catholics and established the Constitutional Church according to its own ideas, the government now backed the radicals who wished to abandon Christianity, and even religion, altogether. In October 1793 the old calendar, with years dated from the birth of Christ and weeks based on the account of the Creation in the book of Genesis, was abolished. Years were now counted from the foundation of the Republic, and weeks had ten days. More and more churches were demolished or despoiled; now constitutional clergy too were deposed, forced to marry and abjure their vocation, imprisoned, deported, and killed; popular attempts to maintain Catholic worship and practices were repressed. The cathedral of Notre-Dame was converted into a Temple of Reason, with a Temple of Philosophy inside, and vast open-air festivals were held, tricked out with numerous classical allusions, in honour of the Supreme Being. By these actions the government ruined the Constitutional Church. Over half of the newly elected bishops and of the lesser clergy abdicated. Huge areas were totally deprived of churches and clergy, and a generation, at least of men, escaped altogether the ministrations of the Church. Eighteen years later, all the young French soldiers in Moscow hospitals during the Russian campaign refused the services of a priest. This was not mere secularization, but dechristianization. The Revolution had reduced Christianity in France to its lowest ebb for more than a millennium.

Since the patronage of court, aristocracy, and Church—even that of the old academies—had all been swept away, culture too was revolutionized. In theory it became democratic. Its most positive achievement was the neoclassical school of painting headed by David, whose vast canvases were intended to glorify the Revolution and associate it with the golden age of republican Rome. But its chief symbol was the Pantheon, where the supposed forerunners of the Revolution, Voltaire and Rousseau, were now reburied. This building, treated then and since as a monument to revolutionary neoclassicism, had in fact been commissioned for the most traditional of reasons: the king, Louis XV, when seriously ill, had made a vow that if he survived he would fund a new church for the great Augustinian abbey of Sainte-Geneviève. Designed by J. G. Soufflot, it was begun in 1757 and was converted into the Pantheon after the Revolution. In architecture revolutionary France was either destructive or derivative. Many great buildings were destroyed or 'vandalized'—the word was invented in 1794. But even so France was left with a vast surplus of grand edifices, mainly ecclesiastical, that were empty and could be converted into the prefectures, town halls, museums, and barracks required by the new regime.

When the frenzy of the Terror abated late in 1794, the Cult of the Supreme Being was jettisoned, and for the next few years fitful and partly successful attempts were made to repair some of the damage done to the Constitutional Church. But some aspects of secularization were still being carried further. The Paris Conservatoire, for example, was founded in 1795 as a musical academy proclaiming grand democratic principles—though what had made its foundation necessary was the wilful destruction of traditional forms of musical education.

Outside France the brutality, extremism, and aggression of the revolutionary regime aroused horror; and governments, fearing that the contagion might spread, restricted the development of the public sphere in their countries by tighter press censorship and measures against movements like Freemasonry. The 'godlessness' and 'atheism' of the *philosophes* were blamed for having inspired the excesses of the Revolution. Hence traditional religion recovered its standing with the upper classes, and in Protestant states the climate favoured movements such as Methodism and the Evangelical movement. But despite these constraints the 1790s outside France were a decade of cultural revolution. In English and German literature, and in German music, Romanticism was coming to maturity. The *Lyrical Ballads* of Wordsworth and Coleridge, published in 1798, in their determined use of simple language and everyday themes, broke away from the elevated tone and subjects of earlier poetry. In Germany Novalis and Herder were announcing extreme Romantic positions: glorifying the individual, especially the genius, and his (very rarely her) self-indulgent outpourings; rejecting all classical rules, welcoming the profusion and incoherence of Shakespeare; exploiting myth, fantasy, and magic. This was the most creative period of what Isaiah Berlin called the Counter-Enlightenment, taking to extreme lengths Rousseau's questioning of the power of reason, his denunciation of scientific progress, his praise of diversity and nationalism. Not everyone succumbed to these tendencies. In Austria the greatest artistic achievement of the decade was Haydn's *Creation* (1798), an oratorio based on an English text, itself founded on the biblical account of Creation, and embodying a natural theology that proved as acceptable in revolutionary Paris as in Catholic Vienna and Protestant London—the embodiment of Catholic Enlightenment. It began with a brilliant evocation of the Light that God created out of chaos, which could be interpreted as referring to Enlightenment. But for Haydn it was all part of the work that he always dedicated to God alone, and for the most part constrained within classical forms. On the other hand, Beethoven's first eleven piano sonatas, written before 1800, announced the advent of a secular-minded genius determined to break out of established musical conventions, an intention that was sensationally realized in his 'Eroica' Symphony composed in 1803–4. The ideals of the French Revolution had helped to inspire the democratic aims of *Lyrical Ballads*, and for a time intoxicated Beethoven. But it was only outside France, where the stultifying reality of revolutionary government did not have to be experienced, that the ideals of 1789 contributed to the advance of Romanticism. France itself was isolated by the Revolution from Romanticism as effectively as from the Industrial Revolution.

As French armies conquered neighbouring countries, many of the measures of the Revolution were transplanted to them. In Belgium, the Rhineland, northern and then central Italy monasteries were dissolved, Church lands sold off, and the Civil Constitution applied. In 1797 Pius VI was driven out of Rome and a democratic republic established there. He died two years later in France, and the conclave to elect his successor had to take place in Venice, by then under Austrian rule. In mainly Catholic south Germany, which was under French influence though it had not been annexed by France, the various governments agreed in 1803 to redraw state boundaries abolishing all ecclesiastical states, to suppress all monasteries, and to seize their lands. This agreement meant that in most of Catholic Europe—France, Germany, Belgium, Switzerland, and much of Italy—the traditional structure of the Catholic Church and its temporal power had ceased to exist. Though the new Pope had been allowed back into Rome, he was virtually a prisoner of Napoleon.

In these countries the Church could never be restored as it had existed under the old regime, with ecclesiastics possessing vast properties and exercising immense secular powers, including sovereignty over more than a score of sizeable states. None of these principalities was revived at the Restoration except the papal state, and the best efforts of Catholics and their governments could not restore more than a fraction of the Church's lands and its old monasteries. This was one side of the legacy of these years to the Church of the nineteenth century: it would be poorer and much less secular—and hence, for all its losses, in some ways better fitted for its main task. But what made its immediate recovery possible in France and its annexed territories was Napoleon's Concordat with the Pope of 1801.

It was apparent from the end of the Terror that Catholicism could not be eradicated in France. 'Our religious revolution is a failure,' reported one of Napoleon's generals, 'people have become Roman Catholic again.' A striking feature of the revival in France was the role played by women in maintaining worship, even in places where men had virtually abandoned it. But the disputes between refractories and constitutionals, and between Catholic and anti-Catholic, kept the country divided and fuelled the continuing civil war. The religious reaction was embodied in the works of René de Chateaubriand, an émigré nobleman returned to France who published in 1801 a fervid novel called *Atala*, designed as part of a larger work to be called *The Genius of Christianity*—one of the few French writings of the period that can be counted as Romantic. By this time Napoleon was First Consul. In the twentieth century Stalin famously asked 'How many divisions has the pope?' Napoleon, more wisely if equally cynically, calculated his support at a 'corps of 200,000 men'. He knew that the civil war could be wound up only by ending the religious schism, and that this could be achieved only with the aid of Pope Pius VII. In 1801 an agreement was struck. Some of the achievements of the Revolution could not be surrendered: toleration, civil marriage, and divorce. Church property could not be recovered. But the Concordat declared Catholicism to be the religion of the majority of Frenchmen and promised the Church freedom of worship. In return the Pope would summon all the French bishops of both camps to resign, and depose those who refused to obey. As Owen Chadwick has written, 'A Pope was forced by a half-Catholic French government, for its social and political purposes, to act in the Catholic Church like a despot.' A wide range of inconvenient questions, like the future of monks and nuns, were not mentioned in the agreement. Napoleon cheated the Pope and added provisions of his own, 'the Gallican Articles', which guaranteed the state control over future appointments of bishops. But, despite all the loose ends, the agreement achieved its aim of reconciling post-revolutionary France to the Church.

On Easter Sunday 1802, in the cathedral of Notre-Dame, the archbishop, Boisgelin, who had preached at the coronation of Louis XVI in 1775, preached again at the ceremony that re-established in France a united Catholic Church, approved by the Pope. *The Genius of Christianity* had just appeared. In the same year Emperor Francis permitted the re-establishment of some of the monasteries suppressed by Joseph II in Hungary. The nineteenth century, in the Catholic as well as the Protestant lands of Europe, would be an 'Age of Religious Revival'.

5

International rivalry and warfare

John A. Lynn

In 1709, at the Battle of Malplaquet, the renowned Duke of Marlborough led a British army buttressed by German and Dutch troops
against strong French forces under the command of the greatest
French general of his day, Claude Villars; in 1815, on the field at
Waterloo, less than forty miles from Malplaquet, an equally
renowned duke commanded British battalions once more supported
by German and Dutch soldiers against another French army with the
greatest French general of his day, Napoleon, at its head. The two
clashes, often seen as events in a 'Second Hundred Years War'
between Britain and France, suggest continuity. However, appearances can be misleading, and this apparent continuity masks fundamental evolution in the character of international relations and the
conduct of war. This chapter examines that evolution, exploring both
why and how European states appealed to arms during the period
1700–1815. Such a broad sweep encompasses a particularly diverse
and instructive spectrum of international contention and also
allows a fruitful comparison of the two French hegemonies—the
first enjoyed by Louis XIV and the second imposed by Napoleon I
—that commenced and completed this era. Among other contrasts
to be exposed, it will be shown that Napoleonic forces differed
fundamentally from those that took the field a century before, that
campaigns became more bloody and decisive, and that by 1815 a
Concert of Europe replaced the older, more contentious balance-
of-power politics of earlier decades. Ultimately, this examination
challenges the old French maxim about change and permanence, for

sometimes the more things seem to stay the same, the more they change.

A detailed description of diplomatic machinations and wars fought during this period would demand far more space than permitted here. As a partial substitute for such a record, Table 5.1 encapsulates some of the important facts in an economical form. Clearly, these were troubled times if measured simply by the number of years that knew warfare; the longest period of peace between major powers lasted only twenty years from the Treaty of Rastatt to the onset of the War of the Polish Succession, but even those two decades experienced three lesser wars.

Rather than following an endless parade of battles and treaties across a violent age, this chapter adopts an analytic method. The treatment of international politics relies upon an international systems approach, in which evolving assumptions and practices shaped relations between European great powers on the continent, at sea, and in their colonial dominions. When discussing armed struggle, the military system—that is, the style of armies and navies, their potentials and limitations, and their capacities to determine the clash of arms—figures large. International and military systems converge in the practice of war, which contrasted sharply from the early and mid-eighteenth century to the high point of Napoleonic victory, 1805–7. In order to demonstrate the actual interplay of the international system, the military system, and the practice of war, this chapter provides accounts of several selected conflicts, although there is no attempt to offer a complete narrative of the entire era.

The old regime, 1700–1789

The international system

Paul Schroeder, the noted historian from whom much of this discussion derives, argues that an international system consists of 'the understandings, assumptions, learned skills and responses, rules, norms, procedures, etc.' that states employ. From 1700 to 1789, the international system shifted from a broad European alliance opposed

Table 5.1 Wars of the European Powers, 1700–1815

War	Dates	Main participants			Treaty(ies) concluding the war	Battle deaths[a]
		1st party or coalition	vs	2nd party or coalition		
Great Northern War	1700–21	Russia, Poland, Denmark, Saxony		Sweden, Ottoman Empire	Treaty of Altranstadt, 1706 Treaty of Pruth, 1711 Peace of Adrianople, 1713 Treaties of Stockholm, 1719–21 Treaty of Nystad, 1721	64,000
War of the Spanish Succession	1701–14	France, Spain, Bavaria, Savoy-Piedmont and Portugal (to 1703)		England, United Provinces, Austria, Prussia, Ottoman Empire, Piedmont and Portugal (from 1703)	Treaty of Utrecht, 1713 Treaty of Rastatt, 1714	1,251,000
Austro–Turkish War	1716–18	Austria, Venice		Ottoman Empire	Treaty of Passarowitz, 1718	10,000
War of the Quadruple Alliance	1718–20	France and Britain, United Provinces, Austria		Spain	Treaty of the Hague, 1720	25,000
Spanish War	1727–9	France and Britain		Spain	Treaty of Seville, 1729	15,000
War of the Polish Succession	1733–8	Russia, Austria		France, Spain, Sardinia	Treaty of Vienna, 1738	88,000
Austro–Russian–Turkish War	1736–9	Russia, Austria		Ottoman Empire	Treaty of Nissa, 1739	38,000
War of Jenkins Era	1739–	Britain		Spain	Merged into War of the Austrian Succession	

War	Years	Belligerents	Belligerents	Treaties	Deaths
War of the Austrian Succession	1740–8	Prussia, France, Bavaria, Spain, Piedmont (to 1743), Saxony (to 1743)	Austria, Britain, the United Provinces, Saxony (from 1745), Russia (from 1746)	Treaty of Breslau, 1742; Treaty of Füssen, 1745; Treaty of Dresden, 1745; Treaty of Aachen, 1748	359,000
Russo–Swedish War	1741–3	Russia	Sweden	Treaty of Abö, 1743	10,000
Seven Years War	1756–63	Prussia, Britain	Austria, France, Russia, Sweden, Saxony	Treaty of Paris, 1763; Treaty of Hubertusberg, 1763	992,000
Russo–Turkish War	1768–74	Russia, Ali Bey of Egypt	Ottoman Empire	Treaty of Kuchuk Kainarji, 1774	14,000
War of American Independence	1775–83	United States, France, Spain, United Provinces (at war with Britain until 1784)	Britain	Treaty of Paris, 1782; Treaty of Versailles, 1783	34,000
War of the Bavarian Succession	1778–9	Prussia	Austria	Treaty of Teschen, 1779	300
Ottoman War	1787–92	Russia, Austria	Ottoman Empire	Treaty of Sistova, 1791; Treaty of Jassy, 1792	192,000
Russo–Swedish War	1788–90	Russia	Sweden	Treaty of Wereloe, 1790	3,000
Wars of the French Revolution	1792–1802				663,000
War of the First Coalition	1792–8	France, Spain (after 1796)	Britain, Austria, Prussia, United Provinces, Spain, Saxony, Hanover, Hesse-Cassel, Piedmont	Treaties of Basle, 1795; Treaty of the Hague, 1795; Peace of Leoben, 1796; Treaty of Campo Formio, 1797	
War of the Second Coalition	1798–1802	France, Spain	Britain, Austria, Russia, Portugal, Ottoman Empire	Treaty of Lunéville, 1801; Treaty of Amiens, 1802	

Table 5.1 continued

War	Dates	Main participants		Treaty(ies) concluding the war	Battle deaths[a]
		1st party or coalition vs	2nd party or coalition		
Wars of Napoleon	1803–15				1,869,000
War of the Third Coalition	1805–7	France	Britain, Austria, Russia, Prussia, Sweden	Treaty of Pressburg, 1805 Treaty of Tilsit, 1807	
Peninsular War	1808–14	France and Joseph's Spain	Spanish, Portugal, Britain		
War against Austria	1809	France, Warsaw, Bavaria, Italy, Saxony, and Russia support	Austria, Britain	Treaty of Schönbrunn, 1809	
French Invasion of Russia	1812	France, Austria, Prussia, Warsaw, Italy, and others	Russia, Britain		
Wars of Liberation	1813–14	France, Bavaria, Saxony, Italy	Russia, Prussia, Austria, Britain, Sweden, and others	First Treaty of Paris, 1814	
Hundred Days	1815	France	Britain, Austria, Russia, Prussia, and other states	Second Treaty of Paris, 1815	
Russo–Turkish War	1806–12	Russia	Ottoman Empire	Treaty of Bucharest, 1812	45,000
Russo–Swedish War	1808–9	Russia	Sweden	Treaty of Frederikshavn, 1809	6,000

Note:
[a] Jack S. Levy (*War in the Modern Great Power System, 1945–1975* (Lexington, Ky., 1983), 88–9; table 4.1) provides figures on battle deaths, which he uses as a marker of the severity of wars. The figures are supplied here only as an index of wars' intensity.

to French hegemony, to an Anglo-French accord, and finally to a predatory balance-of-power system.

As the international system evolved, some constants remained; notably, this was an era in which states struggled for discrete advantage, not to destroy other states or regimes and not to decide great issues of religion or ideology. The most common rationale for war was acquisition or retention of territory. In addition, dynastic considerations—which princely family or individual would occupy a disputed throne—ranked high and precipitated several wars of succession. The struggle for wealth also drove states to confront each other. By the eighteenth century, rulers recognized that commercial wealth quickly translated into military power, and they embraced economic motivations that drove them into disputes over land, population, and commerce, both in Europe and its colonies. States did not undertake major wars for reasons calculated to stir any but a ruler's heart. Religion did not determine foreign policy as it once had, although in certain circumstances religious passion added some level of popular support or inspired particular brutality during a conflict. This was particularly true at the periphery of Europe, when Christian Russia and Austria fought the Muslim Ottoman Empire. Likewise, political ideology was hardly a factor in wars between the major European powers, except for the case of the War of American Independence. But that conflict was only an exception if seen from the perspective of the American rebels; considered from a European point of view, it simply continued the Anglo-French power struggle. Wars devoid of great issues failed to mobilize mass popular support, although kings invested considerable gold and blood in fighting them.

The initial pattern of European conflict during the eighteenth century was a legacy of the seventeenth—the struggle against the hegemony exercised by France under Louis XIV, known as the Sun King. Fears that Louis desired to dominate the entire continent arose early in his regime, when the Spanish publicist Lisola charged Louis with wanting to impose a 'universal monarchy'. Convinced that Louis posed a threat to all of Europe, the Dutch prince William of Orange, stadholder of the United Provinces and by 1689 co-monarch of England with his wife Mary, forged broad European coalitions to oppose Louis in the Dutch War (1672–8), the Nine Years War (1688–97), and the War of the Spanish Succession (1701–14). Although William died just as that last war began, he was its architect. Modern scholarship contradicts William's worst fears, for, after the Dutch War, the Sun King desired only to protect his new frontiers—albeit frontiers he sought to extend somewhat in order to render them more defensible—and, later, to secure part of the Spanish inheritance for his grandson. To be sure, there is no question that France rated as the strongest state in Europe, but it was a hegemon bent more on security than on conquest. In any case, the perceived threat from France convinced rulers to contribute towards a common purpose far more effectively than they would against Napoleon before 1813. During the War of the Spanish Succession, Louis tried to dissolve the alliance by appeals to the narrow self-interest of individual states, but was unable to break the coalition until 1712.

The Treaty of Utrecht ended the long period of French hegemony, and a peace of exhaustion followed. Decades of conflict had bankrupted France, and the increasing might of Britain and Austria reduced France to one of a handful of great powers rather than the king of the hill. After Louis's death in 1715, a strong desire to avoid another general European war inspired the erstwhile enemies, France and Britain, to act in accord against Bourbon Spain to restrain Philip and his second wife, Elizabeth Farnese, from upsetting the political balance. In fact, the period of peace between major European powers that lasted from 1714 to at least 1733, and in a real sense until 1740, would be the longest Europe knew throughout the seventeenth and eighteenth centuries. The leading statesmen of this respite in Anglo-French struggle, Cardinal Fleury of France and Sir Robert Walpole of Britain, tried to avoid enmeshing their countries in major conflict, but they were unable to preserve the peace indefinitely.

The important period of cooperation and accord gave way to a series of major wars that embroiled the great powers until the onset of the French Revolution. In these conflicts, alliances shifted as states jockeyed for position, although a revived Anglo-French struggle provided one constant. The British stood with the Austrians in the War of the Austrian Succession (1740–8), while the Prussians and French battled against them. In 1756, in a change of alignment so startling that it is known as the 'diplomatic revolution', the French allied with their traditional continental enemies, the Austrians, and the British supported the Prussians at the start of the Seven Years War. Lesser powers also bounced from side to side in pursuit of gain.

The balance-of-power machinations that followed the breakdown of the cooperation that characterized the Fleury–Walpole era failed to result in stability and peace, but instead brought a conflict-ridden era. Balance-of-power politics was not simply structural, the result of a situation in which five major states competed within an international arena where none had the power to master the others. The instability of the system rose from attitudes and assumptions, as states pursued their own immediate benefit with disregard for the welfare of the system as a whole. Certain principles and practices defined eighteenth-century balance of power. One state demanded *compensation*, usually in territory, for gains made by another state. Should a state provide another with services or suffer losses because of another's policy, it expected payments, or *indemnities*. Parties contracted *narrowly defined alliances* as means by which to increase their own power. Explicit compensations and indemnities were owed to states that promised support to another in alliance. *Raison d'état* ruled—that is, states acted only in accord with advancing their own interests, all too often of a short-term nature. These principles dictated a fairly ruthless pursuit of self-aggrandizement, but it was subject to some significant restraint. Most importantly, there was a sense that at least the great powers constituted a *European family of states* based on a rough equality. This community was supposed to be regulated by balance, and that at least the major powers had a right to expect compensation and indemnities to maintain it.

Serious and inevitable problems plagued the balance-of-power system. War seemed endemic, for it promised to be the most effective way to gain advantages in a head-on clash of conflicting self-interests. As one Austrian diplomat wrote in 1787, 'But, one will say to me, always more war, always more conquests! This language breathes the politics of the last 34 years. Do we not have enough with what we already possess?' Outright seizures and compensation came mainly in the fashion of trading off or carving up weaker intermediary states. Principalities in Italy changed hands to meet the needs of stronger states. Austria and Russia conquered territory along the northern and western boundaries of the weakening Ottoman Empire. Logically the shaving of intermediary powers could go on only for so long, so the mechanisms of compromise had their limits, as the fate of Poland would demonstrate.

While the deadly game of international politics developed a set of principles and practices during the eighteenth century, old players left the contest, and new players came to the table. The once powerful United Provinces slipped to third-rate status, as the British far surpassed it as a naval and commercial force. In the same manner, the other small state that had made such a mark for itself in the seventeenth century, Sweden, declined sharply.

The rise of Russia to unquestioned great power status during the eighteenth century both reflected and contributed to the fall of Sweden. Before the 1730s, international conflict split into western and eastern compartments, with relatively little interchange between them. While western Europe engaged in the War of the Spanish Succession, the Great Northern War (1700–21) raged in the east, where Sweden fought against the growing power of Russia. Government and military reforms carried out by Tsar Peter the Great strengthened Russia and brought it into the European international community. If the Great Northern War established Russian superiority in northern and eastern Europe, the War of the Polish Succession (1733–8) first brought Russian armies as far west as the Rhine valley, marking Russia as a factor in general European affairs. By the mid-eighteenth century, east European conflict no longer stood apart, compartmentalized from the affairs of the west, and soon Russia dominated its region as a hegemon on the Asian flank of Europe.

Prussia also held a strong hand by the War of the Austrian Succession. In the second half of the seventeenth century, Frederick William, the Great Elector (1640–88), forged a collection of diverse holdings into what would become the Kingdom of Prussia. He unified his state in order to support an army strong enough to defend it. His grandson, King Frederick William I (1713–40) built this force into the largest army per capita maintained by any European monarchy. His son, Frederick II the Great (1740–86), set this formidable army marching into Silesia, and by securing this rich province put Prussia in the front rank of European states.

In addition to lands in Europe, colonial possessions factored into eighteenth-century great power calculations more than in previous periods. Because of its naval superiority, Britain enjoyed an unsurpassed advantage that it would exploit to win its colonial rivalry with France. Until the loss of the thirteen colonies on the North American seaboard in the War of American Independence (1775–83), they had figured largest in British calculations, but soon their loss was made good by conquest in India, where initial success around Madras led to greater gains in Bengal, Bihar, and Orissa, which, in turn, provided the men and money for expanding control of the East India Company over the rest of the subcontinent.

The military system

Just as the international system defined certain parameters of international rivalry during the eighteenth century, the military system determined others. Basic to that military system was the *state commission army*, the prevailing style of land forces from the mid-seventeenth century until the French Revolution. Before the state commission army, forces were assembled from diverse sources, including mercenary bands and irregular bodies of troops raised by local nobles. All too often such earlier armies had displayed little loyalty to the rulers who hired them, and commanders tended to assert an undesired independence. Now, officers received commissions from rulers to recruit standardized regiments that were raised and maintained as stipulated by the state, which closely regulated its army and imposed high standards of obedience and hierarchy on its officers.

State commission armies grew to unprecedented proportions. Between 1635 and 1696 wartime French forces increased sevenfold to a paper strength of 420,000, and peacetime forces increased at an even more impressive rate, yielding the first real standing army, which reached about 150,000 troops. Both wartime and peacetime levels remained relatively constant from that point until the French Revolution. Voluntary enlistment provided the bulk of the necessary manpower for larger armies, although many a 'volunteer' was tricked or bullied into the ranks by unscrupulous recruiters. As manpower needs soared, the French supplemented regular recruitment with a form of limited conscription in the Nine Years War, and other European armies followed suit. After 1733 the Prussians placed a heavier reliance on a new form of limited compulsory service, the canton system, which assigned regiments specific regions from which they could conscript peasants into the ranks. With a marvellously Prussian concern for efficiency, the canton system allowed conscripted peasants to return to the land for much of the year during peacetime, so that agricultural production would not suffer. However, even after the institution of compulsory service, the state continued to recruit a high percentage of volunteers, the majority of them foreigners.

The state commission army was more uniform, obedient, and reliable than earlier forces, but along with these advantages came important problems. For one thing, a state commission army took longer to raise, and this slowed mobilization for war. For another, although greatly improved military administration provided troops with more regular provision of food and other necessities, this rendered armies more dependent on magazines, field ovens, and convoys. This reliance on cumbersome logistics limited mobility, as armies tethered by umbilical cords of supply could not go too fast or too far. Neither volunteers nor those forced to serve in the ranks were expected to feel much devotion to cause or country. Honour may have motivated officers, but they expected little more than obedience of their troops and held them in low repute. The Count of Saint-Germain, French Minister of War, 1775-7, dismissed his common soldiers as 'the slime of the nation'. Frederick the Great stated that he simply wanted an enlisted man 'to be more afraid of his officers than of the dangers to which he is exposed'. Given the limited loyalties of men in the ranks, desertion posed a major problem for armies of this era.

Because the men in the ranks could not be trusted to show enthusiasm or initiative, battlefield tactics emphasized mechanical discipline in tightly ordered formations. Infantry stood shoulder to shoulder in long straight lines three or four ranks deep and fired volley after volley at short range against the enemy, guaranteeing high casualty rates. Cavalry, also packed into neat squadrons, still mattered in battle, and many a fight was decided by the charge of row after row of mounted men. Artillery, the most technical of the combat branches, played an increasingly important role in battle. Marshalling an army for battle in the formal manner of the day usually consumed hours, and, therefore, it was not easy to impose battle on an unwilling enemy.

When it occurred, battle was thus costly and usually indecisive. Louis XIV regarded battles as wasteful and preferred sieges, for success in a siege at least rewarded the victor with possession of the fortress, and many commanders agreed with him. Others, like the Duke of Marlborough and Frederick the Great declared their willingness to fight, but Marlborough engaged in only a few major field battles during a decade in supreme command, and Frederick came to regret the cost of his battle-hungry style of war.

Manœuvre and positional warfare provided eighteenth-century alternatives to battle. Manœuvre transformed war into a chess match, in which skilful threats to an enemy's flank, rear, or supply lines could force a withdrawal. Since war was largely about territory, manœuvre which compelled an enemy to abandon ground promised as great a reward as did victory in battle, and at far less cost. Marshal Maurice de Saxe declared that a truly great commander could win his campaigns without fighting any battles. Positional warfare—that is, the construction, defence, and attack of fortresses and fortified lines— played a major role in seventeenth- and eighteenth-century warfare. Fortresses of this era employed cleverly designed bastions and walls to defy storming by enemy troops and survive bombardment by enemy cannon. In response, attacking forces used all the science and sophistication of geometry to surround, approach, and seize fortresses. Virtually any fortress could be taken, but it might take months to do so. Because armies campaigned for only about six months of the year, from late spring into autumn, the siege of a major fortress could consume most of the campaign season. The existence of fortresses also limited the effect of battle. An army that had won on the field might gain little, as its advance was blocked by a hostile fortress, and defeated troops might find shelter behind friendly walls. The fact that fortifications were the key to territorial conquest and control made positional warfare extremely important.

Naval warfare employed some of the same technology and obeyed some of the same imperatives as land warfare. Cannon, so critical for battle and siege on land, gave contemporary fleets their bite. The broadside-firing, three-masted sailing vessel reached perfection during the eighteenth century, with the largest ships of the line mounting 100 guns. Until the end of the eighteenth-century, naval combat was highly formalistic. In battle, the contending fleets sailed in line ahead, one ship following another, to bring the largest number of guns to bear on the enemy. The two rival lines drew close to each other and fired salvo after salvo, usually at a distance of no more than 50 or 100 yards. Even at close range, however, it proved extremely difficult to sink wooden ships by gunfire alone; a vessel's greatest threat came from being set ablaze. The tactics of line ahead derived not only from the characteristics of the ships but from the need to make naval forces more obedient to the will of the state. The highly skilled but fiercely independent 'sea dogs' of the sixteenth and early seventeenth centuries gave way to more controllable, and often less skilled, captains. Line-ahead tactics may have produced less dramatic results, but they enforced an admiral's will on his fleet and made less demands on the abilities of captains. Thus, navies reflected the same concern for state control that shaped the state commission army.

During the eighteenth century, Europe saw several large armies contend in the field but only one great fleet command the seas. France attempted to challenge British naval dominance after the Seven Years War and enjoyed a decisive, if brief, advantage in American waters during the War of American Independence. However, this was but an exception to the rule. Britain predominated at sea because it could concentrate its resources on the fleet, building and manning more war vessels than could any other European competitor. France, the only major naval rival the British faced during this period, had to split its resources between the army and the navy, with the navy getting decidedly less, but, blessed by its insular position, Britain never had to maintain a large army of continental proportions. Extensive British maritime commerce supplied the great number of trained seamen required to man the king's ships and many of the skilled officers to command them in time of war. The navy also trained its own officers in a system that put a premium on talent, although high birth still had its advantages.

The practice of war

The international and military systems intersected in a practice of war that suited the goals of the international system and the capacities of the military system. This practice, labelled here *war-as-process*, contrasted sharply with *war-as-event* as epitomized by Napoleon's campaigns. Several characteristics defined war-as-process: the indecisive character of battle and siege, the slow tempo of operations, the tendency toward multiple-front wars, the great need to make war feed war, and the considerable emphasis given to ongoing diplomatic negotiations.

Battles did not settle the fate of wars during this period. Certainly, some battles decided particular strategic gambits or ended conflicts on individual fronts, as did the Battle of Blenheim in 1704, but single victories never imposed a general peace. In fact, the eighteenth-century military system was unlikely to produce quick decisive results in war. So, despite Frederick the Great's most impressive triumphs at the battles of Rossbach and Leuthen in the closing months of 1757, the Seven Years War continued until 1763. Moreover, it was not simply that battles were indecisive; the outcomes of individual military engagements or even entire campaigns often seemed almost inconsequential to the outcome of a war.

Both as a product and a cause of the indecisive nature of combat, the operational tempo of war-as-process generally moved at a slow and halting pace. Occasionally there were bursts of rapid marching, such as Marlborough's descent to the Danube in 1704 or Frederick's shifting of forces in 1757. However, in general, campaigns moved deliberately and armies did not go too far. Reasons for this are not hard to find: complicated logistics, the confining influence of fortresses, and pessimism concerning what could be gained by forcing the matter in battle. Operational tempo seemed particularly laggard after major victories, when maintaining the momentum of victory would seem to have promised the greatest rewards.

Primary participants tended to pursue war on multiple fronts, and this limited decisive campaigns and promoted stalemate. The need to engage enemies on several fronts kept a belligerent from marshalling its full military might on any one of them, making it unlikely that the belligerent would have the forces needed to destroy an opponent there. However, if fighting on multiple fronts hampered a state's offensive possibilities, it also buttressed that state's defensive resources, because an army stationed on a more secure front could reinforce one that had fared badly on another. In fact, a common characteristic of the War of the Spanish Succession and the War of the Austrian Succession was the continual shifting of forces from one front to another, aided by the fact that fortresses could buy time for the transfer.

The necessity to make war feed war during long conflicts further contributed to the indecisive character and slow tempo of contemporary military operations. Rather than concentrating on eliminating the enemy's main forces in battle, a Napoleonic goal that would rise to the level of dogma in *On War* by Carl von Clausewitz, armies tended to fight in order to secure resources. To an important degree, forces were expected to support themselves in the field, and planners who conceived of warfare as long and costly looked to the fighting itself as a way of sparing the royal treasury. Contributions—that is, war taxes imposed by armies on occupied or threatened territory—remained a standard part of warfare into the wars of the French Revolution.

Major struggles became long wars of attrition, and in such contests resolving the issues at stake involved the interplay of three factors: battlefield success, resource exhaustion, and diplomatic finesse. With military action so indecisive and the attrition of state resources such a critical factor, diplomacy was not simply the handmaiden of martial triumph. So, even as a succession of victories might seem to push in one direction, diplomacy could move in another, as the weight of attrition became insupportable. Skill in diplomacy could not replace skill in war, but the former was essential to final success. Importantly, not only did diplomacy possess considerable leverage at the end of armed conflicts, but negotiations also began rather early in wars and proceeded for years in symbiosis with military action.

Ruling princes, remote from their common subjects, could conduct war-as-process with its slow pace, high costs, and limited gains, because they need not justify state policy to the general population. Later evolution of governments towards mass support would make the pursuit of war-as-process without popular support politically impossible. In this manner, war-as-process suited both the political nature of the eighteenth-century state and the state commission army it created.

The war of the Spanish Succession

Louis's last war, the War of the Spanish Succession, exemplifies the role of dynastic issues so central to eighteenth-century diplomacy; in addition, this conflict displays the essentially defensive form of French hegemony under the Sun King, the effective European coalition formed against France, and the pattern of war-as-process. This war broke over Europe with the inevitability of a natural catastrophe. Chastened by the colossal human and financial costs of the Nine Years War, Louis laboured to avoid renewed war over what every astute statesman realized would be the coming crisis over Spain. The last monarch in the direct Spanish Hapsburg line, the sickly and impotent Carlos II, would soon die childless. Three candidates held claims to the Spanish crown: a French pretender, initially the Dauphin but later his second son, Philip of Anjou; Archduke Charles, the second son of the Holy Roman Emperor Leopold I; and the young electoral prince of Bavaria. A partition treaty signed by Louis XIV of France, and William III of England, and Leopold in 1698 had sought to avert war between France and Austria by bestowing the lion's share of the inheritance upon the Bavarian claimant. However, his death in 1699 put the issue up for contention again. Louis hoped to circumvent war by a second partition treaty he negotiated with William; it would have awarded Spain and its New World colonies to Archduke Charles and reserved only parts of Italy for the French candidate.

Leopold never agreed to this treaty, and neither did Carlos II, who wished above all else that his entire inheritance remain intact. On his deathbed he bequeathed everything to Philip of Anjou with the proviso that, if the French refused the offer, all would be offered to Archduke Charles. When the rider arrived at Versailles with the will of Carlos II, Louis and his advisers debated what to do, but they really had little choice. War with Austria could not be avoided, but, if he accepted the will of Carlos, Spain would stand with France, and Louis would only have to fight a defensive conflict. However, if Louis abided by the terms of the second partition treaty, he would have to fight an offensive war against Leopold, who would still claim everything for Charles, and Spain would be in the enemy camp. Louis accepted the will for his grandson.

However, even though war with Austria was inevitable, Louis need not have had to confront a Grand Alliance; it was only his mishandling of the crisis that brought about a general war. In fact, Louis's hegemony really aimed at rendering France invulnerable and promoting the interests of the Bourbon dynasty; he did not pursue 'continental dominance' as would Napoleon a century later. If Louis was to have averted a general European war in 1700, he should have acted in a manner designed to calm the apprehensions of European statesmen, particularly William III. Instead, Louis committed a series of acts that, while not unreasonable if taken individually, as a whole made him appear arrogant and, once again, a threat to Europe. While Louis's dynastic goals did not aim at the unification of France and Spain, he refused to remove Philip from the French line of succession, however unlikely it was that Philip would ever come to the throne. Furthermore, Louis insisted on sending French troops to take over the Dutch-held barrier forts in the Spanish Netherlands. In the interest of French commerce, he arranged to have the coveted *asiento* (trading rights over the slave trade to Spain's American colonies) awarded to French merchants. Lastly, when James II died in September, Louis immediately recognized his son as the legitimate king of England. Such moves infuriated William, who inspired much of Europe to join him and Leopold in a Grand Alliance against Louis.

Actual fighting broke out exclusively between French and Austrian armies in Italy during 1701, and Louis hoped to limit the war to this contest. However, as he laboriously geared up his army for war, the anti-French coalition grew to include England, the United Provinces, and the Holy Roman Empire. In 1703 both Portugal and Savoy-Piedmont, which had begun the war as allies of Louis XIV, switched allegiances and joined his enemies. Only Spain and Bavaria remained loyal to France. Soon Louis found himself engaged on several fronts: the Spanish Netherlands, along the Moselle and the Rhine, northern Italy, Spain, naval operations in the Atlantic and the Mediterranean, and a counter-insurgency against Protestant rebels, the Camisards, in Languedoc and Provence that peaked in 1702–4. The rules of multi-front warfare again applied, as he shifted forces and commanders from one front to another as necessity required.

This war witnessed the brilliant career of the Duke of Marlborough, who exercised overall command of British and Dutch troops from 1702 until 1711. He neither lost a battle nor failed to take a city he besieged, yet, for all his much-touted desire to fight battles and eschew sieges, he fought only five battles while conducting thirty sieges. His real contribution to the art of war was not so much his taste for battles as his ability to set and maintain a more lively pace of operations than the deliberate manœuvres characteristic of his day. Thus, in 1704 he undertook the most impressive march of the era, leading English troops down from the Meuse to the Danube in order to counter a Franco-Bavarian offensive there. Joined by the able Austrian general, Eugene of Savoy, he smashed the French at Blenheim in August and drove them back to the Rhine. Bavaria remained under allied control for the rest of the war. The allied victory at Blenheim is often credited with saving Europe from French conquest, but it did not, simply because Louis had no such goals. In 1706 Marlborough again triumphed at the Battle of Ramillies in late May and then maintained an unrelenting operational tempo to take a number of cities and towns in the Spanish Netherlands, denying most of it to Louis and his Spanish allies. But even this juggernaut continued for only two weeks before Marlborough had to stop and await the arrival of his siege artillery in order to attack resolute garrisons. The French responded by dispatching two large bodies of troops from the Rhine to reinforce Louis's army in The Netherlands, and the capable Marshal Vendôme came up from Italy to assume command. So even the brilliance of Marlborough could not win the war for the Grand Alliance in timely fashion after a great victory.

Even during the worst periods of defeat, the French proved successful enough to maintain some hope of eventual success. In 1703 and 1707 Marshal Villars fought highly effective campaigns in the Rhineland, although both these operations, particularly the second, had a great deal to do with making war feed war as French resources dwindled. Louis instructed Villars in 1707 that the levying of contributions ranked as the 'principal and sole object' of his army. Other fronts also promised victory. A Franco-Spanish army won the key battle of the Spanish campaigns at Almanza in 1708, although time alone would reveal how important it was.

Still, the string of defeats inflicted on French forces by Marlborough and Eugene brought Louis and his cause close to collapse in 1709. However, the allies overplayed their hand when Louis asked for their peace terms. He was willing to accept great sacrifices of territory and policy, including the surrender of the Spanish throne to Charles, but Louis refused when the Allies insisted that he use French troops to drive his own grandson from Spain should Philip refuse to go peacefully. The war continued, and the tide began to turn. In September Marshal Villars inflicted such heavy casualties on the allies at the Battle of Malplaquet that, even though Marlborough and Eugene claimed victory once again, Villars could inform his king, 'If God gives us the grace to lose another similar battle, your Majesty can count on his enemies being destroyed.'

Although Marlborough and Eugene continued to gain further successes in 1710 and 1711 by taking French fortresses and compromising their defensive lines, as was so often the fact in war-as-process, campaign victory did not translate into diplomatic success. The death of Emperor Leopold I in 1705 put his first son Joseph on the throne, and, when Joseph I died in 1711, Archduke Charles, the Hapsburg candidate for the Spanish crown, became Emperor Charles VI. At this point, the British had far less interest in fighting to win him an additional throne in Spain. The mounting costs of war also discouraged the British, and a change in ministries from Whig to Tory deprived Marlborough of his command and brought the English and French to terms. After years of peace feelers and unsuccessful negotiations, Louis finally detached the British from the Grand Alliance early in 1712 and brought down the coalition against him.

The Treaty of Utrecht ended the war between France, Spain, Britain, the United Provinces and several other lesser states in 1713. Charles VI chose to continue the war for another year, but concluded peace with France and Spain in 1714 in the treaties of Rastatt and Baden. Britain won Gibraltar and the *asiento* from Spain, and gained Acadia (Nova Scotia), Newfoundland, and Hudson Bay from France, so the British could claim a commercial and colonial victory. However, Louis could justly claim to have won, because his grandson sat securely on the Spanish throne. Charles VI gained possession of the Spanish Netherlands, Naples, Milan, Sardinia, Mantua, and the Tuscan ports as compensation and other lesser powers picked up lands in Germany and Italy. The treaties of Utrecht, Rastatt, and Baden marked a watershed in international politics, because the War of the Spanish Succession had so drained France that it could in no sense maintain its previous hegemony in Europe.

The war of the Austrian Succession

In 1740 war came again as the result of another succession crisis when the male line of the Habsburg dynasty came to an end. Emperor Charles VI had no sons, so he resolved to ensure that his lands would pass intact to his oldest daughter, Maria Theresa. He declared his intentions in the Pragmatic Sanction, and over the years secured agreement to it by making concessions and payments to German princes. Even France was induced to sign. Among major German rulers, only the Elector of Bavaria refused to acquiesce, because he believed that he possessed a stronger claim to the Austrian inheritance. Yet, despite their assurances, when Charles died in October 1740, his neighbours pounced on Austria because they expected the 23-year-old Maria Theresa to be weak. In fact, the young ruler handled herself with resolve and finesse.

Fighting began when Frederick the Great, whose father had

accepted the Pragmatic Sanction, asserted a dubious claim to the rich Austrian province of Silesia, and invaded it in December. The war quickly spread, as Elector Charles of Bavaria launched an army into Bohemia, France dispatched an army to aid its Bavarian ally, and Saxony and Piedmont also joined the assault on Maria Theresa. Despite the mounting odds, she refused to capitulate and, instead, prepared a counter-attack. Britain came to her defence, and she successfully appealed to her Hungarian nobility, who offered military aid and badly needed moral support. In October 1741 she agreed to a truce with Frederick that allowed him to control Silesia but freed her troops to deploy to Bohemia. Although Prague fell to a Franco-Bavarian army, she remained confident enough to dispatch an army into Bavaria and, at the same time, to reopen the war with Frederick over Silesia that December. Her forces triumphed in Bavaria, where they occupied Munich, but they fared worse against Frederick. Therefore, in order to employ her troops against other foes, Maria Theresa reluctantly conceded Silesia to Frederick in the Treaty of Breslau in June 1742.

Maria Theresa may have lost Silesia, but she had survived the initial onslaught and now scored further victories. The Austrians concentrated their efforts against the French and Bavarians in Bohemia, and by January 1743 it was back in Austrian hands. However, as the Austrians retook Bohemia, a French army overran most of Bavaria, where the Elector of Bavaria led another army that joined forces with the French. So, after securing Bohemia, Austrian armies converged on Bavaria, where they defeated the advancing enemies and sent them reeling back. Elsewhere in 1743, Maria Theresa's ally, George II, king of England and elector of Hanover, had taken the field with a polyglot force, known as the Pragmatic army. Campaigning along the Rhine, he defeated a French army at Dettingen in June, the last time a British sovereign personally commanded troops in battle, although there was little consequence to his victory.

Up to this point, France had fought in the war only as an ally of Bavaria, but in April 1744 Louis XV formally declared war on Austria and launched an attack in the traditional battleground of the southern Netherlands, now an Austrian possession. Soon Louis XV cut short this operation and rushed south with troops to resist an Austrian invasion of Alsace and Lorraine. This threat dissolved when, faced with troubles elsewhere, Maria Theresa ordered her army back from French soil. But, although the French offensive in the Austrian Netherlands stalled in 1744, the next year a French army under the command of Marshal Maurice de Saxe triumphed. He won the Battle of Fontenoy, the greatest French victory of the war, and followed this success by a series of sieges that gave Flanders to the French.

After much hard fighting through 1744 and 1745, Maria Theresa finally came to terms with her German adversaries. In 1744 Frederick became alarmed by Austrian success, re-entered the war, and invaded Bohemia in August. Maria Theresa quickly concentrated all her forces against him by recalling troops from France and evacuating Bavaria. When Frederick withdrew from Bohemia, Austrian forces invaded Bavaria once again in January 1745, defeated the surprised Bavarians, and occupied much of the country. Bavaria agreed to terms at the Treaty of Füssen in April. Bavarian defection left Frederick without allies close to hand as he faced an Austrian invasion of Silesia. There Frederick won at Hohenfriedberg, but did not prevent the Austrians and their new Saxon allies from advancing into Prussian territory and threatening Berlin. By driving on the Saxon capital of Dresden, Frederick forced his enemies to turn back and defeated them in battles fought in November and December. Maria Theresa could not recoup this setback, because she realized that she must send more troops to the Austrian Netherlands to resist de Saxe, particularly because the British had to withdraw their forces in order to fight the Scottish Jacobite rising of the 'Forty-Five'. Thus, she cut her losses by finally agreeing again, this time finally, to Frederick's acquisition of Silesia in the Treaty of Dresden signed on Christmas Day 1745, and Frederick left the war for good.

But this was not the end of the conflict. Despite Austrian resistance, de Saxe went from triumph to triumph in the Low Countries in 1746–8, conquering Austrian and Dutch territory to a degree that had eluded Louis XIV. In Italy, French and Spanish forces fought a series of see-saw campaigns against the Austrians. In North America, a British and New England expedition took the French fortress of Louisbourg on Cape Breton Island, while in South Asia the French and British, allied with local Indian rulers, began a series of wars that continued even beyond the return of peace in Europe.

The Treaty of Aachen in 1748 brought the War of the Austrian Succession to an end. Maria Theresa retained all her lands except for Silesia, a favourable result considering the formidable array of enemies that had attacked her. However, she never forgave the Prussian theft of Silesia, and would pursue government and military reforms meant to strengthen Austria for the next round. Prussia, of course, established itself firmly among the great powers. Britain gained significant colonial prizes, although the colonial rivalry between France and Britain would only be finally resolved in the next war. For all its battlefield victories, the French came off with the least, as French colonial losses stood and Austria and the United Provinces received back what de Saxe had conquered.

This war illustrates the predatory nature of balance-of-power politics and the character of war-as-process. Princes who agreed to recognize the Pragmatic Sanction discarded their commitments in the hope of new territory. Alliances formed and re-formed, participants entered and exited, in the hopes of optimizing short-term rewards. The tempo of operations remained restrained, as combatants faced each other on multiple fronts. Outcomes of battle and siege certainly mattered, but they did not necessarily determine the peace, as the return of de Saxe's conquests demonstrated. Throughout the war, continuing diplomatic manœuvres produced a dizzying succession of negotiations, agreements, and betrayals. In the end, the War of the Austrian Succession did not settle the issues contested by the great powers—issues that would soon spark another and even more bloody war.

The Seven Years War

Two fundamental rivalries spawned the Seven Years War—continental enmity between Prussia and Austria and colonial competition between Britain and France. Frederick the Great would have been happy to maintain the status quo, since he held Silesia, but Maria Theresa was determined to retrieve her lost province, punish Frederick for his impudence, and reduce Prussia to the level of a third-rate power. The essential aspects of the Anglo-French conflict did not focus on Europe during this war, but on North America and India, where fighting had begun long before it broke out on the continent. In this imperial showdown, Britain held the great trump in its navy, which would guarantee colonial victory. Beyond these two confrontations, a third theme played out in the war—namely, the emergence of Russia as a major power in central and western Europe.

As tensions increased during the 1750s and potential foes positioned themselves for the coming fight, the surprising diplomatic revolution redefined major alliances. An apparent *rapprochement* between Prussia and Britain, which had been on opposite sides during the War of the Austrian Succession, provided the opening for the Austrian diplomat, Kaunitz, who hoped to isolate Prussia from continental support. To this end, in 1756 he engineered a surprising alliance with France, the traditional enemy of Austria; Russia and Sweden also joined the coalition against Prussia. As shocking as was the change of partners, it accorded with the nature of balance-of-power politics, which demanded flexible and shifting allegiances to maximize short-term advantage. One of the interesting by-products of the diplomatic revolution was to give the Seven Years War a confessional dimension, as Protestant Britain and Prussia confronted Catholic Austria, France and—after 1760—Spain. Religion could still affect popular sympathies in Britain and in Protestant Germany, even if it did not determine foreign policy, for public opinion greeted victories over the French as blows against popery.

The mighty alliance against Frederick the Great appeared overwhelming, especially because Frederick could not expect the British to provide anything beyond subsidies to help defend his territory, although this ally would mount forces in western Germany to fend off attacks on Hanover and Hesse. The unrelenting pressure on Frederick nearly proved to be fatal. Unlike the previous war, the continental campaigns of the Seven Years War centred almost exclusively on Germany, while the Low Countries, Italy, and France (with the exception of coastal raids) were spared the fighting. The French commitment on the continent did not equal its effort in the War of the Austrian Succession, but the Austrians and Russians raised large forces and directed them exclusively at Prussia. Only Frederick's determination, and brilliance, and the endurance of the Prussian army, preserved his state.

Frederick's generalship was extraordinary but far from flawless, and he could not claim, as could Alexander or Marlborough, never to have lost a battle. He won more often than not, but his defeats could be disastrous, most notably at the Battle of Kunersdorf in 1759, where he suffered over 40 per cent casualties and lost 178 cannon to an Austro-Russian army. Still, he came out victorious often enough to resist his enemies until exhaustion and luck rewarded him with an acceptable peace. At times his battlefield success dazzled, as at the Battle of Leuthen, his masterpiece fought in December 1757. With 39,000 troops he defeated an Austrian army of 66,000 by using the cover of wooded hills to march his battalions across the front of the enemy's fortified position so as to concentrate his entire force on the Austrians' left flank. Once there, he attacked and crushed the enemy left, and rolled up the enemy line. But even such a great triumph fell short of winning the war for Frederick. As befitted war-as-process, his victories were not decisive, except in the negative sense that they kept his enemies from crushing him.

Although he was an undisputed master of the contemporary military system and a consummate practitioner of the reigning practice of war, Frederick transformed neither. Still, if he was no revolutionary, Frederick none the less did contribute some important refinements and innovations. His style of warfare was distinctly battle oriented, as befitted a theatre of war where fortresses were by no means as common as they were in the Low Countries. Prussian training was both severe and effective, making the Prussian infantry and cavalry the most proficient in Europe. Their superiority at drill allowed Frederick to manœuvre and deploy faster than any of his foes and, thus, impose battle on his terms. He became known for his 'oblique order', an advance with units in echelon that allowed him to concentrate his power on one flank.

The most impressive change in warfare was the considerable increase in the number of artillery pieces employed in battle by mid-century. At Malplaquet in 1709, for example, Marlborough and Eugene had 100 cannon for 86,000 troops, while Frederick brought 170 guns for 39,000 troops at Leuthen, where his opponents boasted 210 artillery pieces. This multiplication of cannon on the battlefield, made all the more effective by artillery reforms that improved the manufacture and quality of guns, constituted an 'artillery revolution' for which Napoleon is sometimes erroneously given the credit.

By 1761 the allies had worn Frederick down despite his great abilities, but a near miracle intervened to save him from what seemed to be inevitable defeat. Tsarina Elizabeth, an implacable foe of Frederick, died in January 1762, and her pro-Prussian nephew and successor, Peter III, reversed Russian policy by signing a peace treaty with Frederick in May and offering him a Russian corps. Even though Peter soon fell to a coup that put his wife on the throne as Catherine II, later awarded the sobriquet 'the Great', Russia did not re-enter the war against Frederick, so he survived. By the Treaty of Hubertusburg in February 1763, Austria agreed to the *status quo ante-bellum*, leaving Prussia in possession of Silesia.

The consequences of the Seven Years War, both within Europe and around the globe, were colossal. After first seizing and then holding onto Silesia against such towering opposition, Prussia retained and increased its status as a great power while becoming the military paradigm of its day. Yet, Prussian success aided Russia in a back-handed way, because continued rivalry between Prussia and Austria in Germany prevented either from effectively resisting Russia, which therefore enjoyed a virtual free hand against the Ottoman Empire, a dominant position in Poland, and considerable influence in Germany.

In this truly global war, Britain also gained immeasurably because the clash of arms decided important imperial issues in its favour. In North America, where the conflict was known as the French and Indian War, Wolfe's forces took Quebec in 1759, winning Canada for Britain. This secured all of Atlantic North America for the British, although the War of American Independence would soon strip away the richest American colonies. In contrast, triumph in India would not only give the British East India Company short-term rewards but would redirect the imperial energies of Britain in the long term, giving it an Asian empire to replace its American holdings. With astoundingly small forces, the East India Company became a victorious territorial power in South Asia, rather than simply being the manager of a string of commercial outposts. At the Battle of Plassey in 1757, Robert Clive, with 3,200 troops (only a third of them European) defeated a south Asian coalition that fielded an army of 50,000 against him. To be sure, dissension and intrigue riddled that vast army, but Plassey was an important victory none the less. Finalized by Hector Munro's triumph at the Battle of Buxar in 1764, Plassey gave the East India Company the manpower and riches of Bengal, Bihar, and Orissa, a formidable base from which to extend British rule across the subcontinent. By the Treaty of Paris, signed in February 1763, France renounced to Britain all claims to Canada, Nova Scotia, and the Ohio valley, while transferring the Louisiana territory, including New Orleans, to Spain. In addition, the French Compagnie des Indes accepted crippling conditions that restricted it to maintaining a few trading stations on the Indian subcontinent. France had essentially lost its colonial empire outside the West Indies. Beyond all this, the fact that Britain with its Indian domains, and Russia with its vast Siberian possessions, had risen to such importance—an importance that would only continue to grow—meant that Asia now factored into the European state system as never before. But even greater changes would soon overtake the patterns of international rivalry and war.

Revolution and Empire, 1789–1815

Revolutionary change and international continuity, 1789–1802

While the French Revolution of 1789 was not initially an international event, it had important consequences for the way in which states mobilized for and conducted war. Today, historians debate whether the French Revolution restructured society or redefined the language, and thus the concept, of politics; the answer is that it did both. Social reform ended aristocratic privileges such as domination of civil and military offices, ended 'feudal' remnants including dues owed by peasants to lords, and spread landownership among the peasantry and middle classes. Politics came to express the new, more inclusive, society by giving common people legal equality and political rights, including the vote. All this encouraged a strong commitment to revolution, society, and state—in short, patriotism—throughout France. This intense and widespread commitment translated into much more effective mobilization for war, as the citizenry resolved to do whatever was necessary to defend the fatherland (*patrie*) and its new regime.

This intense resolution expressed itself in the creation of a new style of army, the *popular conscript army*. Its ranks would be filled by universal conscription, instituted most dramatically in the revolutionary *levée en masse* decreed in August 1793. In the summer of 1794, this force mustered perhaps as many as 1,000,000 effectives, two and a half times the peak strength of the state commission army of Louis XIV. To support the larger number of troops, the state mobilized the wherewithal of war as never before, requisitioning food, material, and labour to supply its armies. Citizen soldiers inspired by patriotism could not be led in the same way by the same officers who commanded the army before the Revolution. In 1788, 85 per cent of officers had been aristocratic, but by the summer of 1794, only 2–3 per cent were nobles. Commoners in command understood the character and potential of their enlisted men far better than had their aristocratic predecessors.

Along with the popular conscript army, a different practice of warfare began to evolve during the wars of the French Revolution. The dedication and self-confidence of the common soldier made possible new and more aggressive tactics. Infantry formed in fast-moving attack columns, which took advantage of martial enthusiasm, and deployed as skirmishers, which exploited the superior personal initiative of the troops. At the same time, the French did not abandon the traditional line formation, but combined it with columns and skirmishers to produce a tactical flexibility that allowed revolutionary armies to adapt to topography and circumstance in battle better than could any other European army. In addition, confidence in the dedication of the common soldier reduced the fear of desertion, made possible more improvised logistics, and therefore increased the potential for greater mobility and a quicker operational tempo. Battle replaced siege as the most important and prevalent form of clash between major forces, although sieges could still matter at key times. This evolution towards battle should not be exclusively ascribed to the French Revolution, for, as already mentioned, Frederick the Great had made battle the signature of his campaign style at mid-century, and, for a number of reasons, this was a trend likely to continue. However, it is clear that the Revolution greatly accelerated and extended operational trends.

Revolution raised France back to the position of a hegemon on the continent, although not in the same exclusive way that Louis XIV stood above his foes. The revolutionary and Napoleonic period would see three European hegemons dominate European international politics. France played the role of a central hegemon, strong enough to defend and assert itself at the heart of Europe, although it would take several years for its new power position to become obvious. The constantly increasing importance of naval power, trade, and colonies had made Britain a hegemon as well on the periphery of

Europe. The fleet rendered Britain invulnerable to direct attack, while its wealth allowed it to intervene on the continent even though Britain did not possess a large army. By the onset of the Revolution, Russia had established itself as the other peripheral hegemon in Europe. Russia faced little threat from the east or the north after 1721, and sheer distance made it relatively invulnerable to fatal attack from the west. Its large armed forces allowed it to project power into Germany almost at will without assuming much risk.

However, the rise of a new French hegemony did not change the principles of balance-of-power politics until after Napoleon had come to dominate France and Europe. France initiated war in 1792, and while the needs of national defence drove the new regime to a great patriotic effort, after 1794 French strategy concerned territorial conquest as much as revolutionary ideology. Britain was quite willing to back a succession of coalitions against France with a modest investment, while at the same time pursuing colonial advantages in the Americas and South Asia. Russia made but a limited commitment during the wars of the French Revolution, marching an army against France only in 1798–9. Instead, Tsarina Catherine the Great showed far more interest in devouring Poland than in thwarting revolutionary France. European statesmen would not see beyond the dictates of balance of power until after the rapacious Napoleon convinced them that only in concert could they resist his will.

War and Partition, 1792–1795

If the monarchs of Europe hardly looked upon the French Revolution with favour, they were not plotting to attack the new regime outright. No doubt, Britain, Russia, and others were only too happy to turn French weakness and disorder to their own profit, but revolutionary France brought war upon itself. From June 1791, French public opinion regarded war as likely, and the government began to gear up, expanding the size of the regular army and calling for 100,000 new volunteers from the National Guard militia to serve one year of active duty. As the months passed, factions within France hoped to exploit a war for their own political benefit, so, when the new Legislative Assembly debated war in the spring of 1792 few representatives counselled against it. On 20 April the Assembly declared war against the Habsburg Francis II in the hopes of confining the war to a struggle between France and Austria, but Prussia entered the lists against France as well. No one knew that Europe was entering a period of twenty-three years of nearly constant warfare to be ended only at Waterloo.

The popular conscript army mustered by revolutionary France would demonstrate its superiority over the state commission style, but its abilities were not immediately apparent. When French troops first took the field in April 1792 the inexperienced regulars and volunteers ran at the mere sight of the enemy. The mounting threat compelled the government to summon another wave of volunteers that summer. By late summer, the allies launched an invasion under the Duke of Brunswick in command of a Prussian army with Austrian support. He advanced into France and confronted a French army under Kellermann at Valmy on 20 September. The Prussians expected that the French would bolt and run, but they did not; a summer's campaigning had seasoned the troops. After a long preliminary bombardment, Prussian battalions, reputedly the best in Europe, formed for the attack. Kellermann rode out in front of the French line, raised his hat on the tip of his sword, and cried 'Vive la nation!' His battalions echoed back, 'Vive la nation! Vive la France!' The citizen soldiers held firm—patriotism fortified the French line at Valmy, changing warfare forever. After a tentative assault, Brunswick pulled back and in a few days began a retreat during which disease decimated his army.

After Valmy, the French drove the Austrians out of the southern Netherlands and won victories along the Rhine before the end of the year. However, this triumph was short-lived, because the army dissolved over the winter, as volunteers returned home and a breakdown in logistics undermined the army. Austrian and Prussian forces counter-attacked in the spring of 1793 and regained the Netherlands and the Rhineland, while Britain and other lesser states joined the coalition. With the growing crisis, the Parisian government instituted mass conscription, first in a limited form in February and then through the *levée en masse* in August 1793. This act declared that 'all the French are in permanent requisition for the service of an army'. It ordered able-bodied bachelors, aged 18–25, to the front, and this final surge of manpower created the huge and spirited armies of 1794.

French battalions stopped the allied offensive in the summer and autumn of 1793 and then won a string of victories in 1794 and 1795 that drove many of the allies from the war. By defeating the Austrians at Fleurus in June 1794, the French won back the southern Netherlands. Elsewhere, French armies forced the allies back across the Rhine, and conquered both Savoy in the south and the United Provinces in the north. In addition, revolutionary armies, showing considerable brutality, put down the Vendée rebellion, a counter-revolutionary insurgency in the west of France. In response to the parade of triumphs, Prussia made peace with France in the Treaty of Basle, signed in April 1795, while Spain left the war by another Treaty of Basle concluded in July. Other lesser German states made peace at this time, so France remained at war only with Britain, Piedmont, still under attack by French armies, and Austria, the sole great power that had lost significant territory to the French.

The military system had been profoundly transformed by revolution in France; and, in response to these innovations, the practice of war also began an important transition that Napoleon would complete. However, the international system persevered in following the dictates of balance-of-power politics even as France became a new hegemon. The partitions of Poland demonstrate this continuity.

It might seem reasonable to expect that the wars of revolutionary France would have been the overriding concern of continental statesmen between 1792 and 1795, but in fact it was the fate of Poland that occupied top place on the agenda of France's continental enemies. Within the framework of late-eighteenth-century balance-of-power politics, Poland provided the ultimate intermediary state—a vulnerable source of territorial gain and compensation for its great power neighbours.

In this predatory world, the growing power of Russia demanded the sacrifice of Poland. The first partition came in 1772, when partition served the interests of Russia, Prussia, and Austria. Russia, engaged in a highly successful and profitable war against the Ottoman Empire, worried that Prussia and Austria might league together to contest Russian aggrandizement. Partition promised to mollify their opposition. At the same time, Prussia and Austria, both anxious to avoid being compelled by the logic of the balance of power to fight Russia, regarded partition as a way to moderate Russian demands on the Ottomans while at the same time gaining compensation for themselves. Fattened with Polish territory, the three partitioning powers sidestepped a war, although Russia emerged the major winner because it secured its victory over the Ottomans.

Hoping to create a more viable state after the first partition, the Poles attempted political reforms, but Russia would tolerate only a weak and dependent Poland. Austria tried to stabilize the situation through an agreement between the three great powers to respect Polish territorial integrity, but Russia balked. Russian desire to take more from Poland goes a long way to explaining why Catherine did not become involved in the war against revolutionary France, but instead encouraged a Prussian commitment to that war precisely to give Russia a freer hand in Polish matters. In fact, the Prussians' attention was never really focused on the war with France because they were always looking over their shoulder at Poland. A second partition came in 1793, when Russia felt compelled to agree to Prussian demands for another partition in order to keep them from making peace with France. The Austrians were so heavily engaged in the war with France that they could not actively resist the second partition, even though it brought them nothing.

The third and final partition that extinguished the Polish state came late in 1795. Once again, great power lust for Polish territory took precedence over fear of the French Revolution. The Prussians had pulled out of the war at Basle in April, not only because of French success but also because they feared that a growing *rapprochement* between Austria and Russia threatened their ability to make further gains in Poland. Russia now took what it wanted, compensating Prussia and leaving the rest for Austria, which Catherine further mollified with false promises of Russian troops to aid the war against France.

Napoleon's military revolution, 1802–1812

Napoleon ended the wars of the French Revolution by concluding the Treaty of Lunéville with Austria in February 1801 and the Treaty of Amiens with Britain in March 1802. Austria and Britain conceded French possession of the left bank of the Rhine, including the former Austrian Netherlands, and recognized French puppet republics in Holland, Switzerland, and Italy. These treaties could have become a permanent settlement, or at least as permanent as anything ever was in a balance-of-power system. Europe seemed willing to accept the new French hegemony, as long as the French did not threaten either the British or Russian spheres. This would have modified the traditional balance, but it could have continued to operate on the old principles.

However, this was not to be, for to Napoleon peace was simply the continuation of war by other means, and, even before the Treaty of Amiens had been signed, he had begun a series of actions that alarmed the European powers. Napoleon intervened in Swiss and German politics in a way that eroded the European balance by augmenting French might. His reshaping of Italy was an even greater threat to peace because it ran counter to the Treaty of Lunéville. There he transformed the Cisalpine Republic into the more authoritarian Italian Republic, with himself as the president, annexed Piedmont to France, and redistributed Italian principalities to suit his whim. In addition to all this, Napoleon ordered a building plan for the French navy designed to surpass the British in time. These and other actions convinced the British that Napoleon had to be stopped; consequently, they refused to abandon Malta as the Treaty of Amiens required. The escalating dispute between Napoleon and Britain led to renewed war in May 1803.

Napoleon genuinely believed that British betrayal had imposed war upon him, but he defined reasonable international behaviour as capitulation to his desires. His rapaciousness dumbfounded rather than outwitted rival European statesmen, because he operated outside the parameters of the balance-of-power system. Doubtless, that system was intrinsically flawed, but it had a certain predictability, limitation, and *quid pro quo*. Napoleon's policy lacked all of these; moreover, Napoleon had no clear conception of a peaceful and stable Europe, so he had no long-range policy at all. Instead he simply pursued whatever seemed the best way to score the next gain. The mixture of Napoleon's perpetual aggression with his enemies' balance-of-power behaviour produced a fatal alchemy. Napoleon refused to be restrained by their rules, but the rules his rivals followed so promoted selfish action that they could not form the unified front that would have been required to halt the Napoleonic juggernaut. Enjoying relative invulnerability, Britain and Russia pursued independent opposition to Napoleon, an opposition that often put Prussia and, above all, Austria at risk. In such an environment, Napoleon could do as he wished. But his success bore within it the seeds of its own destruction, because victory lured

Napoleon into overextending himself, first in Spain and then in Russia.

Napoleon's triumphs flowed not only from his ambition but from a new and highly effective practice of war, war-as-event, which exploited the battlefield potential of the popular conscript army created by the Revolution. Conscription, transformed into a regularized system by the Jourdan Law of 1798, provided the means by which Napoleon could quickly expand his military forces. Revolutionary tactical innovations, now even more effective when applied by his veteran *grande armée*, gave Napoleon key advantages in battle. Patriotism among the troops still inspired dedication and initiative in combat even though France had turned from Republic to Empire.

War-as-event contrasted sharply with eighteenth-century war-as-process. Unlike the ineffectual battles of time past, Napoleon's victories were decisive, in the sense that battles such as Austerlitz and Wagram each eliminated a major foe from a war. Battle retained its potential to win wars for Napoleon, at least until the débâcle in Russia. Napoleon's armies moved far and fast, a mobility he employed to impose battle on his terms and, after scoring a victory, to multiply its benefits by driving forward at a brisk operational tempo in pursuit or exploitation. Napoleon also utilized local resources, but not in the same manner that former armies had exacted contributions. Napoleonic forces 'lived off the country', but this meant that his troops dispensed with formal logistics and foraged to move rapidly in short wars. Napoleon also made vanquished foes pay the price of his wars, but only after they had been defeated. War-as-event simply moved too rapidly to allow the full exploitation of enemy resources during the campaign, and as a result, Napoleon did not make operational decisions aimed at controlling resource areas. By imposing, winning, and exploiting battle, Napoleon accelerated the course of war and avoided exhausting state resources or political will, so that attrition did not negate operational success until late in his regime. The speed and decision of Napoleonic war-as-event relegated diplomacy to a mopping-up operation, a way of registering a *fait accompli*. It would not be stretching things to say that diplomacy defined war under Louis XIV but that war defined diplomacy under Napoleon.

The apogee of Napoleon, 1805–1807

So impressive were Napoleon's campaigns of 1805–7 that they have served as models of the military art for nearly two centuries. In each of these campaigns, Napoleon was able to deploy his forces on a single primary line of operations against an isolated foe and gain decisive results in surprisingly little time. Such strategic focus was a luxury that Louis XIV had not enjoyed in his last two great wars, when the great powers of his day effectively united to oppose France.

The War of the Third Coalition grew out of the state of hostilities that had existed between Britain and France since 1803. Alarmed by Napoleon's continued aggrandizement, Russia and Austria concluded an alliance in the autumn of 1804, but it was strictly defensive. However, Russia and Britain reached an offensive accord in April 1805 to which Austria agreed in July. Although Prussia had been harmed by Napoleon's policy in Germany, it shied away from committing itself against France. Napoleon ordered the Austrians to disarm and began to shift his troops to the Rhine at the end of August, but in the first days of September Austria struck first by invading Bavaria in the hopes of forestalling a French offensive. Although he faced a coalition, Napoleon could concentrate his army against Austria alone. Russia simply supplied reinforcements for war along the Danube rather than undertaking a separate campaign, and the British fought Napoleon only at sea.

Early in the war, the Royal Navy commanded by Admiral Nelson crushed a combined Spanish and French fleet at Trafalgar in October. During the revolutionary and Napoleonic wars, the British developed more aggressive naval tactics. At Trafalgar, Nelson refused to parallel the enemy fleet in traditional line ahead, but crashed into the French battle line with two columns of ships led by himself and Collingwood. Nelson could be so aggressive because of the great ability of his captains and crews and a style of command that had evolved to expect concord of action, rather than strict adherence to specific commands. In the succeeding battle, of the thirty-three enemy ships, eighteen fell to the British. Victory at Trafalgar cost Nelson his life, but it permanently broke French naval power. However, it cannot be said that Trafalgar saved England from invasion, for Napoleon had already jettisoned his intentions to cross the Channel and had marched away to Germany.

Napoleon marshalled his forces rapidly, and this speed of assembly proved the key to victory in 1805–7. At war with Britain since 1803, Napoleon had maintained a large army without the necessity of deploying it against a continental foe. This odd circumstance gave him an existing army that did not need to go through any lengthy process of mobilization before taking the field. The main body of the *grande armée*, some 210,000 troops, lined up along the Rhine from Strasbourg to Mainz in order to swing east and south and envelop an Austrian army of 70,000 near Ulm. Napoleon gave Marshal Masséna an additional 50,000 men to pin down the 100,000 Austrian troops commanded by Archduke Charles in Italy.

Napoleon's army crossed the Rhine during the last few days of September; Austria capitulated only ten weeks later. The march from the Rhine to the Danube moved so swiftly that his troops left supply convoys far behind and simply foraged for food as they advanced. Swinging around Ulm, the French forced the Austrians there to capitulate on 17 October. After Ulm Napoleon pressed on, because he had resolved to force the Austrians out of the war before the Prussians could be convinced to enter the lists against him. Advancing down the Danube to Vienna, Napoleon drove back the Russian armies that had arrived to aid the Austrians. He wanted to engage the enemy, but they fought well, avoided any traps, and continued to withdraw. By mid-November Napoleon had occupied Vienna, but he needed a decisive battle. This he won at Austerlitz in Moravia, about 70 miles north-east of Vienna. Through manœuvre and clever deceit Napoleon lured the Austro-Russian forces into battle there on 2 December. Appearing to be weak on his right, Napoleon tempted the allies to send most of their centre against the French right, and, when Russian troops were fully committed to the flanking move, Napoleon smashed through the depleted allied centre. Two days after his devastating defeat, Emperor Francis II capitulated to Napoleon. The Treaty of Pressburg, signed in late December, ratified the results of the campaign: Austria pulled out of the war and granted territorial concessions in Germany and Italy. Russia recalled its forces but did not conclude a formal peace.

Prussia's turn to meet disaster came in 1806. Napoleon continued petty aggressions after Pressburg, as he attacked Naples, enforced more concessions in Dalmatia, and increased demands in Germany. He also betrayed Prussia, which had paid a high price to gain

Hanover from France only to discover that Napoleon proposed to offer it back to Britain in exchange for peace. French bullying finally convinced even the weak Prussian king, Frederick William III, to issue an ultimatum on 26 September 1806 demanding that all French troops pull back across the Rhine. With his troops stationed in Germany, Napoleon rapidly assembled an army of 200,000 troops south of the Thuringian Forest and marched north into the flank and rear of the Prussian forces and their Saxon allies. Caught off guard, the Prussians began to retreat west, but the *grande armée* struck them in the midst of withdrawal at Jena and Auerstedt on 14 October. After victory in this double battle, Napoleon hounded the defeated Prussians in a relentless pursuit that captured nearly their entire army by late November, as Frederick William fled to Russia.

Napoleon's campaign against the Russians began in January 1807, when they attacked the French in winter quarters. Halting the initial Russian advance at Eylau in February, the French then besieged and took Danzig. When active campaigning began again in June, Napoleon defeated the Russians at Friedland less than two weeks into the offensive, and the Russians requested a truce. This led to the Treaty of Tilsit, which created the Grand Duchy of Warsaw at Prussian expense and required Prussia to make further territorial concessions to Napoleon's German allies in the Confederation of the Rhine. Prussia also agreed to pay a large war indemnity to France and accept severe limitations on the size of its army. Russia recognized the Grand Duchy of Warsaw and allied with France against Britain. Napoleon also instituted his Continental System at this time. Advertised as a painless way to strangle British commerce by closing the continent to British trade, it in fact sacrificed the well-being of continental economies to French interests and profits.

The victories of 1805-7 marked the apogee of Napoleon. Paradoxically, while these three campaigns have become shining examples of masterful generalship, they were in fact the product of such anomalous circumstances that their promise of short and decisive wars should be regarded as a chimera. Louis XIV's problems in multi-front war-as-process apply to a far wider range of military experience than does Napoleon's good fortune in being able to concentrate all his forces on a single front in war-as-event. Be that as it may, there is no doubt that the campaigns of 1805-7 won for Napoleon a position of unparalleled power.

The Treaty of Tilsit might have consolidated this position as the basis for a permanent settlement, but his ambition led Napoleon to choke on his own success. The next year his overconfidence drew him into Spain, where the French became bogged down in a long war of attrition. Napoleon again vanquished the Austrians at Wagram in 1809, although before this battle the Austrians handed him his first major defeat at Aspern-Essling. In 1812, outraged at Russian independence, Napoleon launched an invasion of Russia with a huge, multinational army, including contingents from Prussia and Austria. Wisely, the Tsar and his generals recognized that they could resist Napoleon simply by withdrawing and waiting for distance and weather to destroy his army. The French reached Moscow, but, when the Russians refused to negotiate, Napoleon was forced to retreat across a frigid wasteland. Between mid-October and the end of the year the *grande armée* died in the snows of Russia, as few of the troops who reached Moscow ever saw home again.

The formation of the Concert of Europe

Defeat in Russia doomed Napoleon. Defections began as the Prussian contingent concluded a truce with the Russians at the end of December and withdrew to stir armed resistance in Germany. The Austrian detachment marched home as well but the Emperor Francis I and his Chief Minister Metternich would not immediately join the new coalition that united Prussia, Sweden, Russia, and Britain in February and March of 1813. At first Napoleon did well in this War of Liberation, but growing allied power and his own dwindling resources forced him to agree to a truce from early June to mid-August. The truce benefited the allies considerably, because, when the fighting resumed, the Austrians joined the allies and tipped the scales against Napoleon. Again, his tactical and operational brilliance won him limited victories, but allied advantages eventually told, and in October 1813 Napoleon suffered a crushing defeat at the Battle of Leipzig, a bloody three-day affair.

Although Napoleon could not maintain his grip on Germany, he refused to negotiate seriously, and turned down surprisingly generous offers of peace after Leipzig. During the winter and early spring of 1814 he held off invading allied columns in a masterful delaying campaign, but he was eventually forced to capitulate in April. The

French throne did not pass to his son, as he had hoped, but to Louis XVIII, the brother of Louis XVI. After Napoleon's return from exile on the Island of Elba in 1815, his attempt to re-establish his regime during the Hundred Days was doomed because he could never convince the European great powers that he would pursue a peaceful policy. His defeat at Waterloo simply put an end to an impossible venture.

The allied victory in 1813–15 came because Napoleon had taught his enemies important lessons. They had adopted the advantages of the new military system encapsulated in the popular conscript army, as Russia, Austria, and, particularly, Prussia undertook military reforms in response to battlefield defeat. Napoleon also demonstrated to Europe the decisive operational potential of war-as-event, and the slower moving war-as-process receded into history. Eventually, Napoleon also taught his enemies the problems inherent in traditional balance-of-power politics, but here he did not instruct them by example, for his enemies learned not by imitating him but by opposing him.

The problem of vanquishing Napoleon differed from the challenge of creating a stable European peace in the wake of his defeat but the answer to the former helped move Europe in the direction of solving the latter. The other great powers finally realized that they could overpower Napoleonic France only by setting aside their own predatory interests and banding together for as long as it was necessary to defeat their common enemy. But, in order to fashion a lasting peace, the great powers would have to go further; they had to reconceive their individual interests and accept that these would be best served in an international system equitable enough to satisfy all the European states in the long run. And this meant prioritizing not one's own immediate benefit but the legitimate interests of other states in the system. This higher conception of international politics evolved during the final phase of the Wars of Napoleon and at the Congress of Vienna.

It is worth noting that sheer exhaustion served as midwife to this new and wiser form of international system, for a tired Europe was looking for good reasons not to fight. The Wars of Napoleon had exacted a terrible price; total military and civilian deaths brought about by war numbered as high as four or five million. Weakened and shaken by such a monumental sacrifice of life and fortune, European powers sought a lasting peace. To this extent the period after the Congress of Vienna resembled that after the Treaties of Utrecht and Rastatt a century before.

The important transformation of international practices is revealed in the fate of two lesser powers, Bavaria and Saxony, both of which had allied with Napoleon and might have been regarded as spoils of war by Austria, Prussia, and Russia. Bavaria deserted Napoleon by the Treaty of Ried signed with Austria in October 1813. Rather than bullying their neighbour to change sides, the Austrians offered Bavaria favourable terms and guarantees, including Austrian troops to serve under Bavarian command to protect Bavarian borders. The Austrians also granted Bavaria continued dominion over territory that Austria might well have claimed. In short, the treaty demonstrated restraint on Austria's part and a recognition of Bavaria's future role in the European international system. During the Congress of Vienna, the fate of Saxony also hung in the balance. Prussia felt justified in demanding all of Saxony as compensation for Prussian sacrifice and leadership in the War of Liberation. At first Prussia received full Russian support, but the Tsar eventually appreciated the need to respect the legitimacy of Saxony and refused to let it disappear entirely. Prussia was allowed to absorb only about two-fifths of the Saxon population, while the rest of Saxon lands remained under the Saxon ruler. The critical role of Russia in this bargain demonstrates another key point about the Vienna settlement—the key roles played by hegemons. The Congress of Vienna was not an affair of equals. Both Britain and Russia enjoyed clear hegemonies that could coexist. The key was that these hegemonies be exercised wisely, not that they be replaced by a gaggle of more evenly matched states. The new coordination between states, known as the Concert of Europe, would have conductors and principle players, rather than being an egalitarian ensemble.

The trinity of the international system, military system, and practice of war all changed in fundamental ways after the onset of the French Revolution. Each of these three evolutions had substantial implications for the future, but the conversion from balance-of-power politics to the more equitable and stable Concert of Europe exceeded the others in importance. This was the most subtle, the most conceptual, yet the most far-reaching of the developments that redefined the trinity after 1789. As a result of progress in international relations, Europe would avoid another war between great powers for forty years and a general war for one hundred. The nineteenth century would not follow the belligerent path of the eighteenth; surely this change for the better ranks as one of the great facts of history.

6

Europe and the rest of the world

P. J. Marshall

Eighteenth-century Europeans were the heirs of two main thrusts of expansion that had begun at the end of the fifteenth century: one to the west across the Atlantic into the Americas; the other eastwards to Asia, for the most part also by sea round the Cape of Good Hope. By 1700 these two thrusts had produced very different results. In the Americas the coming of the Europeans had led to a catastrophic decline in the native population, the conquest of large areas, and the creation of European empires that covered much of the continent from the St Lawrence River in Canada to Chile in the southern tip of South America. In Asia the European presence was still a very limited one. A large volume of trade passed to and from Europe via the Cape of Good Hope, but only relatively small areas had come under European rule. The great Asian empires, those of the Ottoman Turks, the rulers of Iran, the Mughals in India, the Chinese, and the dynasty that controlled Japan, had generally consolidated and extended their dominions during the seventeenth century.

The eighteenth century brought important changes in both western and eastern hemispheres. There was spectacular growth in the population and wealth of most of the European colonies in the Americas and by the end of the century the rule of the metropolitan countries was being challenged by the colonial peoples. In much of what had been British North America and in the rich French West Indian colony of Saint-Domingue, now Haiti, independence had actually been attained. It was shortly to follow over most of the rest of the continent. While the European empires were disintegrating in the

Americas, new empires were being created in Asia. The British had subjugated large parts of India, bringing, it was thought, some forty million people under their rule, and the Russians were pushing south-eastwards overland into Central Asia. A new global configuration was clearly emerging: the Americas would be dominated by new republics, politically independent but still closely tied economically and culturally to Europe; new European empires of rule over non-European peoples would extend into Central Asia and from India to south-east Asia and into Africa.

Europeans outside Europe

Empires in the Americas

Until the very end of the fifteenth century, the native peoples of the Americas lived virtually without contact with the rest of the world. The sudden appearance of Europeans after the first landfall of Christopher Columbus in 1492 had a cataclysmic effect upon them. Populations were wiped out or greatly reduced by new diseases. Even the sophisticated imperial systems built up by the Aztecs in central Mexico or by the Incas in the Andes proved unable to offer effective military resistance to Spanish assaults. The fate of the diminished native populations was either to be incorporated, mostly in subordinate positions as labourers or as peasant cultivators, into European colonies, above all in Peru or Mexico, or to be pushed to the margins of European settlement, as on the long frontier of colonial North America, in northern Mexico, or in the Brazilian interior. In spite of two centuries of disaster, native peoples still played a significant role in the eighteenth-century history of the Americas. In Peru there were periodic Indian rebellions, the most serious being a great revolt in 1780–2 called after the name of its leader, Tupac Amaru. In North America Europeans conducted a huge trade in furs and skins through native peoples and enlisted them as allies in their wars. Nevertheless, people of European origin were relentlessly gaining control over more and more of the continent and its resources.

From the very first contact Europeans had regarded the Americas as a continent subject to their imperial domination. In the Treaty of

Tordesillas of 1494 Spain and Portugal, acting on papal authority, had divided the Americas between them. The Portuguese laid claim to the eastern part of South America, where they were to develop the colonies that had become Brazil by the eighteenth century. The Spanish claimed the rest. They built up a great empire in Central and South America, largely founded on conquered Indian kingdoms. Their claims could not, however, be sustained either in North America or in the Caribbean. During the seventeenth century, French, British, and Dutch infiltration redrew the political map of both regions and the outcome of wars was to redraw it again during the course of the eighteenth century. On the North American continent in 1700 French settlement was established on the St Lawrence in Canada and French claims extended in an arc from the Great Lakes down the Mississippi to Louisiana on the Gulf of Mexico. Along the eastern seaboard of North America was a series of British colonies. After 1763 the French were expelled from North America and the British claimed the whole continent east of the Mississippi. Twenty years later they were to be left with no more than the recently conquered Canada, as their old colonies rebelled and established the new United States of America. The Caribbean in 1700 was a chequerboard of competing empires: Spain retained some of the larger islands but others had passed to the French, the British, the Dutch, and the Danes. War was to produce some redistribution of possessions, with the British gaining at the expense of the French, the Dutch, and the Spanish.

Eighteenth-century American colonies can be divided into three main categories, determined by environment and by the extent to which the indigenous populations had survived. British and French colonies in north-eastern North America, roughly from the St Lawrence to the Chesapeake, had certain obvious similarities. Colonies on the coasts and islands of the Caribbean, including the southern regions of mainland North America and much of coastal Brazil, had evolved in a rather different way, but again with marked similarities. A third category of colonies consisted of those established in the interior of Central and South America.

In the colonies of north-eastern North America, whether they were French or British, the majority of the population was of European origin and worked the land in relatively small farms to raise mainly European crops. The native population had for the most part been either eliminated by war and disease or dispersed away from the areas settled by Europeans. From the European point of view, however, the disease environment was benign and populations reproduced themselves at a rapid rate. In what were known as the British 'middle' colonies, primarily New York and Pennsylvania, natural increase was being supplemented by a very high rate of immigration. Towns such as Quebec, Montreal, Boston, New York, or Philadelphia were centres of trade. They handled the furs obtained through Indians, the fish caught in great abundance off Newfoundland and the shipments of meat, flour, timber, and other farm products to the Caribbean or similar areas in the western hemisphere that concentrated on export rather than on food crops.

From the Chesapeake southwards conditions were favourable for crops for which there was a huge demand in Europe, such as tobacco, indigo, rice, coffee, and sugar. Colonial economies from Virginia to coastal Brazil, and above all in the West Indies, were built on these 'staple' commodities. Colonial societies were shaped by their needs. For the most part these crops were high-cost ones, produced on large blocks of land, called plantations, requiring heavy capital investment and a big labour force. On the West Indian islands dominated by the production of sugar, such as French Saint-Domingue or British Jamaica, there was a huge disparity, sometimes of more than one to ten, between the owners, managers, and their assistants, who were white, and the labour force, which consisted of black slaves.

By the eighteenth century, slavery flourished wherever staple crops were being raised for Europe—that is, from Brazil to Virginia. As the demand for tropical produce grew in Europe, especially in the second half of the century, more and more slaves were shipped out of Africa and put to work in the plantations. Slaves were obtained by Europeans at many points along the West African coast from the Senegal River in the north almost to the Orange River in the south. Since fresh supplies of slaves were deemed essential even to maintain, let alone to expand, the production of tropical staples, West Africa was an integral part of the Atlantic commercial system. Only the Portuguese, however, had what amounted to even a limited imperial presence there. Luanda on the Angola coast was a Portuguese town from which they tried to exercise control over African rulers inland. Elsewhere, Europeans either occupied permanent forts by permission of African rulers or traded from their ships in African ports. In neither case did Europeans obtain slaves directly themselves. They purchased them from African merchants or from those rulers that traded in them, relying on the efficient indigenous commercial systems that were able to meet the ever-increasing demand. The terms of trade were generally determined by Africans rather than by Europeans and prices rose throughout the eighteenth century, as quantities increased, reaching a peak in the 1780s. During the course of the century, the British shipped some three million slaves across the Atlantic, the Portuguese about 1,900,000, and the French about one million.

A slave in the Americas was a chattel, a piece of property, able to be bought and sold and subject to special codes of law. Whether these were enacted by royal authority, as in Portuguese and French colonies, or by local colonial regimes, as in the British colonies, the results were essentially the same. Slaves were at the mercy of their owners and were liable to draconian punishment at the slightest sign of disobedience. The life prospects for Africans in the new world depended less on the European power into whose hands they happened to have fallen than on where they were taken. On the continental land masses, in North America or Brazil, where food supplies were relatively abundant and the labour routines required for the crops were less debilitating, black populations began to reproduce themselves. In the Caribbean, slaves were overworked and undernourished and the birth rate among African women was pitifully low. West Indian plantations, therefore, needed to be frequently restocked by new imports.

Mexico (New Spain) and Peru were the old centres of Spanish colonial power. Mexico City and Lima were still the richest cities in the Americas, with great churches and public buildings. The colonies' wealth was founded on the density of Indian populations, in spite of the high post-conquest mortality, and on great deposits of silver. During the eighteenth century some 90 per cent of the world's silver came from Spanish America—that is, from the Potosi mines in Peru and from Mexico. Silver output grew in both colonies during the century, tripling between 1730 and 1800, with most of the increase coming from Mexico. Silver-mining was only part of a sophisticated Mexican economy with large-scale farming and ranching on great estates called *haciendas* and a considerable amount of manufacturing in small workshops. At the top of the social structure in both Peru and Mexico were old established Spanish élites from families long resident in the Americas, known as creoles, and small groups who had recently come out from Spain as high officials, clergy, and merchants. There were large numbers of people of mixed race in both colonies (nearly a quarter of the population in Mexico) and a great mass of Indians, somewhat more integrated into the rest of society in Mexico than in Peru.

In the late eighteenth century, Spanish colonies, notably Cuba and Venezuela in the Caribbean, were increasingly involved in the growing export of tropical staples from slave-worked plantations. New colonies were also prospering in the far south. Buenos Aires on the River Plate became a major Atlantic port, outlet for Peru's silver and for its own hides and salt beef.

Eighteenth-century Brazil was another colony sustained for a time by mineral wealth. Alluvial gold deposits were discovered in the 1690s in an inland district of southern Brazil called Minas Gerais. This became Europe's most important source of gold until the deposits were worked out by the 1760s. The gold rush drew waves of new Portuguese migrants to Brazil and enabled the southern ports, notably Rio de Janeiro, to prosper. When the gold boom subsided, Brazil remained a rich colony in the later eighteenth century, markedly richer than Portugal itself. Brazil exported sugar, tobacco, hides, and cotton, about a quarter of the supply of raw cotton for the new Lancashire textile industry at one time coming from Brazil,

The European powers pursued generally similar policies towards their American colonies in the eighteenth century: they tried to maintain a degree of metropolitan authority over them and especially to regulate their economies so that their trade contributed to the wealth of the mother country rather than to that of European rivals. This meant that controls were applied limiting access to the colonies to the ships of their own metropolitan power and ensuring that the most valuable colonial exports went to the mother country from whom colonies were also required to receive their imports. If objectives were generally similar, the machinery for trying to attain these ends differed markedly. Ostensibly the most impressive was that of Spain. In Spanish colonies there was a hierarchy of offices, with the king's viceroy at the top, presiding over judges of the courts, who supervised administration as well as doing justice, and local administrators. There were no representative institutions, even for those elements of the colonial population claiming to be of Spanish descent, beyond town councils, who nominated their own members rather than submitting themselves to election. At the other extreme was the British system of colonial administration. Some colonies, which were still the private property of individuals or of corporate bodies, had virtually no agents of royal authority posted in them. Elsewhere there were royal governors and a handful of officials appointed in Britain. Everywhere in the British Empire, however, the power of the governors was countervailed by that of elected local assemblies, representative of property-holders among the white male population. These bodies consciously modelled themselves on the British House of Commons, claiming the right to consent to all local legislation and to control the funds available to the governor. French colonial administration, both in France itself and in Canada and the West Indies, had far fewer checks on it than its British counterpart. Colonies were under the control of governors and officials called *intendants* without the interference of representative bodies. Brazil was under a more relaxed Portuguese version of Spanish colonial administration.

Whether metropolitan authority was obeyed, especially in the first half of the eighteenth century, was likely to depend more on whether it was in the interest of the colonial élites to do so than on the powers wielded by the agents of metropolitan authority. Communications were slow and bureaucratic procedures even slower. Local interests did not need formal representation to exert effective influence over officials. Offices might become the personal property of the holder or be operated by him for his own pecuniary advantage rather than for the service of the Empire. The trade regulations are a very good example of the fragility of colonial government. For the most part it was in the interests of the British North Americans or West Indians to observe them, since Britain offered a bigger fleet of merchant shipping, a larger market for tropical produce, and generally cheaper supplies of manufactured goods than any of its competitors. On the other hand, there were very strong incentives for Spanish colonial populations to disobey the regulations that decreed that they should trade exclusively with Spain. For long periods no Spanish shipping reached the Americas and at the best of times it was available only at certain restricted places. Spain was an inadequate market for the increasingly large quantities of goods being exported from the Americas, and it certainly could not provide the manufactures that its colonists required. They therefore traded widely with the British, the French, the Dutch, and the Portuguese. There was relatively little that authorities in metropolitan Spain could do to stop this trade.

The crisis of the American empires

In the first half of eighteenth century the colonial populations and colonial economies, with exceptions like Brazil in its gold rush, tended to grow slowly. There was generally a kind of equipoise between local interests, whose disobedience usually stopped short of open defiance or rebellion, and metropolitan authority, which was not exerted in ways that encroached too strongly on established privileges and autonomies. Colonial powers fought wars but without doing much damage to one another's empires.

From mid-century, however, the tempo began to change. The volume of trade crossing the Atlantic grew dramatically for nearly all colonies. There was a general rise in population. War in the Americas increased in scale and intensity from the Seven Years War, fought by Britain against France and then Spain, that began *de facto* in the Ohio valley in 1754, two years before the formal declaration of war, and raged across North America and the Caribbean until 1763. The British began fighting their colonial subjects in North America in 1775 and by the end of the war in 1783 the French, the Spanish, and the Dutch had joined in against them, forcing Britain to recognize American independence. Britain and revolutionary France went to war in 1793 and from the following year British expeditions were sent to attack the French and later the Spanish and Dutch colonies in the West Indies.

The increase in the volume of colonial trade and of the scale of warfare in the Americas were closely linked. As the trade became more valuable, so did the contribution that it made to state finances through various forms of taxation, such as customs, the Spanish crown's fifth of silver imports, or the Portuguese crown's fifth of gold and its tobacco monopoly. For the British in particular the colonial trades were an important element in their extremely successful system of public credit. Colonial merchants took up a considerable proportion of the government's loans and it was commonly feared that, were any of the important colonial trades to be lost, a collapse of credit leading to national bankruptcy would ensue. Colonial trades were also deemed vital for the European navies, since their seamen could be diverted to warships when needed. So much was now believed to be at stake that all the European states with colonial empires felt it necessary to strengthen the defences of their own possessions and conversely that they should try to disrupt the colonial trades of their rivals and thus to weaken their capacity to make war in Europe. The success of the British in the Seven Years War, when they inflicted heavy losses on the French and seized Havana in Cuba, the staging post for the Spanish silver fleet on its return to Europe, sent shock waves throughout Europe. Defences must be strengthened and opportunities sought to cut the domineering British down to size by striking a blow at their colonial empire.

This heightened sense of the value of American possessions and of their trade had important consequences for colonial populations. Metropolitan authorities could no longer tolerate laxity of administration or tacit autonomies. Active steps were taken to develop the economic resources of colonies. Commercial regulations must be properly enforced and colonial governments reformed to make them more responsive to orders from home. Proper defensive measures needed be taken. Revenues were raised wherever possible.

Characteristically, it was the Spanish who applied the most rigorous programme of reforms, especially in Mexico after a tour of inspection from 1765 to 1771 by José de Gálvez, who was to be minister responsible for the Indies from 1776 to 1787. The production of silver was increased. Larger sums were raised in taxation and transferred to metropolitan Spain. The commercial system was reformed to allow much wider participation by Spanish ports. Garrisons of regular troops were strengthened. The wealth and privileges of the Church were attacked and the Society of Jesus, which was very influential in the Americas, was abolished altogether. New administrative units and new offices were created. For the most part these and other important positions were now to be filled by men who came out from Spain, not by creoles. The Marquis de Pombal, Portuguese minister from 1750 to 1777, tried to ensure that Portugal rather than Britain benefited from the wealth of Brazil by placing valuable trades under the control of monopoly companies. He too endeavoured to raise royal revenue and to reduce the influence of the Church. The British, in spite of their successes in the Seven Years War, felt it necessary to strengthen the defences of their North American and West Indian colonies and to enforce trade regulations more rigorously. Attempts were made to raise taxes, notably with the ill-starred Stamp Act of 1765, and to bring colonial officials more directly under royal control.

Accelerated economic growth, war, and new interventionist policies by the colonial powers from the 1760s had a profoundly unsettling effect in the Americas. There were outbreaks of violent disorder throughout the continent. In British North America both the frontier communities and the urban poor rioted. In the Caribbean there were slave rebellions of which the most spectacular were in French Saint-Domingue. In August 1791 the slaves rose over much of the northern part of the colony. As the revolt spread, the French revolutionary government supported the slaves against British attempts to annex the colony. The rebels were, however, able to ensure that the new Haiti eventually won its independence from France. In Spanish America there were riots against new taxes in Mexico, an uprising of poor whites and mixed-race people in the colony of New Granada in 1781, and the great Indian revolt of Tupac Amaru in Peru at the same time. A small group of mixed-race mulattos plotted rebellion with slaves in 1798 at Bahia in Brazil.

Faced with violent rebellion by slaves, Indians, or the white poor, the colonial élites generally sided with the metropolitan authorities and indeed expected metropolitan troops to restore order. Their loyalty could not, however, be taken for granted. Were this loyalty to be withdrawn, the empires would not survive.

The evidence of disaffection in the second half of the eighteenth century among people of European origin born in the Americas is unmistakable throughout the continent, even if it found expression in revolt and independence only in British North America by the end of the century. It is clear that in all the colonies there was a sense that the implied compacts of the earlier eighteenth century, whereby approximate obedience was rendered in return for loosely exerted authority, had been broken by the metropolitan governments. Authority was now being rigorously exerted to the disadvantage of creoles throughout the continent. Government was bearing down on them in new ways that they resented. They were having to pay higher taxes and to submit to reinforced commercial regulations that seemed to favour metropolitan interests over colonial ones. Their chances of holding high office or of influencing the course of administration were being diminished. Old landmarks, like the privileges of the colonial churches, were being obliterated.

Increasing assertiveness by the colonial powers went against the grain of what can with some exaggeration be described as growing 'nationalism' by the creole élites. The term 'nationalism' has to be used with extreme caution, because there was virtually no sense in which the peoples of any colony as yet saw themselves as a united nation in the making. There were deep internal divisions between whites, half-castes, Indians, and Africans. The primary loyalty of the élites was still to their king over the water and their country of origin, however remote from their own experience. Creoles often prided themselves on being more loyal to the traditions of the old country than were the ministers whose policies were vexing them. British colonists in the Americas fiercely upheld 'the rights of Englishmen'. Historians have detected increasing 'Anglicization'—that is, identification with what they took to be English culture and values—on the eve of the American Revolution. For Spanish creoles the Americas were not colonies; they were kingdoms of the Spanish monarch, enjoying their own rights and privileges, which were comparable with those of his European kingdoms. They rejected attempts to assimilate them into a more centralized unitary Spain, but they did not reject the monarchy. French planters on Saint-Domingue played with fire in insisting on the outbreak of the Revolution that the colony had the right, as part of France, to representation in the Estates General. The Brazilian élite, who had been favoured rather than excluded by Pombal's reforms, for the most part remained tied closely to Portugal.

Yet if separate nationhood and independence were nowhere seen as desirable or attainable, all over the Americas, people were identifying themselves with the place where by the eighteenth century their families had lived for several generations. They tended to use the Latin term *patria* (country) and to express their pride in it by writing about its beauties, its resources, and its history. This process was carried furthest in Mexico, where creoles were investing themselves with a history distinct from that of Spain. They adopted Indian traditions as their own. Mexico was for them a land with its own Christian culture, manifested in its own miracles, celebrated in the cult of the Virgin of Guadelupe, who had appeared to an Indian girl.

There seem to be several plausible explanations as to why the mainland British colonies should have led the field in open resistance that began in 1775, followed by the Declaration of Independence of 1776 and a war that lasted until 1783. Metropolitan authority was weaker in the British colonies than anywhere else and so attempts, however tentative, to reassert it threatened long-established local autonomies. British creoles were used to ruling themselves and eventually grasped independence with far fewer inhibitions than might have been felt elsewhere. In North America, in spite of increasing numbers of African slaves, the population was more homogeneous than elsewhere. There was a very large body of literate white property-owners, entitled to vote and already politicized, who could easily be mobilized to resist metropolitan authority. The existence of the huge black majority put a curb on the ambitions of the British West Indian whites, a consideration powerfully reinforced for all in the region by the Saint-Domingue slave revolt. Throughout Spanish and Portuguese mainland America, the whites had little experience of effective participation in politcal life, while there were huge populations of half-castes, unassimilated Indians, and black slaves whose reactions to turmoil seemed incalculable.

If overt resistance by the American élites to colonial authority in the eighteenth century was confined to British North America, an increasing sense of their own separate identity and of resentment at newly intrusive colonial power had sapped their loyalty to the empires everywhere. The West Indies and British Canada remained exceptions, but elsewhere the days of the empires were numbered. In the nineteenth century the Americas were to be ever more closely integrated to Europe economically and by great new flows of migrants, but in trying to reassert their political authority the empires had overreached themselves and had become unsustainable.

Asian trade

For the first hundred years after Vasco da Gama's voyage in 1498, the Cape route had been a Portuguese monopoly. Early in the seventeenth century the Dutch and the English had started using the route and the French had followed later. Another far less used intercontinental trading route had also been open since the sixteenth century. This route was used by Spanish ships that crossed the Pacific from Mexico to the Spanish settlement at Manila in the Philippines.

The economic system of the Americas in the eighteenth century was a European creation. Europeans organized the extraction of minerals or the cultivation of land, usually with crops and animals that they had introduced. The situation was entirely different in Asia. There Europeans became participants in Asian economic systems. Their needs constituted only a limited part of vast networks of trade, both by land and by sea. Europeans had as yet introduced nothing of significance. They operated within the framework of Asian states, purchasing crops grown by Asian cultivators or the goods made by Asian artisans, through the services of Asian merchants.

European methods of trading with Asia were well established by the beginning of the century. Intercontinental trade between Asia and Europe was an enterprise requiring a large outlay. Cargoes of goods or bullion had to be consigned to Asia with no expectation of any return for at least two years. The ships employed in the trade were the largest and most expensive merchant ships in the world. Permanent establishments had to be maintained in Asian ports to assemble the cargoes that the ships would take back to Europe. To obtain these cargoes, European agents had to make payments, several months before they could expect delivery, to Asian merchants who would then distribute the money to a mass of small cultivators or artisans. These operations were risky, as well as being costly. Asian trade was therefore conducted on a large scale by bodies capable of raising substantial capital and spreading the risk. These bodies expected to enjoy a monopoly of their country's trade with Asia. In the Portuguese case the trade was directly conducted by a state corporation called the *Estado da India*. The Dutch, the British, and the French, by contrast, entrusted the trade to private East India companies. These were essentially similar bodies. They had close links with their national governments, advancing them money and operating under regulations in return for their monopolies. Their capital, raised from a large body of shareholders, was placed under the management of directors, who appointed agents to serve the companies in the East at 'factories' in Asian ports.

In the sixteenth and early seventeenth centuries the Asian commodities that Europeans had most eagerly competed for had been pepper and the rarer spices, such as nutmeg or cloves. Pepper had attracted Europeans to south-west India and to the Indonesian archipelago. Spices were obtained from certain islands in eastern Indonesia. In the eighteenth century, pepper and spices were still a significant item of trade, but the emphasis had shifted to textiles, cotton cloth, and raw silk from India, and to beverages, tea from

China, which became a major item in the later part of the century, and coffee from Arabia and Java. The funds to purchase Asian commodities were raised in part by the sale of European goods. Before European industrialization in the nineteenth century, however, the companies generally found it difficult to sell such goods in large quantities. They did not meet Asian needs and in any case were likely to be too expensive. There was no alternative to exporting silver bullion on a massive scale. About one-third of the silver imported to Europe from the Americas went straight out again to Asia. Cargoes could also be purchased by profits made from trading in Asia. Europeans were thus actively engaged in the inter-Asian or so-called country trade. Indian textiles, for instance, were shipped to Indonesia, Japanese copper to India, or Chinese silk to Japan. To obtain the range of goods needed for cargoes for Europe and to participate fully in inter-Asian trade, the companies spread their factories around the Indian Ocean and the China Sea, from Basra at the top of the Persian Gulf to Nagasaki in Japan.

European countries competed against one another as fiercely for Asian as for American trade. Lisbon, Amsterdam, London, and Paris all strove to be the main distribution point from which the European demand for Asian goods was met. Exclusive control of Asian trading areas based on European colonial domination and monopolies was for the most part impractical. Europeans traded in Persia, India, China, or Japan on terms laid down by their rulers. These varied from permission to establish permanent factories and even to develop port towns under their own jurisdiction, which could be obtained in India, to living in a sealed-off ghetto in Nagasaki, which was all that the Japanese permitted to the Dutch, the only Europeans allowed any sort of access to Japan. Attempts to extract concessions by force against major Asian states seemed to be impractical, at least until mid-century. Force had, however, long been used at sea, where European gun ships had great advantages, and against the rulers of islands. The Portuguese had tried to disrupt the trade of Asian competitors by naval power from the outset. The Dutch had attacked both the Portuguese and the Asians. During the seventeenth century they had eliminated many of the Portuguese factories and had compelled the rulers of spice-producing areas to grant the Dutch company a monopoly over their harvests. The sources of the rare spices in Indonesia had passed under their control, as had some of the major pepper ports. They had established their rule on the coast of Ceylon and had intervened with military force in dynastic disputes in Java, eventually making the island's rulers tributaries of the company. Neither the British nor the French had as yet followed the Dutch example in deploying force on any scale in Asia.

The first half of the eighteenth century was a relatively stable period in European relations with maritime Asia. The overall volume of trade remained at the level attained in the late seventeenth century, when textiles first became a mass item shipped to Europe. Europeans generally kept the peace with Asians and among themselves. The Portuguese royal enterprise was underfunded by comparison with its competitors and it had been badly mauled by the Dutch. Trade between Portugal and Asia was very restricted. In Asia, however, the Portuguese presence was still a significant one. Rich settlements like Goa in western India or Macao on the China coast survived. There the Portuguese had to some extent been assimilated into Asian society by intermarriage, and considerable communities of Asian Christians had been converted by Portuguese missionaries. The Spanish presence was limited to Manila, which received cargoes of silver from across the Pacific and sent back the ships with Chinese silk and Indian cottons. The French company was a late starter, largely operating in India, where it began successfully to expand its operations from the 1720s. By 1700 the British company was coming out of the shadow of its Dutch rival. It had yielded to the Dutch in the pepper and spice trades, but had pioneered the import of Indian textiles to Europe. In the late seventeenth century there had been a massive increase in the demand for Indian cottons, which became the staple of the profitable trade of the British company. During the century the British were also to develop both the trade in tea from China and a very successful inter-Asian trade, largely in Indian commodities. The eighteenth-century Dutch company was still an impressive body, whose trade continued to grow. It dominated Indonesia by force and had an extensive network of factories throughout Asia. It was, however, over-committed to spices and pepper, for which the European demand was static by comparison with the market for textiles, and the cost of its numerous factories and armed ships was making its operations unprofitable. By the mid-eighteenth century the British were to turn the tables completely on the Dutch and win an unchallenged supremacy among Europeans in Asia.

New empires in Asia

If the first half of the eighteenth century was a period of relative stability for the Europeans in maritime Asia, it was a time of periodic war along Asia's land frontier with Europe. For contemporaries, definitions of 'Europe' and 'Asia' were not altogether clear. There was, however, an increasing consensus that Russia was a European power, whereas the Ottoman Turks were definitely Asiatic. The Turks were ceasing to be the scourge of Christian Europe that they had seemed as late as 1683 and the siege of Vienna. Although there was no clear qualitative difference between their armed forces and those of the Russians and Austrians who opposed them, they were becoming increasingly vulnerable to European armies.

Russia was exerting pressure on the Khanate of the Crimea, which under Ottoman suzerainty blocked its access to the Black Sea. The Turks won a great victory in 1711, but Russian expansion towards the Black Sea and the Caspian resumed, carried forward by a successful war in 1735–9. Further east, Russian penetration of the steppes was a less systematic process. A line of fortified posts was being constructed between the Caspian Sea and the borders of China. Beyond the posts settlers in search of new land and occasional military raids pressed southwards on the nomadic peoples of the steppes. In 1730 a section of the Kazakh people put themselves under Russian protection. Much further north the Russians had crossed Siberia with astonishing speed in the seventeenth century, establishing a trading post on the Chinese frontier, where Russian merchants bought tea for the annual caravans to take back to their homeland.

In the second half of the eighteenth century the Russians won spectacular victories in wars against the Turks, enabling them to subjugate large areas around the Black Sea and to incorporate the Crimea in 1783–4. By then, however, revolutionary changes were happening in maritime Asia, as the British launched their career as empire-builders in India.

The transformation of the British position in India was a very rapid one. In 1745 the East India Company was a thriving trading body in India in control of three now considerable port towns, Bombay, Madras, and Calcutta. In 1765 the British were the *de facto* rulers of Bengal and its adjacent provinces, containing a population thought to amount to at least twenty million people, they had acquired some territory and political dominance in the south-east of the Indian peninsula, and they were extending their influence far up the Ganges valley over the state of Awadh (Oudh).

There has for long been general agreement that these revolutionary changes can be explained by the vulnerability of India brought about by the collapse of the Mughal empire in the early eighteenth century and by the spread to India of the worldwide Anglo-French wars. There is some merit in these interpretations. The ending of Mughal power meant that India was divided into what were effectively independent states and therefore that coordinated opposition to foreign incursions, as would have been attempted in China or Japan, was now impossible. The British and French certainly exploited this situation to fight wars in southern India that with short intervals lasted from 1746 to 1761. To counter the French, the British increased the level of force available to them in India to the point where they could coerce Indians as well. Yet modern historiography finds those explanations by themselves inadequate. Mughal failure had produced not anarchy, but a series of successor states, which were consolidating themselves with some success in the eighteenth century. The first wave of conquest involved infiltration of these states rather than direct assault upon them. It is, therefore, necessary to take account of developments that made infiltration possible.

Some post-Mughal Indian states on the coast had created armies of professional soldiers and administrations that collected a high level of taxation and (not unlike European states) they relied on merchants and bankers for raising part of their revenue and for loans. European soldiers and merchants were able to participate in this new Indian world. They offered commercial opportunities to Indians and engaged in a range of financial transactions with them. The French and British East India companies backed claimants for power within the states with their small but extremely effective corps of Indian and British soldiers. The British won the greatest *coup* when they provided the strike force under Robert Clive that brought down the ruler of Bengal at the Battle of Plassey in 1757 and substituted a British satellite ruler in his place. In return for such services Europeans extracted trading concessions and large sums of money both to pay the costs of their intervention and to reward themselves personally. During the Seven Years War the gains went entirely to the British. By 1765, when the powerless Mughal emperor formally entrusted them with administrative responsibility, the British had already won control of most of the public revenue of Bengal and had greatly expanded their army.

The new British Bengal of Robert Clive and later of Warren Hastings, who held the office of Governor or Governor-General from 1772 to 1785, was built on the foundations recently laid by its independent Indian rulers. Peasants were taxed through a system of Indian intermediaries, enabling the East India Company to dispose of a state revenue already about a quarter of the size of that available to the British state at home. While the higher posts in the government came to be filled by the British members of the East India Company's new civil service, Indians continued to provide the essential expertise needed to conduct the administration. The revenue was chiefly used to pay for an army that not only defended Bengal but enabled the British to intervene in politics elsewhere and eventually to take over other Indian states.

Part of the money raised from Bengal was also used to boost the East India Company's trade. The value of British imports from Asia doubled between 1750/1 and 1772/3, as surplus taxation paid for more Indian textiles or was sent to China to boost shipments of tea. Even so, the full economic benefits of the possession of an empire in India were only slowly realized by Britain. Asia did not become a market for British exports in any way comparable to the Americas until well into the nineteenth century, while Indian textiles, the chief item that the East India Company imported throughout the eighteenth century, were increasingly having to compete with British factory-made goods. Raw materials and foodstuffs to take their place, such as cotton or sugar, could not at first compete with cheaper American sources.

British success in India was disastrous for French trade with Asia; during the late-eighteenth-century wars it was virtually closed down. British success also damaged the Dutch severely. Dutch trade with India was restricted, while their traditional strongholds in Indonesia were vulnerable to British commercial penetration in peacetime and to British attacks in war, as the Dutch Republic was forced to side with revolutionary France. By the end of the century the Dutch Company was insolvent and was wound up.

Of the two arms of the European pincer movement on Asia in the late eighteenth century, the Russians overland and the British by sea, the British were to have by far the greater impact. Russian expansion in Central Asia was still that of an unstable frontier edging forward slowly and unsystematically. In India a power with a dynamic economy and a confident belief in its capacity to improve humanity was now enabled to harness abundant local resources to its ambitions. British power and influence were quickly to spread outwards from India to the Middle East and through south-east Asia to the coast of China.

European perspectives

The benefits of expansion

The growth of European long-distance trade and empires in the eighteenth century obviously had important consequences for non-European peoples. Some profited materially from them. Even the African slave trade enriched the rulers and merchants who supplied the slaves. The trade of the East India companies similarly made fortunes for some Asian merchants, such as the Hong guild who provided tea at Canton or Indian brokers who acted for Europeans. Where Europeans assumed political control, as in the Indonesian spice islands or later in Bengal, the consequences for local merchants and producers were likely to be less benign. Five years after the British takeover, parts of Bengal were devastated by famine in 1770. While there can be no doubt of the severity of the drought that caused the harvest failure, dislocation brought about by the new regime may well have accentuated its effects,

Elsewhere, the adverse consequences are clear. Within the established American colonies Indian populations were recovering from the heavy mortalities of the past, but the living conditions and status of the mass improved little if at all. Those being exposed to new waves of European expansion in North America or Brazil suffered severely. Many Brazilian Indians were, for instance, being enslaved. Africans were enslaved in the eighteenth century on the largest scale in the whole history of the Atlantic slave trade, as the use of black slaves spread throughout the Americas. By the end of the eighteenth century new peoples were at risk. European penetration of the Pacific, following the great voyages of James Cook and Louis-Antoine de

Bougainville, brought the region's peoples into contact with new diseases. The effect was particularly severe among the Australian aborigines, following the establishment of the first British colony in New South Wales in 1788.

What inflicted serious damage on other people did not necessarily bring great benefits to Europe. The eighteenth century saw both accelerated European expansion overseas and increased economic growth in most parts of Europe, most dramatically with the beginnings of industrialization in Britain. There was, however, no simple correlation between the two. Expansion clearly helped to promote economic growth, but its role is a difficult one to unravel from many other elements,

One obvious difficulty in assessing the effect of overseas expansion on Europe is that its impact was uneven both geographically and socially. Direct involvement in oceanic trade and empire overseas was confined to western Europe. Yet even in west-European countries certain sections of society were deeply affected by it, while it impinged on others hardly at all.

Those whose lives were likely to have been most affected were those who actually went overseas. The vast majority of these crossed the Atlantic rather than going to Asia. There was virtually no demand for European labour in Asia, where Indians, Chinese, or Indonesians provided a skilled and adaptable workforce at far less cost than Europeans. The only need was for military labour, but even here local soldiers, especially Indian sepoys, were cheap and abundant. The situation was different in the Americas. Only in Mexico and Peru and partially in Brazil could native peoples be organized for labour on a large scale. Elsewhere labour had to be imported. In the seventeenth century most of the labour came from Europe. All colonies from the West Indies to Canada imported European 'servants', the largest number coming from the British Isles. In the eighteenth century, labour for the plantation belt came overwhelmingly from Africa. There was, however, still a vigorous demand for European labour in North America. Servants—that is, people bound to work for a certain period in return for their passage—were still shipped out. Others travelled on their own in search of work and land, especially to British North America after 1763, when British success in war opened up so much new land. From the beginning of the eighteenth century up to the Revolution some 220,000 British immigrants came from

Scotland and Ireland as well as from England. They were joined by about 100,000 Germans. Brazil imported slaves for its plantations but it also attracted large numbers of Portuguese emigrants, especially after the discovery of gold. Some 600,000 people may have gone from Portugal to Brazil between 1700 and 1760. They constituted the largest outflow of Europeans in the eighteenth century.

It cannot be assumed that all those who left Europe prospered. Mortality among the Portuguese in Brazil and among the soldiers who went to Asia or the West Indies was very high. In North America chances of survival were good and even convicts or servants could eventually expect land on easy terms or work at high wages in a country where labour was scarce. There were also men and women of ambition and substance who went overseas for new opportunities to better themselves. The age of great fortunes made in the Americas through plundering Indian gold and seizing huge landed estates had passed. By the eighteenth century the landholding and urban élites of North America, Mexico, or Peru mostly came from families long settled there. But there were abundant opportunities for new immigrants to make a good living in the service of the colonial governments or their armed forces, in the professions, as merchants, and as planters in the West Indies. Most eighteenth-century Spanish migrants to the Americas seem to have been such people. In Asia the East India companies offered lucrative openings, which expanded spectacularly with the British conquests. For a time India was the new frontier for quick wealth through bribes and plunder. Robert Clive, who left India worth £400,000, probably made the greatest fortune of any European to go overseas in the eighteenth century.

A huge volume of imports from outside Europe poured into European ports during the eighteenth century. The value of silver from Spanish America and gold from Brazil was greater than any other trade, but items of common consumption were imported on a very large scale as well. Sugar was the biggest of these. In the mid-eighteenth century Europe imported about 170,000 tons of sugar a year from the West Indies and Brazil. Tobacco was the most valuable North American commodity, the British colonies of Virginia and Maryland being the world's main producers. Rice, dyestuffs for the European textile industries, fish, furs, coffee, cacao, and hides were also imported across the Atlantic in large quantities. Indian cotton cloth, which had provided Europeans for the first time with a relatively cheap lightweight fabric to substitute for woollen cloth, dominated Asian imports. By the beginning of the eighteenth century the British and the Dutch East India companies were delivering over a million pieces of Indian calico to Europe. Large shipments of raw silk, tea, and coffee, as well as the traditional pepper and spices, also came from Asia.

Impressive as the quantities of imports from outside Europe undoubtedly were, they still need to be kept in proportion. An ingenious calculation has estimated that if the imports were distributed throughout the whole European population at mid-century, each person in a year might have got 3 pounds of sugar, a half pound of tobacco, and enough calico for one pocket handkerchief. Imported commodities and the benefits that the trades brought were not, however, distributed evenly throughout Europe. Colonial imports had a very large role in British and French trade. Fifty-two per cent of British imports and 47 per cent of French ones in 1772 came from Asia and the Americas, the high French proportion being a striking indication of the productive capacity of their West Indian plantations. The proportion of non-European imports for the Dutch was smaller, some 20 per cent in mid-century.

Imports from outside Europe were partly consumed within the importing country and partly re-exported throughout Europe. Mexican and Peruvian silver and Brazilian gold, sugar, and cotton flowed out of Spain and Portugal in return for imports of manufactured goods, mostly from Britain or France. The bullion then entered the money stock of other countries, as with the British sovereign made of Brazilian gold, or was shipped eastwards to pay for Asian or Baltic imports. Other countries re-exported a high proportion of the tropical commodities that they imported. The French captured most of Europe's market for sugar and coffee and the British held the largest share of its tobacco consumption. London and Amsterdam competed more or less neck-and-neck, but with an increasing lead for London, in the race to be the leading centre for the sale of Asian commodities. These movements of imported produce boosted the revenues of governments who taxed them and they enriched the merchant communities and ports that handled them. Eighteenth-century Lisbon maintained some of its old prosperity. Cadiz replaced Seville as the main Spanish port dealing with the Americas. French and British Atlantic ports, Bordeaux, Nantes, Bristol, Liverpool, and Glasgow, flourished greatly. Major financial and commercial centres such as London and Amsterdam also did well out of long-distance trades. Such prosperity had wider economic effects. Capital was accumulated for investment in the domestic economy in projects such as improved communications or the development of towns. Overseas trade stimulated banking and other financial services. Some of the wealth of the ports circulated in the hinterlands that supplied them with labour and food. Even so, the impact of rich port cities was likely to have been a limited one, even in western Europe. No part of Europe as yet depended on basic foods imported from overseas and, until the dramatic rise of cotton manufacturing in Britain at the end of the century, no industry was wholly dependent on non-European raw materials.

The strongest links between worldwide trade and European domestic economies are likely to have been provided by exports rather than by the great flows of imports. Asia remained a relatively limited market for European goods, but the American market grew greatly in the eighteenth century. The old established Spanish colonies had imported goods in return for bullion since the sixteenth century. Although Spain recovered some of it in the late eighteenth century, this trade continued to be a very valuable one for other Europeans, whether the goods passed legally through Cadiz or were smuggled directly into the Americas. The Brazil market grew in the eighteenth century, largely to the benefit of Britain. The most rapid growth, however, was in the British North American colonies, where by the second half of the century some two million relatively prosperous white consumers were buying all sorts of manufactured European goods. This again was largely to Britain's advantage. Those who seek a link between the degradation and misery inflicted on non-European people and Europe's prosperity have a case here. The capacity of North America to pay for its imports on such a scale depended to a considerable degree on its earnings from supplying the plantations of the West Indies. Those plantations depended on the enslaving of Africans. In the later eighteenth century just over half of British domestic exports were going outside Europe, rising to 70 per cent around 1800. The new cotton industry was entirely dependent for its basic raw material on non-European sources and also sold a high proportion of its finished product outside Europe. No other European country was as deeply involved as Britain. French textiles went to Spanish America and also to the Middle East, but markets outside Europe took only between 10 and 20 per cent of total French exports in the later eighteenth century.

Impressive as the figures for Britain may look, it is necessary to put them and the estimates for other countries into the context of economies that remained largely self-contained. Even for Britain, exports, to Europe as well as overseas, may have constituted no more than about 8 per cent of its national income around 1700, rising to about 16 per cent at the end of the century. For other countries the importance of overseas trade in the economy as a whole must have been even lower.

The available evidence therefore suggests that wealth generated from outside Europe cannot have been on a scale in the eighteenth century to bring about of itself transformations in the economic development of individual European countries actively engaged overseas, let alone of Europe as a whole. Individuals and communities, cities and their hinterlands, were certainly enriched greatly. Poor countries such as Spain and Portugal, however, remained poor in spite of their empires from which Europe derived most of its bullion. A great volume of trade with Asia could not prevent the erosion of Dutch manufacturing in the eighteenth century. France had a dynamic plantation economy in the Americas, but its benefits seem to have been confined to limited enclaves within the mother country. Britain had an economy already being driven forward by its agriculture, its manufacturing, and its sophisticated financial system. It was thus supremely well placed to take advantage of opportunities outside Europe, above all those created by the large-scale emigration of its own people to North America. These advantages were taken. They cannot be said to have 'caused' industrialization, but they contributed significantly towards it.

Envisaging new worlds

The process of European expansion meant that peoples outside Europe were exposed to European values as well as to the force of European arms, to European commerce, and to the effects of new crops or new diseases. The cultural exchange was not, however, all one way, although it was inevitably an unequal one. Europeans took their values overseas and, most obviously in the case of Christian missionaries, propagated them vigorously. Very few non-Europeans were in a position to propagate their values in Europe in return. Europe therefore learnt about non-European societies through other Europeans, predominantly through what they wrote about them, but also through attempts visually to represent them.

It hardly needs saying that this was an imperfect way of transmitting knowledge or that preconceptions and misunderstanding of all kinds inevitably intruded. Whatever their deficiencies, accounts of the non-European world were of great interest to educated Europeans in the eighteenth century. A huge volume of material was available. This varied from scholarly attempts to translate texts out of non-European languages or to produce self-consciously scientific accounts that can be seen as forerunners of later ethnography, through an enormous volume of impressionistic travel writing and memoirs of all sorts, to representations of stereotyped figures of 'natives' in fiction, decorations, or on the stage.

By the eighteenth century there was a long tradition of writing about non-European peoples. In the sixteenth century, Spanish clerics had published much about 'the Indies' and their peoples. In the seventeenth century, the Jesuits sent back a huge volume of accounts, notably of China and North America, which attracted much attention. Increased European diplomacy and trade also stimulated many attempts to describe the Islamic lands from the Ottoman to the Mughal empire. During the eighteenth century, British conquests in India resulted in much material being made available about Hindus, including translations from Sanskrit. Systematic expeditions of exploration, either by sea, as in the Pacific voyages, or overland, as in the journeys into Siberia of Peter Pallas, the German naturalist in Russian employment, were characteristic of the later eighteenth century. The dispatch of a large body of scholars and scientists with the French army to Egypt in 1798 was the greatest of such endeavours. Expeditions were instructed to make surveys, to collect specimens and scientific data, and to record precise information about peoples. They were strongly influenced by the Enlightenment assumptions that were evident in so much writing about the non-European world—that is, that a scientific approach was appropriate to human as well as to natural phenomena. Careful study of human beings in all their variety would make it possible to compare societies and to deduce certain principles about humanity in general.

The effect on Europe of increasing knowledge of non-European societies is a highly controversial topic. On the one hand, awareness of the diversity of humanity could pose challenges to European self-confidence. European religion, ways of living, or art could be shown neither to be unique nor necessarily to have universal validity. On the other hand, Europeans collected the data and set the terms of comparison with other people. They therefore tended to assume that Europe was the norm and to measure other people by the degree to which they conformed to that norm. In their depiction of non-European peoples, eighteenth-century Europeans are now often said to have helped to define Europe in terms such as 'advanced' or 'rational' against the non-European 'other', which was 'backward', emotional, and incapable of reason. Opprobrious terms for other people, such as 'barbarian' or 'heathen', are ancient in European languages, but it is sometimes argued that the Enlightenment with its claims to scientific exactitude endowed prejudice with an apparent objectivity and that this has set the terms for the way in which 'the West' has tried to order and intellectually to dominate the world ever since. At their crudest, Enlightenment views of European superiority are accused of providing the rationale for colonialism.

Holding up the non-European mirror to Europe did not always show Europe in a flattering light. Unflattering comparisons were in part a deliberate ploy by those disaffected with contemporary Europe. Religious freethinkers delighted to compare what they regarded as Christian bigotry and priestcraft with the reason and tolerance of Chinese Confucianism or of philosophical Brahmins. This was a tactic particularly favoured by Voltaire. Critics of the arbitrary practices of European rulers and of their predilection for war compared them with Chinese emperors who single-mindedly pursued the public good. Those who disliked the artificiality of contemporary manners invoked 'noble savages' in North America or the Pacific as models for an alternative lifestyle. What were called 'Chinoiserie' styles of alleged Asian designs were in vogue for those who wanted a lighter alternative to the formality of baroque or neoclassicism.

All this was based on at best a very superficial awareness of non-European cultures. A deeper awareness could, however, produce genuinely creative responses. Serious study of the texts and myths of other religions alongside those of Christianity might or might not be subversive of orthodox Christian beliefs, but it enhanced some

Europeans' understanding of the phenomenon of religion far beyond the crude iconoclasm of Voltaire. This deeper understanding of religion was part of what has been called 'the oriental renaissance', Europe's response to Hindu and Buddhist texts. These are said to have been most influential in early nineteenth-century France and Germany and to have had a profound effect on German idealism and on European romanticism in general.

There was a radical edge to the Enlightenment view of the world that stressed essential similarities across humanity as a whole. If all men were essentially similar, then principles of common humanity and basic human rights must be applied to the victims of European conquests and above all to those that were being enslaved to maintain the labour force for colonial economies. For the radicals, the expansion of Europe was a record of crimes and these crimes were getting progressively more heinous. The fullest expression of this view was the *Histoire philosophique et politique des deux Indes* (*The Philosophical and Political History of the East and West Indies*) of the Abbé Guillaume-Thomas Raynal, the first version of which appeared in 1770 and whose later editions included contributions by the great *philosophe* Denis Diderot. Denunciation of slavery and the slave trade in France was a more or less élite cause. In Britain it was a popular one, being inspired there less by a secular than by a Christian sense of common humanity and obligation to God's fellow creatures.

If the Enlightenment helped to undermine European acceptance of slavery, its later critics who have seen it as generally reinforcing a European sense of superiority over non-European peoples have some justification. Europeans in earlier centuries had seen themselves as distinguished by being the custodians of Christian truth. For eighteenth-century Europeans that was still the case, but, for west-European intellectuals at least, Europe enjoyed an eminence over the rest of the world for secular reasons as well. It was becoming increasingly common to compare different societies by trying to assess their position on a scale of evolution that was deemed to have universal applicability. The highest point on the scale was occupied by 'commercial' societies. European societies were at the commercial stage and indeed progressing towards ever greater refinement, whereas Asian societies, such as India or China, were deemed to be failed commercial societies, ceasing to make progress. Other non-European societies were yet to attain that stage; they were agriculturists, pastoralists, or hunters (colloquially 'savages'). European superiority over them was based not merely on their economic capacity, but on their rationality, their political arrangements, and their military power. Although this conclusion was rarely stated explicitly, such a degree of superiority could be seen as constituting a claim to exercise authority over other people. Enlightened writers often criticized existing empires for their abuses. Reforming ministers tried to reinvigorate their empires by rationalizing administration, moderating the evils of slavery, and substituting free trade for monopoly and blatant exploitation. Such programmes were not intended to bring about the end of empires. Only a tiny minority wanted that.

The eighteenth-century expansion of Europe gave its intellectuals much new and striking material about other human beings. 'I have always thought', wrote Edmund Burke in 1777, 'that we possess at this time very great advantages towards the knowledge of human Nature. . . . Now the Great Map of mankind is unrolld at once; and there is no state or Gradation of barbarism, and no mode of refinement which we have not at the same instant under our View.' Yet it would be difficult to argue that this great abundance of material fundamentally altered European views of the world. Rather it served to reinforce existing ones. Europeans' sense of their own superiority was not seriously challenged, even if the range of European thought and European art and literature was enriched at the margins.

This also seems to have been characteristic of the economic impact of worldwide expansion during the eighteenth-century. Wealth was generated in abundance for certain groups within European society. These riches did not, however, transform the balance of wealth or of power among the European nations. It could not lift Spain and Portugal into the first rank of states nor prevent the decline of the Dutch. When France resumed its dominant role in Europe in the revolutionary and Napoleonic period, its immensely valuable colonial possessions were no longer available. Britain was the great gainer outside Europe, but these gains went to strengthen what was already the most advanced economy in Europe

If Europe was not transformed by its activities overseas in the eighteenth century, this does not mean that those activities have not left a deep and enduring mark on the world. Nearly seven million

Africans taken across the Atlantic bore that mark. The legacies of the eighteenth century include both the emergence of the United States of America, shortly to be followed by the Latin American republics, and the beginning of the greatest of all European colonial ventures, the subjugation of India by Britain with all its implications for the rest of Asia and later for Africa.

Conclusion: the French Revolution and beyond

T. C. W. Blanning

The very words 'French Revolution' and 'Napoleon' conjure up a world of movement, violence, excitement, and heroism. The storming of the Bastille, the executioner holding aloft the guillotined head of Louis XVI, Bonaparte at the bridge of Arcole, Nelson dying on *HMS Victory*, the Old Guard shouting defiance at Waterloo—the images of action crowd in with an evocative power matched by few episodes before the horrors of the twentieth century. So many of the signs and symbols that make up the modern semiosphere stem from this period: flags, such as the tricolour for France (the red and blue colours of Paris separated by the white of the Bourbons), or the black–red–gold for Germany (the colours of the Lützow Freikorps' uniforms); headgear, such as the Phrygian cap of liberty for the revolutionaries, or the floppy black berets of their German opponents; decorations, such as the Légion d'Honneur (instituted by Bonaparte in 1802), or the Iron Cross (instituted by Frederick William III of Prussia in 1813); even monumental architecture, such as the Arc de Triomphe, begun in 1806, or the Brandenburg Gate, completed in 1791.

Nor should these signs be confined to visual artefacts. They should also include linguistic symbols, such as 'left' and 'right' (which derived from the seating arrangements in the National Assembly), 'Jacobin' and 'Girondin', 'sans-culotte' and 'chouan'. They should also include the political concepts that were turned into slogans for mass consumption, such as 'liberty, equality and fraternity', 'unity and indivisibility', 'the fatherland in danger', 'liberty or death', 'war to the châteaux, peace to the cottages'. They could also be set to music, as in the revolutionary '*Ça ira!*' ('It'll be OK') or '*La Marseillaise*' (whose original title—'Battle-Hymn of the Army of the Rhine'—also reveals its origins) and the counter-revolutionary '*Réveil du peuple*' ('Awakening of the People') or '*Richard, o mon roi!*' ('Richard, oh my King!'). Moreover, all these semiotic codes were bound together to form political myths of enduring power, such as the revolutionary volunteers stopping the Prussian invaders in their tracks at Valmy in the autumn of 1792, prompting no less a spectator than Goethe to observe to his companions that 'a new epoch in the history of the world' was beginning before their very eyes, or the Prussians' War of Liberation against their French occupiers in 1813 when 'the King called and all came running'.

The counterpoint to all this frenetic activity was formed by the ponderous pace of change in other, more impersonal fields of human activity. As we have seen, in economics the current historiographical emphasis is all on continuity. Change there was, in all sectors, but it was slow in pace and uneven in distribution. The 'agricultural revolution', the 'commercial revolution', and the 'industrial revolution' all turn out to owe more to conceptual neatness than to empirical data. As Sheilagh Ogilvie concludes, even the newest addition to the revolutionary vocabulary—'the industrious revolution'—was 'evolutionary rather than revolutionary, and far from universal throughout Europe'. The French Revolution and Napoleon did little, if anything, to accelerate the pace of economic change, not even in France. The verdict of William Doyle in *The Old European Order* was bluntly unequivocal: 'economically the Revolution was a disaster for France.'

Nor did it seem to do much to hasten social change. In his chapter, Christof Dipper identifies as the main sources of dynamism the irresistible increase in population and the rather less inevitable expansion of the market. Yet for most Europeans, including the French, the Revolution's impact came in the shape of almost continuous warfare between 1792 and 1815, which had a negative effect on both, by killing large numbers of people and disrupting markets. It is estimated that the wars cost France alone 1.4 million casualties, while its overseas commerce was virtually eliminated by British maritime supremacy. According to the figures of Jacques Dupâquier, France emerged in 1815 with a low male/female ratio (down to 0.857 from 0.992 in 1790) and a falling share of Europe's population. The Marxist–Leninist view that the French Revolution was the explosive culmination of a long process that made the bourgeoisie 'the mistress of the world' (Albert Soboul) is difficult to sustain when the performance of the seat of revolution is compared with other countries. In the course of the nineteenth century, France fell behind the USA, Germany, Austria–Hungary, and Russia in terms of population; was overtaken by the USA, Germany, and Great Britain in terms of industrial production and in terms of income *per capita* by Switzerland, The Netherlands, Belgium, Scandinavia, and several parts of the British Empire as well. Moreover, it has become something of a truism to observe that France after 1815 was run by the same sort of mixed élite of noble and commoner *notables* as had ruled the roost before 1789.

In two senses, however, the revolutionary experience did have a major impact on Europe's economy and society. In the first place, it led to a massive increase in the pretensions and power of the state. The need to raise, finance, and motivate armies and navies of unprecedented size forced even the more conservative regimes both to expand their bureaucracies and to use them more intrusively. In Prussia, the best but not the only example, this military imperative created a reform movement whose achievements were flawed but real. Sheilagh Ogilvie has stressed that industrialization needed a strong state to overcome privilege and Christof Dipper has identified the state as the main enemy of the society of orders, so this was a development with important social implications. Secondly, the French Revolution created a social vocabulary with political consequences. It was after 1789 that words such as 'bourgeois' and 'aristocrat' took on their modern meanings. The linguistic ammunition for the great debates of the nineteenth century was manufactured by the French revolutionaries—and their opponents.

A similarly mixed legacy can be found in European culture. Louis Réau believed that, for the historian of art, the significance of 1789 was 'almost zero'. Neither of the dominant tendencies (in both cases, 'movement' would be too exclusive a word) in the visual arts— neoclassicism and Romanticism—derived from the events of 1789–1815. The style of Jacques-Louis David, the neoclassicist and revolutionary artist *par excellence*, was formed in the academies of the old regime. His two greatest history paintings—*The Oath of the Horatii* and *Lictors bringing to Brutus the Bodies of his Sons*, painted in 1784 and 1789 respectively—were pre-revolutionary. So were the defining moments in the development of Romanticism, such as Rousseau's moment of inspiration on his walk to Vincennes in 1749, Horace Walpole's nightmare in 1765, or Goethe's encounter with Strasbourg cathedral in 1770. The most radical architecture was already in place by 1789, in the shape of Claude-Nicolas Ledoux's *barrières*, the customs houses built around Paris in the 1780s for the 'General Farm', the old regime's detested tax collection agency. They were promptly demolished by the revolutionaries, who in general destroyed more buildings than they erected.

The Revolution certainly politicized art, most brutally during the Terror, when the Opéra's repertoire, for example, was purged of any works that portrayed kings in a favourable light or were in any way offensive to republicans. That meant, of course, the prohibition of virtually all *opera seria*, including such apparently innocuous works as Gluck's *Iphigénie en Aulide*. It was a policy that reached its *reductio ad absurdum* when the actor Arouch was guillotined for calling out on stage 'Long live our noble King!', even though he was simply following the script of Calderón's *Life is a Dream*, written in 1635. It proved easier to exclude than to create: the number of overtly revolutionary works in any genre to have stood the test of time is very small. Only David's secular pietá *À Marat*, painted as a memorial to his dead friend, springs readily to mind. At the close of his substantial study *A Cultural History of the French Revolution*, Emmet Kennedy concluded starkly: 'The Revolution did not leave a culture of its own behind largely because it negated the culture of the old regime rather than creating a new one.' Opponents of French military expansion were rather more productive. In paintings such as Goya's *The Execution of the Third of May 1808*, dramas such as Heinrich von Kleist's *Hermann's Battle*, poems such as Körner's *Lützow's Wild, Audacious Pursuit*, and even musical compositions such as Beethoven's 'Battle' Symphony, hatred of French hegemony found durable expression.

But culture, of course, is not just about individual works of art. Taking the long view, we can see that the upheaval of 1789–1815 left a deep imprint on both institutions and values, intensifying existing forces and initiating new. In particular, it gave a massive impetus to secularization. The vitality of religion and its undimmed power to mobilize support were demonstrated again and again during the revolutionary–Napoleonic period, by the rising in the Vendée in 1793, by the reconquest of Naples by Cardinal Ruffo and his *armata cristiana* in 1799, by the militancy of the clergy of Spain in 1808 and of the Tyrol in 1809, and so on. Yet, relatively speaking, religion and the churches were pushed away from the centre. If it was a movement of long standing, dating back at least to the Reformation, it was greatly accelerated by the Revolution. In one country after another, material expropriation and ideological challenge negated the churches' claim to axiomatic pre-eminence and relegated them to being just another set of interest groups: very important interest groups certainly, but interest groups just the same. Into the space they vacated, there moved secular voluntary associations and, above all, the state. It was a development that brought the sacralization of culture as a secular substitute for revealed religion, expressed visually in the creation of temple-like museums, art galleries, theatres, opera houses, and concert halls. In the sonorous words of Schiller: 'The temples remained sacred to the eye of the beholder long after their Gods had become figures of fun. The lost dignity of mankind was redeemed by art and has been preserved in architecture.'

This process both drove and was driven by politics. After a brief honeymoon period, when it greeted the Revolution with *Te deums*, the Catholic Church adopted an oppositional stance as fierce as it was implacable. So the new state responded by abandoning the traditional trappings of legitimacy and inventing its own secular substitutes. In the place of the cross it adopted the liberty tree, in the place of the confraternity it instituted the political club, in the place of the pilgrimage it organized the political march, in the place of the creed it imposed the oath to liberty, equality, and fraternity, in the place of the church service it introduced the political rally. The political process was both secularized and sacralized, reaching a climax with the great festivals of year II (1793–4) when Robespierre and his 'pageant master' David assembled huge crowds on the Champs de Mars for collective acts of secular worship. These looked forward not so much to the popular demonstrations of the nineteenth century as to the totalitarian rallies of the twentieth.

They also announced the arrival of a new kind of legitimacy. Of course other regimes had incorporated popular participation of some kind into their constitutions, notably Britain, Switzerland, and the city republics of the Holy Roman Empire, but all had also relied heavily on tradition too. None, not even the newly independent United States of America, believed that their arrangements could or should be exported to the rest of the world. It was the rational universalism of the French Revolution that made it so novel and so alarming. Its seminal document, the Declaration of the Rights of Man and the Citizen of 26 August 1789, addressed *all* men and *all* citizens, not just those residing in France. In the years that followed, the revolutionary regimes became increasingly nationalist, as most Europeans failed to respond with sufficient enthusiasm to their appeals, and increasingly authoritarian, as many French failed to respond with sufficient enthusiasm to their appeals, but the principle of popular sovereignty remained as the bedrock of the new regime's legitimacy and its most durable achievement. So many French people participated directly in politics after 1789, voting in elections, joining clubs, going on demonstrations, attending pageants, that any future return to the divine-right authoritarianism of the old regime could only be temporary. As Lynn Hunt concluded in her influential study *Politics, Culture and Class in the French Revolution:* 'The chief accomplishment of the French Revolution was the institution of a dramatically new political culture . . . Revolution in France contributed little to economic growth or to political stabilisation. What it did establish was the mobilising potential of democratic republicanism and the compelling intensity of revolutionary change.'

For international politics, popular sovereignty implied both national sovereignty and self-determination. As principles justified by reason and nature, they took precedence over such historical considerations as prescription (in this sense meaning 'uninterrupted use or possession since time immemorial') and treaty rights. Their explosive potential appeared to be realized in November 1792, when the National Assembly's Edict of Fraternity promised assistance to 'any people seeking to regain its liberty'. Yet this proved to be only a very brief phase in the history of the Revolution's relations with the rest of the world. Within six months, the reluctance of those other peoples to be forced to be free and military problems combined to prompt an about-turn towards 'France first' and 'Revolution in one country' in a manner later repeated by the Bolsheviks. For the rest of Europe, it was not French principles but French power, delivered in the unattractive shape of the French army, that was the transmitter of the Revolution. The experience generated a counter-nationalism that provided popular support for conservative regimes, especially in Britain, Belgium, Spain, and Germany.

The massive expansion unleashed by the Revolution's liberation of the state was exemplified by the declaration of total war on 23 August 1793 (often referred to inadequately as the *levée en masse*), when every living creature and inanimate object was conscripted for the war effort. The result was the largest armed force hitherto assembled in Europe—probably comprising 800,000 men, perhaps as many as a million. With it the French were able to conquer western, southern, and central Europe, experiencing downs as well as ups but winning all the decisive battles on land. In the process, they destroyed the Holy Roman Empire, that undynamic but by no means moribund polity that had held together the German-speaking peoples for the best part of a millennium. Yet, although the revolutionaries brought to the conduct of international relations a new energy and ruthlessness, they did not change its essence. Like the old regime powers, they were still operating within a traditional balance-of-power culture characterized by predatory expansion. It was only when Napoleon injected such a dysfunctional degree of aggression that the system could change. At long last, the old regime powers began to see that only a fundamental change of attitude towards each other and the way they resolved their disputes could save them from further self-destructive laceration. It was a conversion that was to lead to almost a century of peace, punctuated only by conflicts that were as short as they were infrequent.

Paradoxically, the great victories achieved by the armies of the Revolution and Napoleon brought to a spectacular end almost two centuries of French hegemony in Europe. With insufficient resources to achieve terrestrial and maritime supremacy simultaneously, the French gave the British an opportunity to establish hegemony overseas that they were quick to seize. By 1815 the British had established such a lead that they could not be challenged, let alone caught. General Bonaparte's attempt to redress the balance with his Egyptian expedition in 1798 not only ended in disaster, it also brought Russia into the war for the first time, and with almost fatal consequences. On the continent, Bonaparte's vaulting ambition imposed such a degree of overexertion that every success he gained served only to make his eventual collapse more certain. France emerged from the debris of his empire still a great power, not least because of the sensible moderation of the victors, but the writing was on the wall for those who could read it. In particular, the destruction of the Holy Roman Empire was a massive step towards the eventual unification of Germany. As the next volume in this series will demonstrate, in 1815 France's day was done and the century of Britain and Germany was beginning.

Further Reading

Politics

On Britain, H. T. Dickinson, *The Politics of the People in Eighteenth-century Britain* (London, 1995), and F. O'Gorman, *Voters, Patrons and Parties: The Unreformed Electoral System of Hanoverian England, 1734–1832* (Oxford, 1989), provide stimulating and often controversial introductions to British politics. For France, a combination of James B. Collins, *The State in Early Modern France* (Cambridge, 1995), Daniel Roche, *France in the Enlightenment* (Cambridge, Mass., 1998), W. Doyle, *The Oxford History of the French Revolution* (Oxford, 1989), and Geoffrey Ellis, *The Napoleonic Empire* (London, 1990), should be consulted. Jonathan Israel, *The Dutch Republic: Its Rise, Greatness, and Fall, 1477–1806* (Oxford, 1995), is a mine of information. On Germany and the Habsburg Monarchy, see John Gagliardo, *Germany under the Old Regime 1600–1790* (London, 1991), Charles Ingrao, *The Habsburg Monarchy 1618–1815* (Cambridge, 1994), and T. C. W. Blanning, *Joseph II* (London, 1994). On Poland, the most authoritative account is now J. Lukowski, *Liberty's Folly: The Polish–Lithuanian Commonwealth in the Eighteenth Century, 1697–1795* (London, 1991). The best history of Sweden in the period is Michael Roberts, *The Age of Liberty: Sweden, 1719–1772* (Cambridge, 1986). On Russia, three distinguished works are Simon Dixon, *The Modernisation of Russia 1676–1825* (Cambridge, 1999), Lindsey Hughes, *Russia in the Age of Peter the Great* (New Haven, 1998), and Isabel de Madariaga, *Russia in the Age of Catherine the Great* (London, 1981). H. M. Scott (ed.), *Enlightened Absolutism* (London, 1990), contains a collection of stimulating essays on an important subject, including good essays on Italy and Spain.

Society

An excellent general survey of the nobility is Jonathan Dewald, *The European Nobility 1500–1800* (Cambridge, 1996). More specialized are the articles in H. M. Scott (ed.), *The European Nobilities in the Seventeenth and Eighteenth Centuries*, 2 vols. (London, 1995). Controversial but concise and stimulating is Guy Chaussinand-Nogaret, *The French Nobility in the Eighteenth Century: From Feudalism to Enlightenment* (Cambridge, 1985). On the urban world, see Jan de Vries, *European Urbanisation 1500–1800* (London, 1984). Good on the peasantry are Tom Scott (ed.), *The Peasantries of Europe: From the Fourteenth to the Eighteenth Centuries* (London, 1998), P. M. Jones, *The Peasantry in the French Revolution* (Cambridge, 1988), and Richard J. Evans and W. R. Lee (eds.), *The German Peasantry: Conflict and Community in Rural Society from the Eighteenth to the Twentieth Centuries* (London, 1986). On the large and growing underclass, see Olwen Hufton's classic study *The Poor of 18th Century France* (Oxford, 1974). On the peasantry of Russia and much else besides, the standard work is now Janet M. Hartley, *A Social History of the Russian Empire 1650–1825* (London, 1999). On Germany, see Eda Sagarra, *A Social History of Germany 1648–1914* (London, 1977). On Italy, there is Stuart Woolf, *A History of Italy 1700–1860: The Social Constraints of Political Change* (London, 1979). On the more advanced societies of western Europe, see John Brewer and Roy Porter, *Consumption and the World of Goods: Consumption and Society in the Eighteenth Century* (London, 1993), and Roy Porter, *English Society in the Eighteenth Century* (London, 1982). On gender issues and the role of women, there is an excellent general account in Merry E. Wiesner, *Women and Gender in Early Modern Europe* (Cambridge, 1995), and a more substantial treatment in Olwen Hufton, *The Prospect before her: A History of Women in Western Europe*, i. *1500–1800* (London, 1995).

The Economy

On the pre-industrial European economy, the best general textbook is still Jan de Vries, *The Economy of Europe in an Age of Crisis, 1600–1750* (Cambridge, 1976), which has a particularly good discussion of agriculture in chapter 2. For an up-to-date survey of research over the intervening two decades, engagingly presented, see Robert S. DuPlessis, *Transitions to Capitalism in Early Modern Europe* (Cambridge, 1997). A rare central and east European emphasis is provided in Peter Kriedte, *Peasants, Landlords and Merchant Capitalists: Europe and the World Economy, 1500–1800* (Leamington Spa, 1983; German original, 1980). On the European economies during industrialization, a classical perspective is provided by the chapters by experts on various European economies in Carlo M. Cipolla (ed.), *The Fontana Economic History of Europe*, iii. *The Industrial Revolution* (London, 1973). For an alternative approach, which focuses on regions rather than nation states, see Sidney Pollard, *Peaceful Conquest: The Industrialisation of Europe 1760–1970* (Oxford, 1981). On European agriculture, there is still no general work to rival the magisterial survey by B. H. Slicher van Bath, *The Agrarian History of Western Europe, A.D. 500–1850* (London, 1963; Dutch original, 1959). On European industry before the factory, with chapters on most parts of the continent, see Sheilagh Ogilvie and Markus Cerman (eds.), *European Proto-Industrialisation* (Cambridge, 1996). On the 'first' (i.e. British) Industrial Revolution, see Roderick Floud and Donald McCloskey (eds.), *The Economic History of Britain since 1700*, i. *1700–1860* (2nd rev. edn., Cambridge, 1994), and Joel Mokyr (ed.), *The British Industrial Revolution: An Economic Perspective* (Boulder, Colo., 1993), especially the excellent 'Editor's Introduction'. On long-distance trade, see Ralph Davis, *The Rise of the Atlantic Economies*

(London, 1973). An economist's treatment of finance, which sets the changes of the eighteenth century in the context of developments between the medieval period and the twentieth century, is Charles B. Kindelberger, *A Financial History of Western Europe* (London, 1984). On the transformation of the European urban system, the basic work is J. De Vries, *European Urbanisation 1500–1800* (Cambridge, Mass., 1984).

Religion and culture

The best general account of religion in the eighteenth century is now W. R. Ward, *Christianity during the Old Regime* (Cambridge, 1999), which is especially good on Protestantism. On the Catholic Church, see also R. Po-Chia Hsia, *The World of Catholic Renewal 1540–1770* (Cambridge, 1998), and John McManners, *Church and Society in Eighteenth Century France*, 2 vols. (Oxford, 1998). On religion during the revolutionary–Napoleonic period, see Owen Chadwick, *The Popes and European Revolution* (Oxford, 1981), and T. C. W. Blanning, 'The Role of Religion in European Counter-Revolution, 1789–1815', in Derek Beales and Geoffrey Best (eds.), *History, Society and the Churches: Essays in Honour of Owen Chadwick* (Cambridge, 1985). Difficult but rewarding is the immensely influential book by Jürgen Habermas, *The Structural Transformation of the Public Sphere: An Inquiry into a Category of Bourgeois Society* (Cambridge, 1989). A more accessible collection on the same theme is Craig Calhoun (ed.), *Habermas and the Public Sphere* (Cambridge, Mass., 1992). On the Enlightenment, the best introduction is Dorinda Outram, *The Enlightenment* (Cambridge, 1995), which has a good bibliography. It should be complemented by Roy Porter and Mikulas Teich (eds.), *The Enlightenment in National Context* (Cambridge, 1981). One of the best books on French culture in the period is the unjustly neglected J. Lough, *An Introduction to Eighteenth Century France* (London, 1960). Dena Goodman's *The Republic of Letters: A Cultural History of the French Enlightenment* (Ithaca, NY, 1994), is excellent on the social context, stressing especially the crucial role played by women. The best introductions to the visual arts of the eighteenth century are Matthew Craske, *Art in Europe 1700–1830* (Oxford, 1997), Michael Levey, *Rococo to Revolution: Major Trends in 18th Century Painting* (1966), and Hugh Honour, *Neo-Classicism* (Pelican, 1968); of architecture, David Watkin, *A History of Western Architecture* (2nd edn., London, 1996); of music, Neil Zaslaw, *Man and Music: The Classical Era. From the 1740s to the End of the Eighteenth Century* (London, 1989), and Giorgio Pestelli, *The Age of Mozart and Beethoven* (Cambridge, 1984). On the baroque, the best introduction is John Rupert Martin, *Baroque* (London, 1977). The astonishing surge of German cultural activity is described by Victor Lange, *The Classical Age of German Literature 1740–1815* (London, 1982). A distinguished introduction to the popular culture of the period is Peter Burke, *Popular Culture in Early*

Modern Europe (London, 1978), and see also R. W. Scribner, *Popular Religion in Germany and Central Europe* (London, 1996).

War and international relations

Geoffrey Parker, *The Military Revolution: Military Innovation and the Rise of the West, 1500–1800*, (2nd edn., Cambridge, 1996), is a very important study that set off a virtual industry of works on the military revolution, subject to some criticism but of great value. In *The Rise of the Great Powers, 1648–1815* (London, 1983), Derek McKay and H. M. Scott, provide a highly valuable, well-balanced introductory diplomatic history. John A. Lynn, *The Wars of Louis XIV, 1667–1714* (Harlow, Essex, 1999), is the only military history of these wars as a whole available. M. S. Anderson, *The War of the Austrian Succession, 1740–1748* (Harlow, Essex, 1995), is essentially a diplomatic history of this convoluted war, with little military detail. Paul Kennedy, *The Rise and Fall of British Naval Mastery* (London, 1976), is a good introduction to British naval history, although it extends well beyond this period. T. C. W. Blanning's two complementary studies *The Origins of the French Revolutionary Wars* (London, 1986) and *The French Revolutionary Wars, 1787–1802* (London, 1996), provide a broadly conceived and authoritative diplomatic and military history of these crucial conflicts. Jean-Paul Bertaud, *The Army of the French Revolution: From Citizen-Soldiers to Instruments of Power* (Princeton, 1988), is the finest single volume on the army of revolutionary France. T. C. W. Blanning, *The French Revolution in Germany* (Oxford, 1983), charts the destructive impact of the French armies and the resistance they encountered. David Chandler, *The Campaigns of Napoleon* (London, 1966), is still the best detailed picture of Napoleon as a general, although it should be used with care. Paul W. Schroeder, *The Transformation of European Politics, 1763–1848* (Oxford, 1994), is the new classic on the history of international relations in this period with a profoundly thought-provoking approach and towers above the rest.

Europe and the rest of the world

J. H. Parry, *Trade and Dominion: The European Overseas Empires in the Eighteenth Century* (London, 1971), is a useful general account. There are valuable chapters on eighteenth-century Spanish and Portuguese America in vols. i and ii of Leslie Bethell (ed.), *Cambridge History of Latin America*, 11 vols. (Cambridge, 1984–95). Stuart B. Schwartz and James Lockhart, *Early Spanish America* (New York, 1983), is an overview. A succinct introduction to the West Indies, the 'plantation belt', and the slave trade is Philip D. Curtin, *The Rise and Fall of the Plantation Complex: Essays in Atlantic History* (Cambridge, 1990). Among many introductory accounts of British North America are

John J. McCusker and Russell Menard, *The Economy of British America, 1607–1789* (Chapel Hill, NY, 1985), and Gary B. Nash, *Red, White, and Black. The Peoples of Early North America* (3rd edn., Englewood Cliffs, NJ, 1992). Holden Furber, *Rival Empires of Trade in the Orient, 1600–1800* (Minneapolis, 1976), deals with the trade of the East India companies. C. A. Bayly, *Indian Society and the Making of the British Empire*, and P. J. Marshall, *Bengal: The British Bridgehead, Eastern India, 1740–1828 (The New Cambridge History of India*, pt. II vols. i and ii; Cambridge, 1987–8) describe the making of the new British Indian Empire. For the movement of people, see Nicholas Canny (ed.), *Europeans on the Move: Studies on European Migration* (Oxford, 1994). Two valuable collections of essays on the economic consequences of overseas expansion are Hans Pohl (ed.), *The European Discovery of the World and its Economic Effects on Pre-Industrial Society, 1500–1800* (Stuttgart, 1990), and James D. Tracy (ed.), *The Rise of the Merchant Empires: Long-Distance Trade in the Early Modern World 1350–1750* (Cambridge, 1990). Europe's cultural engagement with the world is assessed from the British point of view in P. J. Marshall and Clyndwr Williams, *The Great Map of Mankind: British Perceptions of the World in the Age of Enlightenment* (London, 1982). Edward Said, *Orientalism* (London, 1978), is a very influential general account. Anthony Pagden, *European Encounters with the New World: From Renaissance to Romanticism* (New Haven, 1993), has a chapter on the Enlightenment.

Chronology: the 'Long Eighteenth Century', 1688–1815

(See also Table 5.1, Wars of the European Powers, 1700–1815.)

1688 The 'Glorious Revolution' in England deposes James II.
The Nine Years War begins.

1689 Tsar Peter I ('the Great') seizes power in Russia.

1690 William III of England defeats James II at the Battle of the Boyne.
John Locke, *An Essay Concerning Human Understanding* and *Two Treatises on Government*.

1693–5 First Brazilian gold strike.

1694 Bank of England founded.
University of Halle founded.

1696 Peter the Great captures Azov from the Turks.

1697 Augustus, Elector of Saxony, is elected King of Poland.
Austrian army commanded by Prince Eugene defeats the Turks at Zenta; reconquest of Hungary completed.
Treaty of Ryswick ends the Nine Years War.
Pierre Bayle, *Historical and Critical Dictionary*.
Consecration of St Paul's Cathedral, London.

1699 Peace of Karlowitz ends war between Austria and the Turks.

1700 Great Northern War begins.
Death of Charles II of Spain.

1701	Act of Settlement establishing Hanoverian succession in England.
	War of the Spanish Succession begins.
	Elector Frederick III of Brandenburg becomes King Frederick I of Prussia.
1702	First national daily newspaper founded in England.
1703	Peter the Great founds St Petersburg.
1704	Battle of Blenheim.
1707	Union of England and Scotland.
1708	Vauban, *Projet d'une dixième royale.*
1709	Peter the Great defeats Charles XII of Sweden at the Battle of Poltava.
	Battle of Malplaquet.
	Louis XIV suppresses the Jansenist convent of Port-Royal.
	Darby produces coke-smelted cast iron at Coalbrooke in Shropshire.
1709–10	Meissen porcelain manufactory established in Saxony.
1711	Shaftesbury, *Characteristicks of Men, Manners, Opinions, Times.*
	Exterior of the Palace of Schönbrunn completed.
1712	Newcomen develops the first commercially successful steam engine (used in coal mines).
1713	Treaty of Utrecht: Britain makes territorial gains in North America and West Indies and acquires the right to supply slaves to Spanish empire.
	The papal bull *Unigenitus* condemns Jansenism.

1714	Treaty of Rastatt ends the War of the Spanish Succession.
	Death of Queen Anne; succession to the English throne of the Elector of Hanover as George I.
1715	Death of Louis XIV.
1715–16	Failed Jacobite rising in Britain.
1716	War between Austria and the Turks.
	Corps des Ingénieurs des Ponts et Chaussées begins to develop the French road system to be the finest in Europe.
1717	Establishment of the first Grand Lodge in London begins the modern history of Freemasonry.
1718	Death of Charles XII; beginning of Swedish 'Age of Liberty'.
	Murder of Tsarevich Alexei of Russia.
	Treaty of Passarowitz ends war between Austria and the Turks.
1719	Defoe, *Robinson Crusoe.*
1721	Treaty of Nystad ends the Great Northern War.
	Montesquieu, *Persian Letters.*
	Russian edict makes it possible to assign groups (or entire villages) of serfs to certain factories.
1723	Frederick William I of Prussia establishes the General Directory.
1725	Death of Peter the Great.
	Vico, *New Science.*
	Blenheim Palace completed.
1726	Swift, *Gulliver's Travels.*
1729	J. S. Bach, *St Matthew Passion.*

1730	Failed attempt to impose accession charter on Empress Anna of Russia.
	Russian protectorate declared over part of Kazakhs.
	The papal bull against Jansenism *Unigenitus* is incorporated in French law.
1731	Protestants expelled from Salzburg emigrate to Prussia.
	Holy Roman Empire issues law trying to restrict guild powers (proves largely ineffectual).
1732	Hogarth, *A Rake's Progress*.
1733	War of the Polish Succession begins.
	Frederick William I of Prussia introduces the 'canton system' of conscription.
	Pergolesi, *La serva padrona*.
	Alexander Pope, *An Essay on Man*.
	Kay's flying shuttle doubles woollen weavers' output.
1734	Voltaire, *Lettres philosophiques*.
1736–9	War between Russia, Austria, and the Turks.
1738	John Wesley's conversion experience begins the history of Methodism.
1739	Beginning of Anglo-Spanish war in Caribbean.
1740	Deaths of Charles VI, Frederick William I, and the Tsarina Anna.
	Frederick II invades Silesia; War of the Austrian Succession begins.
	Richardson, *Pamela*.
1741	Handel, *Messiah*.
1742	Treaty of Breslau ends the First Silesian War between Prussia and Austria.

1743	Paul's spinning machine is first used with water power.
1745	Treaty of Dresden ends the Second Silesian War between Prussia and Austria. Battle of Fontenoy.
1745–6	Failed Jacobite rebellion in Britain.
1746	French capture Madras; beginning of Anglo-French wars in India.
1747	William IV's Orangist 'revolution' in the Dutch republic. Muratori, *Of the Well-Ordered Devotion of Christians*.
1748	Montesquieu, *The Spirit of the Laws*. Treaty of Aachen ends War of the Austrian Succession. Excavations begin at Pompeii.
1749	Horace Walpole begins the construction of Strawberry Hill. Buffon, *Natural History*. Fielding, *Tom Jones*.
1751	First volume of the *Encyclopédie*, edited by Diderot and d'Alembert.
1753	Pope grants abolition of fifty-three feast days to help Catholic countries compete with Protestant rivals.
1754	Beginning of Anglo-French hostilities in North America, merging after 1756 into worldwide Seven Years War.
1755	Pombal establishes monopoly company for part of Brazil trade. Lisbon earthquake. Winckelmann, *Thoughts on the Imitation of the Greeks*.

Samuel Johnson, *A Dictionary of the English Language*.
Rebuilding of the Benedictine Abbey of Ottobeuren
completed.

1756   The 'diplomatic revolution'—i.e. the alliance of France
and Austria.
Seven Years War begins, as does the Third Silesian War.

1757   Attempted assassination of Louis XV.
Battle of Plassey: British coup in Bengal.
Battle of Rossbach.
Battle of Leuthen.
Sainte-Geneviève (the Panthéon) begun.
Sankey Brook canal, the first modern canal, links the St
Helen's coalfield with the Mersey.

1758   David Hume, *An Enquiry Concerning Human
Understanding*.

1759   British take Quebec.
Battle of Kunersdorf.
Jesuits expelled from Portugal.
Voltaire's *Candide*.
British Museum opened.

1760   Greuze, *The village betrothal*.

1761   Duke of Bridgewater's canal links the Worsley mines with
Manchester.

1762   Murder of Tsar Peter III of Russia, accession of Catherine
II ('the Great').
Execution of the Protestant Jean Calas.
Jean-Jacques Rousseau, *The Social Contract*.
British take Havana, Cuba.
French legislation partly frees rural industry from guild
domination.
Gluck, *Orfeo ed Eurydice*.

1763   Treaty of Paris ends Seven Years War.

Treaty of Hubertusburg ends Third Silesian War between Prussia and Austria.

Hontheim *alias* Febronius, *On the Condition of the Church.*

Hargreaves's spinning jenny enables one operator to work several spindles.

1764   Jesuits expelled from France.

Beccaria, *On Crimes and Punishments.*

1765   Stamp Act: British attempt to tax American colonies.

British East India Company given *diwani*—revenue administration of Bengal.

Watt invents the separate condenser, solving the weakness of the Newcomen steam engine.

Publication of the *Encyclopédie*, edited by Diderot and d'Alembert, completed.

1766   Serious rioting in Madrid forces Charles III to flee.

Louis XV issues rebuke, known as the Flagellation, to the Parlement of Paris.

Expulsion of Jesuits from Spanish empire.

1767   Catherine the Great's *Instructions to the Legislative Assembly.*

1768   Bougainville at Tahiti.

The Royal Academy founded, with Sir Joshua Reynolds as its first president.

1769   Cook at Tahiti on first voyage.

Garrick's Shakespeare Jubilee at Stratford-on-Avon.

Arkwright's water frame improves the productivity of spinning.

1770   Raynal, *Histoire philosophique et politique des deux Indes.*

1771	Maupeou's revolution remodels French parlements.
	Pope abolishes another twenty feast days to improve productivity of Catholic countries.
1771–2	Famine in central Europe; potato begins to be widely introduced.
1772	Gustav III's coup ends Swedish 'age of liberty'.
	First partition of Poland.
	Warren Hastings becomes governor of Bengal.
1773	Suppression of the Jesuit Order by Pope Clement XIV.
	Boston Tea Party.
	Goethe, *The Sorrows of Young Werther*.
1774	Death of Louis XV, accession of Louis XVI, recall of the old parlements.
	Herder, *Another Philosophy of History Concerning the Development of Mankind*.
	Swedish chemist Scheele discovers chlorine.
1775	First metalled road built in Prussia.
1776	Declaration of American Independence.
	Joseph II creates a National Theatre at Vienna.
	Adam Smith, *The Wealth of Nations*.
	Gibbon, *The History of the Decline and Fall of the Roman Empire*.
	Turgot's edict on the suppression of guilds in France.
	Wilkinson installs the first Watt steam engine in an iron furnace.
1778	War of the Bavarian Succession.
1779	Treaty of Teschen.
	Adam Smith's *The Wealth of Nations* is translated into French.

1780   The Gordon riots in London.

          Beginning of Tupac Amaru's revolt in Peru.

          Joseph II becomes sole ruler of the Habsburg Monarchy on
          the death of his mother, the Empress Maria Theresa.

          The Ruhr river in western Germany is made navigable.

1781   British defeated at Yorktown in Virginia.

          Kant, *Critique of Pure Reason.*
          Schiller, *The Robbers.*

          Serfdom is abolished in the Habsburg Monarchy but
          labour services are left almost unaffected.

1782   British naval victory over the French at the Saintes in the
          West Indies.

          French and Spanish siege of Gibraltar fails.

1783   Recognition of the independence of the United States of
          America.

          Montgolfier brothers' first balloon flight.

          Watt's steam engine is first used to drive forge hammers
          for the British iron industry.

          Brügelmann sets up first copy of Arkwright's water frame at
          Ratingen in the Rhineland.

1783–4   Russian annexation of the Crimea.

1784   Spanish administrative reforms introduced into Peru.

          Cort perfects the puddling process for converting pig iron
          into wrought iron in a reverbratory furnace.

          Guilds abolished in the Austrian Netherlands (Belgium).

1785   Jacques-Louis David, *The Oath of the Horatii.*

          First Boulton and Watt steam engine is erected in a Belgian
          coalfield, at Jemappes.

1785–6   Berthollet experiments with chlorine for bleaching cloth.

1786	Spanish administrative reforms introduced into Mexico.
	Death of Frederick the Great.
	Frederick William II creates a National Theatre at Berlin.
	Mozart, *The Marriage of Figaro*.
	Steam power is first applied to cotton-spinning.
	Feudalism abolished in Denmark.

1787	Assembly of Notables meets at Versailles, thus beginning the 'pre-Revolution'.
	Dutch patriots defeated by the stadholder William V and his Prussian and British allies.
	Ottoman Empire declares war on Russia.
	Mozart, *Don Giovanni*.
	Cartwright develops the power loom (remains economically unviable until 1822).

1788	Louis XVI agrees to convene the Estates General.
	Sweden invades Russia.
	Founding of first British colony in Australia.
	Mozart's symphonies 39–41.

| 1788–9 | Regency crisis in Britain. |

1789	MAY	Meeting of the Estates General.
	JULY	Fall of the Bastille.
	AUG.	Promulgation of the Declaration of the Rights of Man.
	OCT.	The royal family and the National Assembly brought to Paris.
	NOV.	Expropriation of the Church begins.
		Leblanc invents process for deriving soda from sea salt.

1790		Death of Joseph II, succeeded by his brother Leopold II.
	JULY	Civil Constitution of the Clergy.
		Burke, *Reflections on the Revolution in France*.
		Mozart, *Così fan tutte*.

1791 MAY New Polish constitution.

JUNE Louis XVI's flight to Varennes.
Beginning of Saint-Domingue slave revolt.
Mozart, *The Magic Flute*.
Tom Paine, *Rights of Man*.
Revolution government abolishes all guilds in France.
Brandenburg Gate completed.

1792 Death of Leopold II, accession of Francis II.

APR. Wars of the French Revolution begin.

AUG. France becomes a republic.

SEPT. Massacres in Paris.

SEPT. Battle of Valmy.

1793 JAN. Execution of Louis XVI.

MAR. Counter-revolutionary revolt in the Vendée begins.

APR. Committee of Public Safety established.

AUG. *Levée en masse.*

SEPT Terror begins.
Second partition of Poland.
Last witch executed in Poland.
Central Museum of the Arts opened in the Louvre.
Revolutionary government in France abolishes all seigneurial claims, restrictions, and obligations.

1794 JULY Battle of Fleurus.

JULY Fall of Robespierre.
Prussian *Allgemeines Landrecht* (General Legal Code) promulgated.

1795 British occupation of Dutch colonies.
Third partition leads to the extinction of the Polish state.
Treaties of Basle end wars between France and Prussia and France and Spain.
Belgium annexed to France.
Crompton's spinning mule is adapted for power.

| 1796 | Bonaparte conquers northern Italy. |

Catherine the Great of Russia dies; with the accession of her son, Paul I, Russia suspends its role in the First Coalition.
Trevithick begins to apply steam power to traction.
Edward Jenner introduces vaccination against smallpox.

| 1797 | Treaty of Campo Formio ends war between France and Austria. |

| 1798 | General Bonaparte leads an expedition to conquer Egypt. |

Battle of the Nile, a British fleet commanded by Nelson destroys Napoleon's fleet.
Irish rebellion.
War of the Second Coalition.
Wordsworth, *Lyrical Ballads.*
Coleridge, *Lyrical Ballads.*
Malthus, *Essay on the Principle of Population.*
Haydn, *Creation.*
Aloys Senefelder invents lithography.

| 1798–9 | Tennant and Macintosh invent bleaching powder for cloth. |

1799 MAR.	War between France and Austria resumes; Russia enters the war on the side of Austria; the French are expelled from Italy.
OCT.	Bonaparte returns from Egypt.
NOV.	Bonaparte seizes power in France.

Collapse of Dutch East India Company.
First water-driven spinning mule is set up in Saxony.

| 1800 | Battle of Marengo, Bonaparte defeats the Austrians. |

Battle of Hohenlinden, Moreau defeats the Austrians.
Friedrich von Hardenberg *alias* Novalis, *Hymns to the Night.*
Alessandro Volta demonstrates first electric battery.

| 1801 | Treaty of Lunéville ends war between France and Austria. |

Assassination of Paul I, accession of Alexander I.

Bonaparte's Concordat with the Pope.

Act of Union unites Great Britain and Ireland.

1802   Treaty of Amiens.

Chateaubriand, *The Genius of Christianity*.

1803   War resumes between France and Britain.

France sells Louisiana to the USA.

Imperial Recess decrees sweeping territorial changes in
Germany, which ensure French domination.

Widespread secularization of monasteries in Germany.

Beethoven's Third Symphony, 'Eroica', composed (first
performed 1805).

1804   Francis II, Holy Roman Emperor, proclaims himself also
Emperor of Austria as Francis I.

Bonaparte proclaims himself Emperor Napoleon I, is
crowned by the Pope Pius VII.

Code Napoléon enacted.

1805   Bonaparte reorganizes Italy under direct French control.

AUG.   The third coalition consisting of Britain, Austria, Russia,
and Sweden is formed against France; war resumes on the
continent.

OCT.   Austrian army capitulates at Ulm.

OCT.   Battle of Trafalgar.

DEC.   Battle of Austerlitz; Napoleon inflicts a crushing defeat on
an Austro-Russian army.

DEC.   Treaty of Pressburg; Russia withdraws from the war.

1806 MAR.   Napoleon makes his brother Joseph King of Naples.

JUNE   Napoleon makes his brother Louis King of the
Netherlands.

JULY   Napoleon reorganizes Germany as the 'Confederation of
the Rhine'.

AUG.   Formal end of the Holy Roman Empire when the Emperor
Francis II abdicates and becomes Francis I of Austria.

OCT.   Prussia declares war on France.

OCT.   Battles of Jena and Auerstedt, Prussia defeated.

1807   Russia rejoins war as Prussia's ally; indecisive campaign in Poland.

JUNE   Decisive French victory at Battle of Friedland.

JULY   Treaty of Tilsit ends war; France and Russia enter alliance. Portuguese royal family flees to Brazil.

Fichte, *Addresses to the German Nation.*

Caspar David Friedrich, *The Cross in the Mountains.*

Britain abolishes the slave trade.

Humphry Davy isolates sodium and potassium from their compounds.

1808   Napoleon imposes his brother Joseph as King of Spain; Spanish people rise in revolt, assisted by the British army.

Rome occupied by French troops.

Goethe, *Faust*, Part I.

1809   APR.   War resumes between France and Austria.

MAY   Austrians defeat Napoleon at the Battle of Aspern-Essling.

JULY   Napoleon defeats the Austrians at the Battle of Wagram.

OCT.   Treaty of Schönbrunn ends war between Austria and France. Papal States annexed to France.

1810   Napoleon marries the Archduchess Marie Louise, daughter of the Emperor Francis I.

Napoleon annexes the Netherlands to France.

Napoleon annexes the north-western coast of Germany.

Revolts against Spanish rule in Venezuela and Rio de la Plata (future Argentina).

1811   'Luddite' machine-breaking riots in Britain.

1812   Battle of Salamanca, defeat of French in Spain by army commanded by the Duke of Wellington.

Goya, *The Disasters of War.*

JUNE   Napoleon with his German and Italian satellites invades Russia.

SEPT.   Napoleon fights the indecisive Battle of Borodino and enters Moscow a week later.

OCT.   Napoleon's retreat from Moscow begins.

DEC.   Remnants of Napoleon's army leaves Russia.

Henry Bell's *The Comet*, the world's first commercial steamship begins operations on the Clyde.

1813 FEB.   Treaty of Kalisch between Prussia and Russia.

JUNE   Wellington defeats the French at Vittoria, prompting King Joseph to flee to France.

AUG.   Austria declares war on France.

OCT.   Napoleon is defeated at the Battle of Leipzig and loses control of Germany.

DEC.   Prussian army under Blücher begins the invasion of France.

Colombia declares independence from Spain.

Rossini, *Tancredi*.

1814 MAR.   Allies abandon attempt to negotiate with Napoleon and conclude Treaty of Chaumont for wartime and post-war alliance.

MAR.   Wellington captures Bordeaux.

APR.   Napoleon abdicates, is exiled to the island of Elba; Louis XVIII returned to French throne.

SEPT.   General negotiations for a comprehensive peace settlement begin at Vienna.

Uruguay declares independence from Spain.

1815 MAR.   Napoleon returns from Elba

JUNE   (18th) Battle of Waterloo; Napoleon abdicates and is exiled to St Helena.

JUNE   Congress of Vienna completes restructuring of Europe.

SEPT.   Russia, Austria, and Prussia form the 'Holy Alliance'.

NOV.   Britain, Russia, Austria and Prussia form a Quadruple Alliance to maintain the Vienna settlement.

NOV.   Second treaty of Paris reduces France to frontiers of 1790.

Humphry Davy invents miner's safety lamp.

Maps

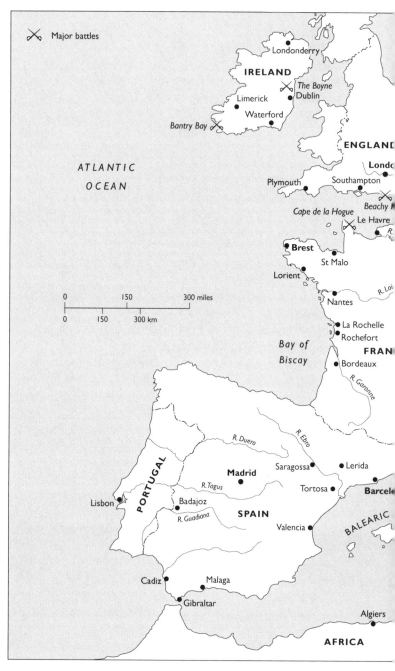

Map 1 Europe in 1715.

NORTH
SEA

BALTIC
SEA

R. Niemen

Texel

Sole
Bay

alais
Dunkirk

Amsterdam

R. Rhine

R. Vistula

Warsaw

POLAND

Berlin

Kunersdorf

Antwerp

Ostend

Brussels

Cologne

Rossbach

Leuthen

Dresden

Hohenfriedberg

ille

enain

Ramillies

Koblenz

Halplaquet

Mainz

Paris

Verdun

Metz

LORRAINE

ALSACE

BAVARIA

Vienna

Pressburg

HUNGARY

Valmy

Teul

Blenheim

Stuttgart

Kehl

R. Danube

Raab

Ofen
(Buda Pest)

TRANSYLVANIA

Munich

Salzburg

FRANCHE COMTE

Montbeliard

Berne

SWITZERLAND

R. Drave

R. Rhône

Lyons

SAVOY

Milan

R. Save

Turin

R. Po

Belgrade

OTTOMAN EMPIRE

gnon
Papal
tate)

Pinerolo

GENOA

Genoa

Nice

Marseilles

Toulon

CORSICA

ADRIATIC SEA

Rome

NAPLES

SARDINIA

MEDITERRANEAN SEA

Stromboli

Palermo

SICILY

Messina

Augusta

Map 2 Europe in 1789.

SWEDEN

Helsinki

St Petersburg

Stockholm

Gotland

Riga

Dvina

BALTIC SEA

RUSSIA

Moscow

Neman

Vilnius

MERANIA

Danzig

EAST PRUSSIA

POLAND

Warsaw

Vistula

S I A

ILESIA

Oder

gue

REP. OF
KRAKOW

Krakow

Dnieper

RAVIA

Vienna

THE HABSBURG
EMPIRE

Dniester

Buda ••Pest

MOLDAVIA

HUNGARY

Belgrade

WALLACHIA

Bucharest

BLACK SEA

BOSNIA

SERBIA

Danube

OTTOMAN

BULGARIA

MONTE-
NEGRO

Sofia

THRACE

Constantinople

ALBANI

MACEDONIA

EMPIRE

Adriatic Sea

Aegean
Sea

MOREA

Athens

E A

Crete

Rhodes

Cyprus

Map 3 Europe in 1815.

NGDOM
OF
WEDEN

● St Petersburg

● Stockholm

● Moscow

Borodino 1812

BALTIC
SEA

openhagen

Tilsit

●Smolensk

RUSSIAN EMPIRE

Friedland 1807

Danzig

Königsberg

PRUSSIA

lin

Vistula

Warsaw

GRAND DUCHY
OF WARSAW

Oder

●Kiev

Dnieper

AXONY

Dniester

Wagram
1809

Austerlitz
1805

Vienna

Pressburg

Buda

Pest

AUSTRIAN EMPIRE

Danube

BLACK SEA

ILLYRIAN PROVINCES

KINGDOM
OF
NAPLES

Naples

OTTOMAN EMPIRE

Constantinople

IONIAN IS.
(Gr. Br)

Athens

KINGDOM
OF
SICILY

MALTA
(Gr. Br)

CRETE

CYPRUS

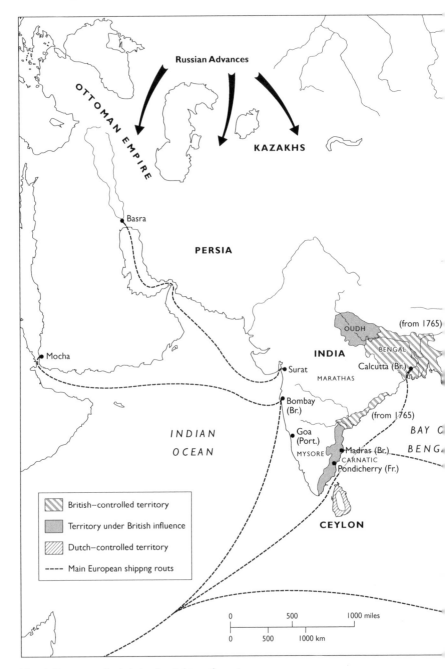

Map 4 Europeans in Asia in the eighteenth century.

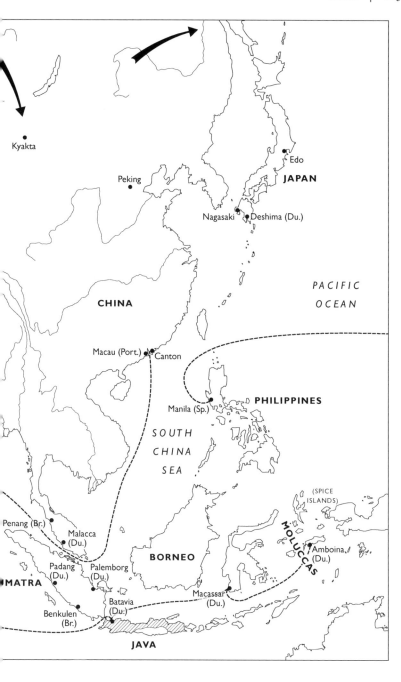

Kyakta

Peking

JAPAN

Edo

Nagasaki Deshima (Du.)

CHINA

PACIFIC OCEAN

Macau (Port.) Canton

Manila (Sp.) **PHILIPPINES**

SOUTH CHINA SEA

(SPICE ISLANDS)

Penang (Br.)

Malacca (Du.)

BORNEO

MOLUCCAS

Amboina (Du.)

Padang (Du.)

Palemborg (Du.)

MATRA

Macassar (Du.)

Benkulen (Br.)

Batavia (Du.)

JAVA

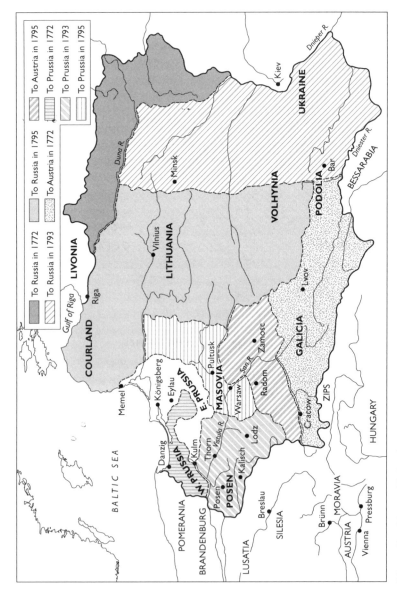

Map 5 Partitions of Poland.

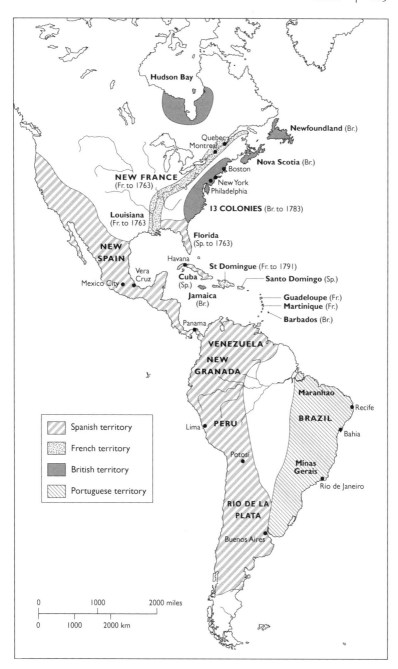

Map 6 The Americas in the eighteenth century.

Index

.